Collingwood and the Crisis
of Western Civilisation

British Idealist Studies Series 2: Collingwood

Collingwood and the Crisis of Western Civilisation

Art, Metaphysics and Dialectic

Richard Murphy

ia

IMPRINT ACADEMIC

Published in the UK by Imprint Academic
PO Box 200, Exeter EX5 5YX, UK

Published in the USA by Imprint Academic
Philosophy Documentation Center
PO Box 7147, Charlottesville, VA 22906-7147, USA

ISBN 978 184540 1061
A CIP catalogue record for this book is available from the
British Library and US Library of Congress

www.imprint-academic.com/idealists

Contents

Abbreviations

Works by Collingwood:

RP	Religion and Philosophy (1916)
TC	*Truth and Contradiction* (1917)
FFH	'A Footnote to Future History' (1919)
SM	*Speculum Mentis* (1924)
PAE	'The Place of Art in Education' (1926)
AM	'Art and the Machine' (1926?)
EPM	*An Essay on Philosophical Method* (1933 and 2005)
NMS	'The Nature of Metaphysical Study' (1934)
MM	'Method and Metaphysics' (1935)
MGM	'Man Goes Mad' (1936)
RI	'Realism and Idealism' (1936)
PA	*The Principles of Art* (1938)
A	An Autobiography (1939)
EM	*An Essay on Metaphysics* (1940 and 1998)
NL	*The New Leviathan* (1942 and 1992)
IN	*The Idea of Nature* (1945)
IH	*The Idea of History* (1946 and 1993)
EPA	*Essays in the Philosophy of Art* (1964)
EPH	*Essays in the Philosophy of History* (1965)
EPP	*Essays in Political Philosophy* (1989)

Works by Ortega y Gasset:

RM	*The Revolt of the Masses* (1932)
HS	*History as a System* (1941 and 1962)
MU	*Mission of the University* (1946 and 1963)
MP	*Man and People* (1957)
MC	*Man and Crisis* (1958)
DA	*The Dehumanization of Art* (1968)

Acknowledgements

I would like to express my gratitude to Professor David Boucher, whose assistance and encouragement throughout my work on this book (which began as a PhD thesis under his supervision) have been invaluable. I also wish to thank him for the opportunity to revise the thesis in this form.

I am particularly indebted to Dr. Mark Evans for his helpful comments and useful advice. Also Professor James Connelly deserves thanks for his helpful suggestions and Professor Roland Axtmann for his insightful critical comments.

The R.G. Collingwood Society generously provided me with financial assistance during my study and for this I am very grateful.

Thanks are due also to my friends (both nearby and further afield) and my colleagues in the Department of Politics and International Relations at Swansea University, who in a variety of ways have contributed to the formulation of my thoughts and the completion of this work.

I also want to thank my family: my brother, Brian, and my sister, Eimear. This book is dedicated to my parents, Roger and Emily Murphy, who contributed greatly with their continuous encouragement and support.

Introduction

The importance of R.G. Collingwood ought to be understood in the context of the legacy of romanticism and the development of historical thinking in the late nineteenth and early twentieth centuries. The emergence of 'historicism' and the influence of Romanticism meant a change from regarding philosophy as the pursuit of abstract transcendental truths towards regarding truth and meaning as immanent, historically contextual, and contingent. This critical development, in both philosophy and Western culture more generally, occurred in response to what was perceived as a profound crisis in Western civilisation. Collingwood was one of the thinkers that provided a key positive contribution to these movements, and developed a response to the crisis.

The transition towards a greater appreciation of historicity and contingency, brought about by the influence of Romanticism and historicism, meant that philosophy comes to be understood to a greater extent as philosophy of cultures and civilisations. It is in this context that the notion of 'crisis' ought to be understood: at any given time, a culture or civilisation may undergo conditions of relative strength or vigour and of relative crisis or decadence.[1] Also, although the focus of this study is primarily on Collingwood, similar philosophies were developed by Ortega y Gasset and Croce, and in

[1]   In investigating Collingwood's treatment of the theme of the crisis of the West, I am assuming that it is to some extent a valid concern. I make the assumption that there is such a thing as 'the West' or 'Western civilisation', although the boundaries between what is and is not the West may be ambiguous and debatable, and the contents of Western culture in fact overlap with those of non-Western cultures. Also, I am assuming that the West has a history and that therefore it can undergo conditions of relative strength or decadence. Furthermore, I am treating as plausible Collingwood's view that there is, if not a unity, an intimate relation of philosophy to practice. Philosophy on this view is not simply the apprehension of eternal transcendent truths, but to some extent descriptive of a world in flux. The starting assumptions of this thesis therefore are themselves of a 'historicist' nature.

the course of the book these affinities, especially with Ortega, will help to shed light on Collingwood's philosophy.[2]

The theme of the crisis of civilisation pervades Collingwood's work, and although this theme has been mentioned by some commentators on Collingwood's philosophy, it has not been discussed in much detail. David Boucher asserts that the later published works of Collingwood reflect his lifelong preoccupation with identifying and combating the enemies of civilisation, by coming to a better self-understanding (Boucher, 2000: 186). Collingwood was prolific in formulating theories about what ailed civilisation and, as Boucher rightly points out, Collingwood's diagnoses, prognoses, and remedies are best viewed as explorations into various aspects of the disease, constituting complementary, rather than alternative, theories (Boucher, 1989: 231).

Boucher refers to an explosion and proliferation of 'crisis' literature in the period between the two world wars in Europe, where civilisation was described as being in a state of severe crisis, or even experiencing its final death throe.[3] Similarly, William M. Johnston remarks that Collingwood belonged to that generation of inter-war thinkers who felt called upon to interrogate the entire tradition of the West in search of its *raison d'être*. In the case of Spengler and Freud, this interrogation yielded evidence of decline and collapse. In the case of Collingwood and Croce, on the other hand, the scrutiny was pursued with the avowed hope of finding fresh sources of rejuvenation. Unlike Spengler, Johnston explains, Collingwood never doubted that the West could recover its creative energies (Johnston, 1967: 139–41). However, it was throughout the late nineteenth and early twentieth centuries, and not just in the inter-war years, that this theme was important. The theme of the crisis of Western civilisation is prominent in late nineteenth- and early twentieth-century philosophical, social, political, literary and artistic discourse.

---

[2]   With regard to the theme of the crisis of Western civilisation in general, Dilthey, Nietzsche and Max Weber are particularly important. Other important thinkers were Bergson, Spengler and Freud.

[3]   For example, E.H. Carr described the whole period as 'the Twenty Years' Crisis', Paul Valéry refers to a 'crisis of the mind', Karl Mannheim refers to a 'crisis in our intellectual life', Albert Schweitzer to a 'collapse of civilization', Peter Drucker to a 'revolution which threatens every concept on which European civilization has been based', and Edward Carpenter to an 'intensified manifestation of Disease – physical, social, moral' (Boucher, 1989: 231). Another interesting account of crisis literature in inter-war Europe is provided by Michael Adas in *Machines as the Measure of Men: science, technology, and ideologies of Western dominance*, Ch. 6 (1989).

What I propose to do here is briefly to outline what Collingwood saw as the crisis of Western civilisation, and its Romantic and historicist context, and then to explain the order of enquiry. To put it very briefly, the crisis of civilisation, for Collingwood, is an over-reliance on abstractly rationalistic forms of thinking. The solution is the cultivation of forms of emotional expression, and to think historically and dialectically.

The theme of the crisis of civilisation is strongly present in Collingwood's philosophy of art, where he argues that civilisation is in crisis because of the suppression of emotion. In the 'Fairy Tales' manuscript (written in 1936–37), this same suppression of emotion is blamed for an obsession with utilitarianism and the failure to understand the primitive survival of emotion in contemporary civilisation. The suppression of emotion is exemplified in the suppression of art proper by amusement art and the ill effects of industrialisation, and by the destruction of the countryside. In his theory of logic and metaphysics Collingwood regards Western civilisation as being under threat from natural science and the effects of positivism and utilitarianism. Here dialectical and historical thinking are seen as a solution. Both of these aspects of the theme of the crisis of civilisation and its solution coincide in Collingwood's account of morality, politics and civilisation.

In *Speculum Mentis*, following the Romantic tradition, Collingwood identified the crisis of civilisation as being the detachment of the forms of experience, art, religion, science, history, and philosophy, from one another. The solution to this spiritual fragmentation is the reunion of the forms of experience 'in a complete and undivided life' (SM, 36). Following *Speculum Mentis*, Collingwood argued that civilisation was threatened not only by the separation of the forms of experience from one another, but the emergence of one which threatened to suffocate the rest. The foundations of civilisation were being undermined by the natural-scientific, or positivist, tendency to undervalue or deny the importance of other forms of experience. As Boucher puts it, the civilisation generated by an excessive deference to natural science is a utilitarian one in which emotion is denied or suppressed; art is perverted into an artificial stimulant to the senses; the mystical content of religion is eliminated, leaving only a rationalistic code of morals, devoid of the substance from which it emerged; and psychology claims to be a science of mind, leaving its legitimate realm of the psyche, or the science of feeling, and claiming instead the entire workings of mind as its province (Boucher, 1989: 232–3).

The various attacks on civilisation are manifestations of 'irrationalism' and one aspect of irrationalism in philosophy is a pre-occupation with psychology. For Collingwood psychology is non-criteriological, and history, not psychology, is the science of mind. Also, philosophies such as positivism and realism, by elevating natural-scientific knowledge to a status which reduces all knowledge of ethics and morality to the level of mere beliefs and superstitions, facilitated the growth of irrationalism (cf. Boucher, 1989: 237–40). I agree with Boucher's judgement that although fascism failed in its revolt against civilisation, all those other elements which Collingwood identified as insidiously eroding the foundations of modern European civilisation have become, on the whole, accentuated rather than alleviated (Boucher, 1989: 241).

As I have indicated, Collingwood's idea of the crisis of civilisation derives from Romanticism and historicism. His concern with the suppression of emotion and emphasis on the importance of art are Romantic in origin, and, as a historicist, Collingwood argues that dialectical and historical thinking are a solution to the crisis of civilisation. Demonstrating the inter-connectedness of Romanticism and historicism, then, Collingwood's philosophy of art and of the idea of a union of the forms of experience complements his theory of dialectical and historical thinking. As with art, where we express and become conscious of our emotions, through a historicist philosophy we achieve self-knowledge at the level of thinking.

Collingwood inherited, and continued, from the Romantic tradition the critique of industrial society: a tradition including John Ruskin, Friedrich Nietzsche, and the modernist writers, T.S. Eliot, D.H. Lawrence, and Ezra Pound. Regarding his historicism, Collingwood has close affinities with Croce and Ortega y Gasset. Hence Collingwood is an important point of connection between these parallel traditions. His philosophy connects the romanticism of John Ruskin with the historicist and dialectical thought of Ortega y Gasset and the Italian Idealists. As a note of caution, however, at this point, the term 'historicism', as I will explain in the first chapter, has a variety of meanings. What is important to emphasise at this stage is that, in the sense in which it is being used here, historicism is *not* equivalent to relativism.

Collingwood's philosophy, which places historicity at the centre of philosophical understanding, along with Ortega y Gasset and the Italian Idealists, also foreshadowed some of the principal developments of twentieth-century philosophy. The crisis of modernity, and the attempt to overcome it through the development of an alternative model for thinking to the one provided by natural science, is central to most of twentieth-century continental philosophy, for example, Heidegger, critical theory, existentialism, and hermeneutics. One common point of origin for the above-mentioned movements is Nietzsche. Nietzsche is also significant for his influence on literary modernism and the legacy of Romanticism in the twentieth century. Thus, although Nietzsche does not exert any direct obvious influence on Collingwood, Collingwood's investigation of the crisis of civilisation participates in a stream where Nietzsche is central. The philosophy of Nietzsche, therefore, serves as an illuminating foil or contrast to Collingwood in the course of this study.

Instructive comparisons could also have been made in this book between Collingwood and thinkers such as Adorno, Benjamin and Heidegger, particularly regarding the relation between art and technology. However, the actual comparisons (particularly in the area of the philosophy of art) are mostly with Ruskin, Orwell, Lawrence, Pound, Eliot and Ortega y Gasset. The justification for comparing Collingwood with Orwell, Lawrence, Pound and Eliot is that they are all to some extent (like Collingwood) influenced by Ruskin and are part of the English Romantic tradition (see Williams, 1993), where Ruskin is a leading figure. These comparisons enhance our understanding of Collingwood by enabling us to see him in a wider context, where he plays an important role in drawing together key themes from Romanticism and modernist theories of art into a cohesive and systematic philosophy in order to provide a compelling response to cultural crisis in the modern West.

The comparisons that I make between Collingwood and Ortega y Gasset are more extensive. The importance of Ortega (from the perspective of this study) is the pivotal role he occupies as a 'crisis' thinker in the early twentieth century and his Nietzschean concern with promoting the conditions for an 'aristocracy of culture', which is central to the crisis of Western civilisation as I understand it in this book. John T. Graham, for example, describes Ortega as 'the most challenging of all crisis theorists, past and contemporary' and as 'a pioneer of systematic crisis theory' in the twentieth century (Graham, 1997: 208 and 217). Also, as I have argued, Ortega plays a key role in the development of historicist thought in the early twentieth century. The comparison with Ortega, therefore, illuminates Collingwood's concern with the crisis of civilisation and his attempt to overcome the rationalism of modernity with a theory of art and culture and a theory of historical and dialectical thinking.

In the use of Ortega's philosophy as a comparison with Collingwood's, there is, to follow Collingwood's own argument in *An Essay on Philosophical Method*, an affirmation and a denial. In *An Essay on Philosophical Method* (which I will examine in more detail in Part Two of this book) Collingwood argues that, in philosophy, affirmation and denial imply one another. Concrete affirmation involves the negation of definite ideas that one regards as inadequate (EPM, 106–7). This principle of concrete affirmation and concrete denial is explored by Joseph Levenson, who explains that '… an idea has its particular quality from the fact that other ideas, expressed in other quarters, are demonstrable alternatives' (Levenson, 1965: xii–xiv).

Hence, (in order to provide a fuller understanding of the crisis of the West) the aim of this book is to situate Collingwood's philosophy in a wider context than Idealism.[4] This context will be wide enough to illuminate both the Romantic and historicist aspects of Collingwood's thought. The attention devoted to examining Ortega's philosophy in comparison with Collingwood is an affirmation of the importance of historical thinking in the solution to the crisis of modernity. However, there is also a denial: the investigation is not so wide as to take into account the whole of twentieth-century philosophy. To write an account of 'crisis' thought in twentieth-century philosophy as a whole would go beyond the confines of this book, which is specifically a critical analysis of Collingwood's philosophy. Ortega, as a point of comparison, is important for the particularly historicist solution that he provides to the crisis of civilisation.

Examining Collingwood's philosophy through the theme of the crisis of the West, then, requires an awareness of the broader context of his work (although there are limits to this broader context). It involves taking a slightly broader perspective than that taken by other commentaries on his philosophy, and perhaps this broader emphasis is, to some degree, faithful to Collingwood's advice to scholars to 'write not about me but about the subject' (A, 118–9). For Collingwood, it was an appropriate task for philosophy to respond to the crisis of civilisation because, as he argued in *Speculum Mentis*, 'all thought exists for the sake of action' (SM, 15). Collingwood's historicist conception of reality and his *rapprochement* between theory and practice leads to the view that philosophy can help to effect

---

[4]   I will, however, occasionally consider Collingwood's affinities with Italian Idealism in the course of this book. These affinities which have been discussed by many commentators on Collingwood's philosophy: for example, Connelly discusses Collingwood's affinities with Italian Idealism in 'Art Thou the Man: Croce, Gentile or de Ruggiero?' (1995).

far-reaching transformations in a civilisation or culture. In his *Auto-biography*, Collingwood speaks of using philosophy as 'a weapon' to change the world (A, 153).[5] (In his view that philosophy is transformative, Collingwood resembles Nietzsche.)

As Collingwood points out in 'The Present Need of a Philosophy', part of the business of philosophy is to show that whatever ills exist in human institutions are within the scope of human will to solve (EPP, 166–70). The abstractions that imprison us are our own creations, extensions of our own subjectivity.[6] This view of the transformative role of philosophy on practice is also expressed by Ortega y Gasset: 'For philosophy to rule it is sufficient for it to exist; that is to say, for the philosophers to be philosophers' (RM, 115n).

In Collingwood's works subsequent to *Speculum Mentis* (published in 1924), the theme of the crisis of civilisation is most explicitly present in Collingwood's philosophy of art. Hence Part One of this book will concentrate primarily on the philosophy of art. I then proceed in Part Two to discuss Collingwood's dialectical account of logic and metaphysics. Part Three will be dedicated to his theory of politics and civilisation, where Collingwood's dialectical philosophy is put into concrete form and overlaps to some extent with his philosophy of art. Part Three, then, will also attempt to draw together some of the conclusions from the first two parts.

Chapter One places Collingwood's concern with the crisis of modernity in the context of Romanticism and the emergence of historicism in the late nineteenth and early twentieth century. I argue that Collingwood's philosophy is very much a part of the tradition of both Romanticism and historicism. Additionally, this chapter discusses Collingwood's early formulation of his conception of the crisis of the West in *Speculum Mentis*, published in 1924, and in his 1919 lecture, *Ruskin's Philosophy*. In *Speculum Mentis* his solution to the crisis is 'unity of mind' and, in *Ruskin's Philosophy*, 'historicism'. I also point out that Collingwood's conception of the 'unity of mind' corresponds to the Romantic idea of 'culture', an idea promoted by John Ruskin, and in the twentieth century by

[5] Collingwood's view of the transformative potential of philosophy is evident in his assertion in *Speculum Mentis* that: 'An engineer whose engine will not go does not plead that Nature's stores of energy are exhausted; but the social reformer who cannot get society to obey him is too ready to explain the fact by accusing his age of spiritual poverty. He ought to know better. He ought to know — or his licence as a prophet ought to be taken away — that the spiritual energy pent up within the breast of his own boot-and-knife boy is enough to overthrow empires if the word were spoken that released it' (SM, 21).

[6] As Derek Sayer points out, mechanisation is but a metaphor for forms of our own sociality and subjectivity (Sayer, 1991: 155).

D.H. Lawrence, T.S. Eliot, and José Ortega y Gasset. For Ortega, like Collingwood, the unity of the forms of experience is just one part of a philosophy where historical and dialectical thinking are seen as a solution to a crisis of modernity. Following *Ruskin's Philosophy* and *Speculum Mentis*, Collingwood came to place greater emphasis on the philosophy of art and on historical and dialectical thinking, which became inter-related aspects of a solution to cultural crisis.

According to Collingwood, it is in aesthetic activity that we first begin to apprehend the world. Hence, in art, and the subversion of our artistic life, we find the first evidence and symptoms of the crisis of civilisation. In Chapter Two I explain that Collingwood's conception of art as a starting point for a critique of contemporary civilisation and a solution for its ills depends on a distinction between art and craft. Collingwood argues that Western civilisation is in crisis because of a suppression of emotion, symptoms of which are the predominance of values associated with industrialisation, the replacement of art proper with amusement, and the suppression of magic and the emotional aspects of religion. Collingwood's solution to the problem is a theory of art as the expression of emotion.

Chapter Three explores Collingwood's conception of art as a solution to the crisis of civilisation more deeply. For Collingwood, art is identified with consciousness and language, and provides the data upon which intellect can build. Art, then, creates the world, by becoming conscious of it. In doing so, art is the revelation of truth and provides an antidote to cultural crisis, and to what Collingwood calls the 'corruption of consciousness'. In developing the conception of art as a solution to the crisis of modernity, I suggest that Collingwood is consciously working within the Romantic tradition. The idea of art as having a regenerative effect on civilisation is strongly present in the works of Ruskin, Nietzsche, D.H. Lawrence and Ezra Pound.

Chapter Four demonstrates that the creation of the world through art is a continuous process and is constrained by collaboration between the artist and the wider community. The artist is the spokesperson of his or her audience, and art is the community's medicine for the corruption of consciousness. I argue that the dialectical interaction between innovation and tradition in Collingwood's philosophy of art is complemented by the philosophies of art put forward by Eliot and Ortega y Gasset and prefigures Collingwood's dialectical account of logic and metaphysics.

In Part Two, Chapter Five, I examine Collingwood's dialectical conception of philosophy as a solution to the crisis of civilisation, precipitated by the inadequacy of the Platonic philosophy of being. I discuss his 'revolution' in logic, beginning with his modification of the coherence theory of truth in his early manuscripts and leading to his conception of the scale of forms in *An Essay on Philosophical Method*.

Collingwood's dialectical logic is inextricably linked with an ontological claim that reality is dialectical. Hence his reform of logic also implied a reform of metaphysics. Metaphysics, for Collingwood, as I explain in Chapter Six, is an historical science and provides an account of the constellations of absolute presuppositions upon which 'science', or systematic and orderly thinking, proceeds. In his later work, Collingwood characterised dialectical logic as the logic of question and answer. The meaning of a set of absolute presuppositions, I contend, can only be fully understood in the context of the complex of questions and answers that it gives rise to.

Chapter Seven discusses what Collingwood regarded as the threat to his historical metaphysics from reactionary traditional philosophy and irrationalism. I also demonstrate how Collingwood's philosophy responds to the cultural crisis by reconciling normative thinking with historical change. For Collingwood, I suggest, the advancement of science and civilisation are not safeguarded by metaphysics alone: metaphysics needs to be supplemented by a broader philosophy of history which gives an account of the sciences and practices that absolute presuppositions have given rise to and thus determining if progress has occurred. The criteria for value and truth, then, are located not in an ideal transcendent world, but in a 'way of life', considered in its widest context. This chapter also discusses Ortega y Gasset and Nietzsche who, like Collingwood, also responded to the crisis of modernity by advancing philosophies which placed value less on fundamental principles or individual judgements in themselves, but on their ability to generate vitality and enhance life as a whole.

Part Three examines how Collingwood's solution to the crisis of Western civilisation in terms of logic, metaphysics and the philosophy of history manifests itself in the practices of civilisation and politics. In Collingwood's view, theory and practice are intimately related. In Chapter Eight I demonstrate how Collingwood's dialectical philosophy reveals itself in a historicist phenomenology of mind and in an account of morality as duty. Duty in practical reason corresponds with history in theoretical reason. Comparisons and contrasts with Ortega and Nietzsche are also explored.

Chapter Nine demonstrates how Collingwood's philosophy leads to a reform of social contract theory. In response to the abstractions of social contract theory, Collingwood puts forward a dynamic and dialectical conception of liberalism. In this chapter I also examine Collingwood's argument that civilisation is a dialectical process. Collingwood's dialectical and historicist account of liberalism is compared with that of Ortega: a comparison that allows us to understand Collingwood's political theory as playing a salient role in a wider twentieth-century historicist response to cultural crisis.

In Chapter Ten it is demonstrated that Collingwood's account of civilisation leads to a dialectical critique and response to the negative effects of capitalism. The growth of a distinction between rich and poor, and the suppression of emotion that contemporary capitalism promotes are an element of barbarism in civilisation, something that would be corrected by Collingwood's dialectical conception of civilisation and by his philosophy of art. I also demonstrate that Collingwood's critique of modernity for its over-reliance on rationalistic and dogmatic philosophies, and his proposed solution to the problem in the form of dialectical thinking and the cultivation of forms of emotional expression, are evident in his discussion of education and bureaucracy. Collingwood's views about the dialectic of political life here are shown to be complemented by de Ruggiero and Ortega y Gasset, and are contrasted with the ideas of Nietzsche and Weber.

In the Conclusion I sum up the central arguments of each part of the book, demonstrating how each aspect of Collingwood's response to cultural crisis develops into a cohesive and compelling philosophy. This includes further discussion of how an appreciation of Collingwood's role in the wider contexts of historicism and Romanticism, especially through the comparison with Ortega y Gasset, add to our understanding of Collingwood, these philosophical movements and the condition of contemporary Western civilisation.

Part One

Art and the Crisis of Civilisation

Chapter One

Romanticism, Historicism & the Unity of the Forms of Experience

In the course of this book, I will argue that Collingwood's diagnosis of and solutions to the crisis of Western civilisation ought to be situated in the context of Romanticism and historicism. Therefore, in order to prepare the ground for forthcoming chapters, the purpose of this chapter is to outline what I understand by the terms 'Romanticism' and 'historicism'. Also, this chapter will outline Collingwood's treatment of the theme of the crisis of civilisation in his early career. In particular, I will discuss his view that the ills of modernity are due to the fragmentation of the forms of experience from one another and that the solution to the problem is their re–union in a complete and undivided life.

The legacy of Romanticism is discussed by Larmore under the headings of 'imagination', 'community' and 'irony and authenticity'. For Romantics the mind is understood in terms of its creative power, and our sense of reality is inseparable from the creative imagination. Through imagination we transform what we are given in experience. The Romantic imagination, Larmore asserts, is both creative and responsive. Kant was influential for Romantic thought because of his view that the mind is essentially active, not merely registering but structuring what we call reality. As Larmore puts it, 'The mind responds to the world only by at the same time creating its own forms of understanding' (Larmore, 1996: 23).

A second important aspect of Romanticism is the theme of community. Our deepest beliefs cannot be chosen upon reflection, for we have no sense of what is valuable, and so no adequate basis for choice, without them. We must regard them as felt convictions, which set the terms of the choices we make and which are embodied in the way of life that is ours, and such allegiances express our sense of belonging (cf. Larmore, 1996: 38). For Herder, we must strive for the right balance between critical reflection and belonging. This is connected to pluralism: the ultimate sources of objective value are not one, but many (Larmore, 1996: 40).

For Romantics, contrary to Enlightenment rationalism, reason cannot take the place of belonging, of identifying with an ongoing way of life, as the source of our moral substance. Our deepest convictions are the sustaining basis of our critical reflection. This new conception of reason receives its most profound expression in the philosophy of Hegel. For Hegel, the human spirit makes its advances not by rising to a standpoint outside a given way of life but only by thinking within it, attending to its internal contradictions and failed aspirations. According to Larmore, 'Hegel's philosophy, taken as a whole, is doubtless a grandiose and implausible construction. But if we strip from it his confidence that History harbours an inner logic, geared towards inevitable progress, then it shows itself to be the very paradigm of the new conception of reason that the Romantics introduced. It has been an inspiration to all those thinkers ever since, in movements as otherwise diverse as American pragmatism and the Frankfurt School, who have sought to work out a less metaphysical, more social conception of reason' (Larmore, 1996: 48). The Romantic philosophy of belonging represents a further step in intellectual clarity. The Romantic conception of reason, Larmore points out, also represents an *innovation*. Traditionalism does not mean 'recovering' a pre–Enlightenment form of thought: it is itself modern. The community to which we affirm our belonging, therefore, is not simply given, but is also reconceived and imagined (Larmore, 1996: 60–61).

Another key aspect of Romanticism according to Larmore's account is irony, or 'the disquiet of never feeling fully at home' (Larmore, 1996: 70), whereby we hold back from identifying completely with what we nonetheless affirm. Contrary to Hegel, Larmore asserts, irony is not the absence of commitment, but is necessary for commitment. The mature mind needs to be able to stand back from a belief or practice and look at it from the outside. Recognising that our deepest convictions are a leap of faith rather than objects of rational choice is to look at these commitments ironically (Larmore, 1996: 81–82).

A different way of being an individual, according to the Romantic legacy, is the idea of authenticity. Authenticity, Larmore argues, means not acting with an eye to social convention — not that we act unaffected by it (Larmore, 1996: 90). Charles Taylor traces the emergence of the 'ethic of authenticity' to Rousseau and Herder. Rousseau articulated the idea that I am free when I decide for myself what concerns me, rather than being shaped by external influences. Subsequently Herder put forward the idea that each of us has an original way of being human and gave a new importance to being true to oneself, something which only each individual can articulate and discover (Taylor, 1991: 27–29).

Although Larmore has distinguished three aspects of Romanticism, it is evident that these are inter–connected. For example, the idea of authenticity overlaps with the Romantic theme of community. Taylor points out that human life is fundamentally 'dialogical' in character (Taylor, 1991: 33). We become full human agents, capable of understanding ourselves through dialogue with others who matter to us and the ideal of authenticity depends upon this dialogical feature of our condition. To define ourselves, we have to take as background some sense of what is significant, and this means taking into account history, nature, society, and 'the demands of solidarity' (Taylor, 1991: 40).[1]

The emergence of the ethic of authenticity is also inter–connected with the Romantic emphasis on the role of the creative imagination. Taylor points out that previously the artist could draw on publicly available reference points, but since the end of the eighteenth century these reference points no longer hold for us. The decline of an old order with its established background of meanings made necessary the development of new poetic languages in the Romantic period (Taylor, 1991: 83–84). There was a change from a mimetic to a creative conception of poetry and this was not merely a critical philosophical phenomenon. The modern poem, Taylor points out, must both formulate its own cosmic syntax and shape the poetic reality that the cosmic syntax permits. 'Nature', which was once prior to the poem and available for imitation, now shares with the

---

[1] The development of one's identity through dialogue, partly overt and partly internalised, with others gives an importance to recognition (Taylor, 1991: 48).

poem a common origin in the poet's creativity. The Romantic poets and their successors make us aware of something for which there are as yet no adequate words (Taylor, 1991: 85). Each new 'order' can become ours only through being ratified afresh in the sensibility of each new reader (Taylor, 1991: 87).

It can be argued, following Taylor, that this subjective turn in post–Romantic art does not rule out the fact that authenticity connects us to a wider whole. I suggest, however, and this is where my interpretation differs from Taylor's, that this wider whole is human community, not an objective and transcendent 'nature'. This point takes our discussion to the subject of 'historicism'.

As Boucher points out, historicism does not have a determinate meaning but, nevertheless, a number of broad features can be attributed to the concept. The essence of historicism is a stress upon the contextual nature of understanding human beings. According to Boucher,

> The term historicism, then, has been used in many contradictory ways. It is used to refer to anyone who may believe that an historical study of an event offers a valid form of knowledge; to stigmatise those who love the past for the sake of the past; to denigrate those who refuse to pass moral judgements on past actions; to ridicule those who have perceived grandiose patterns in history; to disapprove of those who espouse any form of mild or radical relativism; to sneer at those who see history in terms of constant progress. It describes those who are firmly committed to an independent and autonomous discipline of history, and those who would transform it into something else. (Boucher, 1985: 18)

Dilthey is widely regarded as one of the main initiators of historicism. As Bruce Haddock points out, sustained criticism of the conception of historical knowledge as a monolith susceptible of understanding according to a method common to all the empirical sciences first began to emerge in Germany with Dilthey, who distinguished between *Geisteswissenschaften* and *Naturwissenschaften*. Hegel was the philosophical patriarch of the movement, and in Italy, with Benedetto Croce, a radically reconstructed Hegel became the fountainhead of a new historicism which asserted the supremacy and logical priority of historical knowledge (Haddock, 1980: 154). Collingwood, as a follower of Croce, was a leading philosophical exponent of the new idealism.

As Rubinoff explains,

> Against the dogma of positivism there arose in the nineteenth century, under the banner of historicism, various attempts to rescue the human and social sciences from the domination of the natural sciences. For most

historicists their quarrel with positivism had serious existential implications concerning the foundations of culture itself (Rubinoff, 1970: 345).

They believed that the very survival of a culture depended upon its ability to resist the dehumanising effects of positivism. Rubinoff refers to Droysen, Nietzsche, Croce, and Ortega y Gasset, all of whom regarded positivism as a threat to European culture. It was in the spirit of the historicist assault on positivism that Collingwood, at various points in his career, described positivism as a threat to science and civilisation and saw history as the antidote (Rubinoff, 1970: 346).

The foundations of historicism, therefore, can be located in the radicalisation of the Hegelian tradition which occurred in the latter half of the nineteenth century. According to Eugene F. Miller,

> The world, or nature, came to be understood in terms of flux, change, or becoming rather than fixity, permanence, or being. Knowledge was now conceived in terms of creation rather than discovery. Worldviews and theories were seen as individual or social creations, which are shaped decisively by sub rational forces. It was denied that the human mind can grasp the character of 'reality' or 'nature' in any final, objective, or absolute way. The position which I have described was developed comprehensively by Friedrich Nietzsche in the 1800s. Yet a number of other thinkers at that time and in the decades that followed came to similar conclusions, often independently of the influence of Nietzsche or of each other (Miller, 1972: 796).

This position, Miller argues, was expressed by the American pragmatists, in England by Collingwood and Wittgenstein, and in France by Bergson, Sartre and Merleau–Ponty, and it gained wide acceptance in Germany through the influence of Nietzsche, Dilthey, Spengler, Mannheim, and Heidegger (Miller, 1972: 797).

The consciousness of history and 'becoming', then, are central characteristics of our world sense today. As Collingwood argues, natural science had appeared to be the eighteenth century's model discipline, so in the contemporary world society tends to see in the historical perspective the archetype of its approach to reality (IH, 209 and 232). John T. Marcus remarks that the historically oriented outlook is marked by the consciousness of a distinctive dimension to man's being. Bergson and Heidegger, for example, found the essence of man's consciousness in the 'historicity' of the awareness of self:

> Thus the historical sense, whether understood or only felt, becomes synonymous with the ontological quality of man. And the distinctive dimension of the human condition reveals itself to be the identification of man's being with the process of his becoming (Marcus, 1962: 31).

Miller makes a number of points to characterise historicism. Firstly, historicism claims that there is no direct awareness of pure sense–data. It agrees with Kant that we apprehend sense–data only as unified and structured by *a priori* principles or categories of the mind. The experience of which we are aware has already been selected and shaped by the mind itself. Secondly, whereas Kant thought that the principles of understanding are constant from one epoch or society to another, historicism follows Hegel in asserting that the very ordering principles or categories of the mind have varied with the succession of epochs and cultures. Each epoch develops a characteristic view of the world in its totality; and essential differences will be found from one epoch or culture to another in the presuppositions, values, and categories upon which cognition is based. All knowledge is perspectival in character and arises not so much from discovery of the real character of nature as from social or individual creation (Miller, 1972: 800). Another characteristic of historicism, as Rader points out, is that it posits an affinity of art and history, and this is the case with 'the best representatives of the historicists': Croce, Collingwood, and Dilthey (Rader, 1967: 158).

Collingwood's emphasis, therefore, on historical thinking as a solution to the ills of modernity was part of the broader phenomenon of historicism. In this Collingwood differed from the earlier British idealists, to whom he owed much. The earlier British idealists failed to display a strong understanding of history and hence, like Oakeshott, Collingwood attempted to derive fresh inspiration from the new generation of Continental idealists and neo–idealists (cf. Boucher, 1985: 50).

For Collingwood, history and the study of human affairs had become the central preoccupation of the present age, and this was paralleled by the priority of historiography and philosophy of history in twentieth–century thought, which had a practical as well as a theoretical basis. Commenting on the First World War in his *Autobiography*, Collingwood remarked on the contrast between success in controlling situations which were part of the physical world and failure to control situations in which human beings are elements. By the late 1930s the triumph of natural science seemed to go hand in hand with the gradual destruction of civilisation. Collingwood's solution to this problem, as Rubinoff points out, was to seek a proper understanding of the human mind.[2] However, unlike behaviourism and positivism, which treated the human mind as if it were a mere

---

[2]   Here I am drawing upon Lionel Rubinoff's *Collingwood and the Reform of Metaphysics* (1970: 4).

species of nature, history, according to Collingwood, was the genuine science of the human mind. It is only through history that we can grasp the fact that human activity is free (IH, 315, 319–20).

However, historical thought which apprehends the fact of freedom is itself a necessary condition of the existence of that freedom. The historical process 'is a process in which man creates for himself this or that kind of human nature by recreating in his own thought the past to which he is heir' (IH, 226). As Collingwood argues in *The New Leviathan*, it is in the world of history rather than in the world of nature that man finds the central problems he has to solve (Rubinoff, 1970: 4). Collingwood argued that just as the chief business of seventeenth–century philosophy was to reckon with seventeenth–century natural science, so the chief business of twentieth–century philosophy is to reckon with twentieth–century history (A, 78–79). According to Collingwood in 'The Present Need of a Philosophy':

> As the seventeenth century needed a reasoned conviction that nature is intelligible and the problems of science in principle soluble, so the twentieth needs a reasoned conviction that human progress is possible and that the problems of moral and political life are in principle soluble. In both cases the need is one which only philosophy can supply. What is needed today is a philosophical reconsideration of the whole idea of progress or development, and especially its two main forms, 'evolution' in the world of nature and 'history' in the world of human affairs. What would correspond to the Renaissance conception of nature as a single intelligible system would be a philosophy showing that human will is of a piece with nature in being genuinely creative; that social and political institutions are creations of the human will, conceived by the same power which created them, and essentially plastic to its hand; and that whatever evils they contain are in principle remediable. In short, the help which philosophy might give our 'dissatisfied, anxious, apprehensive generation' would lie in a reasoned statement of the principle that there can be no evils in any human institution which human will cannot cure (EPP, 169).

As Rubinoff explains, Collingwood also saw the sciences of mind as historical because he repudiated all theories which presuppose the conception of mind or human nature as a fixed and unchanging substance. Reality is a 'dialectical' process of change, and the being of mind, if it is to be found at all, is to be found only in its acts, as art, religion, science, history, philosophy, and so on (Rubinoff, 1970: 6).

However, despite its emphasis on process and becoming, and on the contextual nature of understanding, historicism ought to be distinguished from relativism. According to Rubinoff, historicism of the radical variety implies that while history teaches us that there have been changing views, it cannot teach us whether the change was sound or whether the rejected view deserves to be rejected, without presupposing what it denies — namely that there are eternal objective truths.[3] Rubinoff refers to Leo Strauss's argument that historicism asserts that all human thoughts and beliefs are historical, but historicism is itself a human thought and hence can only be of temporary validity. Historicism, according to Rubinoff, claims to have brought to light a truth valid for all thought and for all time (Rubinoff, 1970: 361). Similarly, Miller claims that historicism is essentially relativist because, for historicism, there is no supra–temporal truth which can be grasped from above the historical stream (Miller, 1972: 801). Marcus declares that by the twentieth century historical relativism and the abandonment of transcendent ideals had led to a sense of collapse of the moral order and the impossibility of any order of values (Marcus, 1962: 39).

Contrary to Rubinoff and Miller, I suggest that historicism is agnostic on the question of whether or not there are eternal truths and claims that truths ought to be apprehended as being within historical contexts. Historicism presupposes that its own position is to some extent 'true'. But it is true only in comparison with other philosophies within the same process of development. Boucher rightly argues that Collingwood was a historicist in believing that in the context of a complex of circumstances the historical understanding must conclude that things could not be other than what they were. But he was prepared to pass judgement on whether one set of circumstances was better than another, and was thus not a relativist (Boucher, 1995a: 22). My point is that the criteria for this judgement themselves ought to be viewed as being immanent to the complex of circumstances or the historical process. This distinction between historicism and relativism will be explored in more detail in Part Two.

Romanticism and historicism, then, obviously overlap one another. This is evident in what H. Stuart Hughes calls the 'emerging critical consciousness' of the early twentieth century (Hughes, 1959: 9). Hughes argues that in the time–span of the forty years from the *fin de siècle* to the beginning of the 1930s, the major innovators were the last in a long succession of system–builders descending from

[3]   Rubinoff distinguishes between transcendental historicism and radical historicism. Transcendental historicism means that philosophical truth, while it is historically grounded, is nevertheless absolute and trans-historical. Radical historicism is the tendency to interpret the whole of reality in historical terms and, according to Rubinoff, radical historicism leads to scepticism (Rubinoff, 1970: 359).

Aristotle, but they introduced a period of specialisation. They had drawn no clear line between literature and social science, but their rigour precluded the formation of successors in their own image. For these thinkers, the problem of consciousness became crucial, and emotion became central. Man, they came to see, was guided in his conduct by supra- or infra-rational values, and this also applied to the scientific observer (Hughes, 1959: 15–16). The work of this 'generation of the 1890s', Hughes argues, risked falling into radical scepticism, and encouraged an anti–intellectualism to which the majority of them were intensely hostile. The greatest of these thinkers fought to salvage as much as possible of the rationalist heritage, and shifted the axis of that tradition to make room for man as something more than a logically calculating animal (Hughes, 1959: 17).

According to Hughes, in what he calls 'the generation of the 1890s', the towering figures of the era were Sigmund Freud, Max Weber and Benedetto Croce, and Wilhelm Dilthey is seen as a precursor (Hughes, 1959: 20). A critique of the Enlightenment was one of the central tasks that social thinkers of the early twentieth century set themselves. However, the hostility of these thinkers, especially Weber and Croce, was directed not so much against the eighteenth–century tradition in its original guise as against its late nineteenth–century reincarnation—in travestied form—as the cult of positivism (cf. Hughes, 1959: 29). Hughes points out that, in the intellectual revolution that took place in the decade of the 1890s and the one succeeding it, the basic assumptions of eighteenth- and nineteenth–century social thought underwent a critical review from which there emerged the new assumptions of our own time (Hughes, 1959: 33). It was seen by some as the *fin de siècle* or the end of an era. In the work of Freud, Weber, Croce, Durkheim, Sorel and others there was an attack on positivism, and naturalistic explanations of human conduct were seen as radically insufficient (Hughes, 1959: 37).

Hughes also argues that in the twentieth century imaginative literature came to play a more serious and self–conscious role in the enunciation of values than was the case in the two preceding centuries. The major novel or play has devolved the task of making concrete and thereby more readily approachable the abstract insights of philosophers and social scientists. In the twentieth century, according to Hughes, philosophy has tended to be replaced by social science on the one hand, and imaginative literature on the other, and the 'generation of the 1890's' are a part of this transition (Hughes, 1959: 21–25). Imaginative writers of the early twentieth century,

such as Gide, Mann, Hesse, Proust and Pirandello, occupied themselves with themes similar to those that troubled social theorists. The
sense of living under high tension, Hughes explains, was common.
They had a conviction that they were living in historical circumstances in which all fixed norms were lacking: the old ethic had collapsed, and a new one was yet to be found (Hughes, 1959: 364).

The principal themes of this book also overlap with some of the
central concerns of philosophy in the latter half of the twentieth century. Historicism employed distinctive methodologies, distinguish-
ing the human sciences from the natural sciences, including the
procedure of understanding, or *verstehen* (cf. Hughes, 1959: 187),
and the methodologies of historicism have become intimately
related to hermeneutics. As well as being a historicist, Collingwood
is directly related to the hermeneutic tradition, and has had a considerable impact upon the continental hermeneutic tradition, with
Bultmann, Gadamer, Pannenburg, Lonergan and Ricoeur indebted
to him (cf. Boucher, 1995a: 17).

According to Parker, Collingwood can also be seen as providing a
solution to some of the problems raised by postmodernism. Parker
argues that while the postmodernist critique of modernism implicates earlier idealists, this is not the case with Bradley, Oakeshott
and Collingwood. Similarities between modern idealism and
postmodernism are, according to Parker, 'very strong' (Parker, 2000:
224). For Parker, Collingwood's attack on the realist doctrine that the
subject or knower of knowledge could not affect the object or known
could help postmodernism in the struggle against relativism
(Parker, 2000: 229).

In his concern with the crisis of modernity, therefore,
Collingwood is both a Romantic and a historicist, and this chapter so
far has attempted to provide an introductory overview of these
movements. As our exploration of the theme of the crisis of civilisation in his philosophy unfolds in more detail, Collingwood's place in
the context of these movements will become clearer.

At this point, I want to turn to a discussion of Collingwood's treatment of the problem of the crisis of civilisation in his early philosophy. In the early part of Collingwood's career, his Romanticism,
historicism and concern with the ills of modernity manifest themselves in a preoccupation with the unity of the forms of experience.
In this, as I will explain, Collingwood was influenced by his father,
W.G. Collingwood and John Ruskin. Collingwood had also inherited a concern with unity of mind from the British and Italian Idealists and from Hegel.

As Boucher indicates,

> In Hegel's mind, we understand a part only by looking at it as part of a whole. The early stages of something are only properly understood when they are seen as the early stages of something more fully developed (Boucher, 1997: xix).

The British Idealists imported Hegel's rejection of all dualisms. They subscribed to Hegel's insistence on the unity of experience and

> ... sought to demonstrate that there could be no absolute divisions, for example, between mind and nature, nature and environment, or the individual and the state. Each includes something of the other and their opposition is overcome in a unity, not one that obliterates differences, but one that is a genuine unity in diversity (Boucher, 1997: xi).

One of the central claims, then, in Collingwood's early philosophy is that Western civilisation has reached a point of crisis because of the detachment of the forms of experience from one another. In *Speculum Mentis*, published in 1924, he argues that it is the special problem of modern life that, on the one hand, there is an unsatisfied demand for art, religion and philosophy, and, on the other hand, there is a crowd of artists, philosophers and ministers of religion who can find no market for their wares. The producers and consumers of spiritual wealth are out of touch (SM, 20). There is a difference between our age and earlier ages, a special *maladie du siècle* which is endemic among us and which we can detect if we compare our society with that of former times, for example, the Middle Ages (SM, 22–23). Medieval man had a firm grip on what we may call the unity of mind: no mental activity existed in its own right and for itself. Art worked hand in hand with religion, and religion hand in hand with philosophy. There was no separation between secular art and religious art (SM, 27).

However, Collingwood argues,

> Art, religion and philosophy are not really the same thing: there are differences between them which need not appear as long as they are at a comparatively low level of development, but appear all too sharply when they reach maturity (SM, 29).

To reach full development, art, religion and philosophy must separate and go each its own way. This separation occurred in the Renaissance, and meant freedom for all the different activities of the mind from interference by each other. The medieval unity of the mind, however, also included freedom, the freedom of occupying an ordained place, in which there is no conflict, 'a positive freedom, like the freedom of a child at play' (SM, 30).

The freedom of the Renaissance is a negative freedom, bought at the price of internal conflict. Religion of the Reformation and the counter–reformation adopted a puritanical and philistine attitude to art and to thought, but reached a new pitch of religious intensity (SM, 31). Art played at reverting to paganism and became irreligious, but also gave birth to a galaxy of great artists. Yet, Collingwood argues, Renaissance art is overshadowed by brooding tragedy:

> Nothing is more typical of the Renaissance than the quality of its laughter: the way in which for Shakespeare the dreadfulness of life lurks among the rose leaves of the lightest comedy, or the way in which Molière jokes like a man who watches himself dying by inches and has nothing left to do but laugh at his ridiculous body (SM, 32).

According to Collingwood, religion cannot live without art and philosophy. But now that art and philosophy have parted company from religion, it cannot employ them. Therefore it invented neo–Gothic and neo–Scholasticism, as it is incapable of keeping up with the advance of art and thought as it did in the Middle Ages (SM, 33). Art, religion and thought have each tended to become a specialised activity, pursued by specialists, and have lost touch with the people:

> Today we can be as artistic, we can be as philosophical, we can be as religious as we please, but we cannot ever be men at all; we are wrecks and fragments of men, and we do not know where to take hold of life and how to begin looking for the happiness which we know we do not possess (SM, 35).

For Collingwood, then, the answer is to re–establish the unity of experience:

> What is wrong with us is precisely the detachment of these forms of experience — art, religion, and the rest — from one another; and our cure can only be their complete reunion in a complete and undivided life (SM, 36).

However, the advance from the Middle Ages to the Renaissance was a real advance, and a re–union must allow for the full development of each form of experience, unlike in the Middle Ages. This answer is

> … the fundamental principle of Christianity that the only life worth living is the life of the whole man, every faculty of body and soul unified into a single organic system. Incarnation, redemption, resurrection of the body, only repeat this cardinal idea from different angles (SM, 37).

Unity of the forms of experience can be achieved either positively, by bringing every activity into harmony, or negatively, by suppressing all but one. The former was the medieval way, the latter that of the Renaissance. 'Our solution, then', Collingwood argues, 'can only be in principle the Christian solution; but it must not be the naïve Christianity of the middle ages or the self–mutilated Christianity of the Renaissance, but something in which the good of both these is preserved, the bad destroyed' (SM, 38). In this he claims to be following and working out the Romantic movement,

> ... purifying it, perhaps, of some things that are worthless today, but happy if we can attain anything like the clearness of vision and closeness of thought which they attained, and anxious above all not to pose as repositories of a new revelation, or vendors of any new–fangled philosophical patent–medicine, but to say once more, in words suited to our generation, something that everybody has always known (SM, 38).

The ideal of a many–sided intellectual life, and the unity of the forms of experience, was something Collingwood inherited from John Ruskin, mediated through his father, W.G. Collingwood. However, as William M. Johnston argues, Collingwood in *Speculum Mentis* seems to differ from Ruskin in the demand for greater precision in philosophy. For Collingwood, philosophy is the most effective tool for seeking unity of mind. Ruskin's exhorting of others to pursue a variety of activities gives way to a delineation of the principal activities which the mind pursues (Johnston, 1967: 96).

Collingwood describes five forms of experience in *Speculum Mentis*: art, religion, science, history and philosophy, proceeding in a scale from the most primitive to the most elaborate. Concurrently with the rise of each form of experience, there emerges a type of dogmatic philosophy based on it. Each one shares the limitations of their corresponding form of experience and serves to justify its one–sidedness. True philosophy emerges only after the other four forms of experience and their corresponding philosophies have come into existence. The task of true philosophy is to expose the limitations of the other forms of experience (see Johnston, 1967: 97).

Johnston argues that Croce is the contemporary thinker whom the early Collingwood most resembles. Croce's philosophy of culture began to take shape when, turning from Marxism to aesthetics, he set himself the task of trying to set out the chief modes of operation of the mind or spirit. Croce's 'philosophy of spirit', whereby he attempts to describe the spheres of experience, had great significance for the early Collingwood, and Collingwood's *Speculum Mentis* was his attempt to improve upon Croce. It was Croce who resurrected this approach to philosophy in the early twentieth century (Johnston, 1967: 75–76).

However, Croce distinguishes sharply between theory and practice, something which Collingwood criticises in 'Croce's Philosophy of History', as it violates his basic principle that the mind is indivisible. According to Johnston, Collingwood went much further than Croce in the effort to unite thought and life, and in so doing he was following a tradition quite removed from anything which Croce had experienced in Italy, namely the educational ideal of John Ruskin (Johnston, 1967: 83–84).

Not only is unity of mind an important part of what Collingwood regards as the solution to the crisis of Western civilisation, but artistic expression and historical thinking are also important. Collingwood had already described Ruskin as an apostle of the ideal of unity of mind in an earlier lecture, *Ruskin's Philosophy*, delivered in 1919.[4] Ruskin is described as an unwitting Hegelian. However, in *Ruskin's Philosophy* Collingwood also demonstrates the connection between the unity of mind and historicism.

Collingwood argues that a man's philosophy is a central thread on which his actions are strung, a constant purpose, or a consistent point of view running through all his work. There are 'certain central principles which the man takes as fundamental and incontrovertible, which he assumes as true in all his thinking and acting' (EPA, 10). These principles form a 'ring' of solid thought — often they are in motion, but a motion seldom perceptible by the naked eye. The ring is formed by a number of different ideas or principles, welded together by some force of mutual cohesion. This central core of convictions is, for the most part, unknown to us, and we do not know what the convictions are which constitute it. According to Collingwood, 'The fact seems to be that a man's deepest convictions are precisely those which he never puts into words' (EPA, 11). The business of the philosopher is to probe into the mind and uncover people's ultimate beliefs.

As Johnston points out, the emphasis on judging a person by premises inherent in both his or her words and deeds characterised Collingwood throughout his career. The nucleus of the later theory of philosophy as question and answer is here (Johnston, 1967: 59). It might be added that *Ruskin's Philosophy* also anticipates the later theory of absolute presuppositions (cf. Connelly, 2003: 117).

---

[4]   Although originally published in 1919, *Ruskin's Philosophy* was reprinted in Collingwood's *Essays in the Philosophy of Art*, (1964) edited with an Introduction by Alan Donagan; abbreviated as EPA. It is to this copy of *Ruskin's Philosophy* that I will refer.

According to Collingwood in *Ruskin's Philosophy*, 'One of the most remarkable facts about the history of thought in the middle nineteenth century is the conflict between two methods of thinking which I shall call the Logical and the Historical' (EPA, 12). The Logical method of thinking proceeds on the assumption that every individual fact is an instance of some eternal and unchanging principle, some law to which time makes no difference; and that the general law is more important than the particular fact. The aim of knowledge, therefore, is to discover these general laws. To explain a fact is to show what law it exemplifies. The task of the statesman is so to govern his country that its national life shall so far as possible obey and exemplify the eternal principles of justice and the natural rights of man.

This type of thought leads to a contempt for facts, a habitual intolerance, and a tendency towards monotony and rigidity in mental work. These qualities are conspicuous during the seventeenth and eighteenth centuries, the 'age of rationalism'. Political theorists of the time, Collingwood contends, believed in systems of eternal and immutable rights, from which political institutions drew their validity, and art critics believed in the 'unities' of the stage and in a rigid adherence to classical forms (EPA, 13–14).

Where the logical mind looks for general laws, according to Collingwood, the historical mind looks for individual facts, and it explains these facts by appealing not to laws but to other facts. Faced with the problems of political life, it tries not so much to determine the natural rights of man as to get at the rights and wrongs of this particular war, controversy or proposal. This type of thought is the reverse of everything we mean by the word doctrinaire (EPA, 14). Hence its natural inclination is always toward tolerance; for it respects facts to such an extent as to suppose that nothing can ever have existed unless it had something to say for itself.

The historical habit of thought was coming into existence in the early nineteenth century, and its rise was shown in a growing interest in the Middle Ages, and growing freedom with regard to art–forms (as shown by the difference between Pope and Browning). Also, there was a growing scepticism with regard to the permanence of political structures (EPA, 15). Logic in the nineteenth century was different from that of the seventeenth and eighteenth centuries, which was the old scholastic logic of formal correctness, consistency, clarity and definiteness in thinking. The logical mind distorted history. Collingwood argues:

No one can be a true historian till he realizes that truth is many–sided and not to be attained by the pursuit of logical consistency; till he has discovered that he cannot be both an historian and, in the old sense of the word, a logician. But this very fact led to the rejection of the old logic, and the growth of a new logic whose whole being was rooted in history; so that just as logicism produced its own school of history, historicism created for itself a logic (EPA, 16).

By Ruskin's time, according to Collingwood, historicism was beginning to show itself as the philosophy of the future. The teaching in which it was systematically expressed, that of Hegel, superseded all previous philosophies. Of this historical movement Ruskin was a whole–hearted adherent. He had the same outlook on the world, the same instinctive attitude towards reality, which made Hegel rewrite logic in terms of history (EPA, 17).

Collingwood argues that the historicism of Ruskin has 'a whole cycle of unmistakable consequences'. The first and most important is the belief in the unity or solidarity of the human spirit. For Ruskin, the art of a particular person or nation is connected with questions of morality, religion, politics, and so on. 'If there is something visibly good or bad in the art of a certain people at a certain date, he always assumes that there must have been corresponding virtues and vices in their moral and political life' (EPA, 18). Each form of human activity is an expression of the whole self. This principle of the unity and indivisibility of the spirit can be shown to proceed from the historical trend of his philosophy. The logical habit of mind takes the historical fact of, say, ancient Greece, and analyses this fact into abstract conceptions such as art, religion, political institutions and so on. The historical habit of mind, on the contrary, takes the historical fact of ancient Greece as a whole, and regards this fact as ultimately real. Thus, for the historical mind, Plato and Phidias both expressed the Greek spirit. For the logical mind, Plato belongs to the eternal company of philosophers, and Phidias to the equally eternal and equally exclusive army of artists. This principle of the unity of the spirit constitutes a breach with the trend of eighteenth century philosophy and a point of contact with Hegel, in whose philosophy it was a cardinal axiom.

For Collingwood, the second point in which Ruskin's thought shows a historical tendency is the emphasis which he lays upon historical causes: 'In the hands of a logically minded person, history becomes a mere succession of events, fact following fact with little or no internal cohesion. To a historically minded person, on the contrary, history is a drama, the unfolding of a plot in which each situation leads necessarily to the next' (EPA, 19). Ruskin had a strong interest in the causes of national prosperity and decay, an interest which forced him to devote much of his life to political and economic speculation.

The third characteristic is Ruskin's tolerance, in the sense of feeling the rightness and value of things which lay outside his own personal system of ideals. Ruskin passionately admired many things in medieval art and medieval life, but never wished to reinstate the Middle Ages, nor to copy their characteristic features (EPA, 20–21):

> This tolerance is the surest mark of the historical as opposed to the logical mind; and here, in this imaginative sympathy with the past, as opposed to idolatrous worship of one phase of the past, Ruskin's kinship with Hegel strikingly appears. For the Hegelian treatment of history depends on the principle that every historical phase has its own individual character, ideals and virtues, and that every phase alike should be an object of admiration, none of imitation (EPA, 22).

A fourth characteristic of Ruskin's mind which shows his kinship with Hegel is his attitude towards the logical problem of contradiction. Collingwood argues:

> The old logic lays it down that of two contradictory propositions one must be false and the other true. To contradict yourself, on this view, is a sign of mental confusion: the wise man never contradicts himself. The alternative view starts from the axiom that there are two sides to every question, and that there is right on both sides; from this, the inference is drawn that truth is many–sided and that self–contradiction may easily be a mark not of weakness but of strength—not of confusion, but of a wide and comprehensive view which embraces much more truth than the one–sided consistency of the logicians (EPA, 22).

Ruskin adopted and defended the second of these views. Collingwood cites from Ruskin's Cambridge Inaugural Lecture:

> I have never met with a question yet, of any importance, which did not need, for the right solution of it, at least one positive and one negative answer, like an equation of the second degree. Mostly, matters of any consequence are three–sided, or four–sided, or polygonal; and the trotting round a polygon is severe work for people any way stiff in their opinions (EPA, 22–23).

Ruskin believed that by contradicting himself he got nearer the truth. According to Collingwood,

> Both in Hegel's case and in Ruskin's, the recognition of this principle is associated with a sympathetic understanding of history; and, as we have already seen, the one is hardly possible without the other. The history of a struggle—and all history is the history of struggles—cannot be written by a man who believes that one party must have been right and the other wrong (EPA, 23).

Ruskin's historicism, however, accentuated his opposition to the philosophers of his day (EPA, 24). Collingwood argues that English Kantians, such as Sir William Hamilton and Coleridge, interpreted Kant's philosophy as a thoroughgoing example of the logical view of contradiction, namely that of two contrary propositions one must be false. Also, the Kantians firmly believed in the reality of distinctions within the mind. Ruskin thought of art, religion, and politics as 'alternative manifestations of the same indivisible spirit, acting and reacting on each other with perfect freedom'. The Kantians on the contrary believed that the mind had 'a number of different faculties which worked, to all intents and purposes, in so many watertight compartments', and they distinguished between the theoretical and practical functions (EPA, 25–26).

The ideas of the English Kantians were popularised so as to dominate the thought of the Victorian age. According to Collingwood,

> During the whole of the central and later Victorian period it was usual for educated and thoughtful Englishmen to believe as a matter of course that the mind has two faculties, the theoretical and the practical, and that the theoretical was fundamentally unreliable, while the practical was always trustworthy (EPA, 26).

Hence,

> it became the fashion to despair of solving difficult intellectual problems, while moral problems of at least equal difficulty were held to be soluble without hesitation, by the employment of the faculty called conscience which you had only to obey and all would be well.

This combination of intellectual scepticism with moral dogmatism

> made the Victorian Englishman appear in the eyes of the world as a prig and a Philistine, religious in it, and proud of his ignorance, confident in his sense of justice and 'fair play' … It was the same fallacy that underlay the typically Victorian suggestion that the doctrines of Christian belief should be given up as being incapable of proof, while the Christian ethics should be preserved, as the best ethical system in existence (EPA, 27).

Ruskin, therefore, was at cross–purposes with his age.

Collingwood argues that Ruskin used his belief in the unity of mind as a philosophical weapon. His synthetic habit of mind laid stress on resemblances and connections between problems, which resulted in a frequent appeal to argument by analogy (EPA, 30). Collingwood cites a passage from Ruskin in *Modern Painters*:

> There are laws of truth and right in painting, just as fixed as those of harmony in music or of affinity in chemistry. Those laws are perfectly ascertainable by labour, and ascertainable no otherwise. It is as ridiculous for any one to speak positively about painting who has not given a greater

part of his life to its study, as it would be for a person who had never studied chemistry to give a lecture on affinities of elements; but it is also as ridiculous for a person to speak hesitantly about laws of painting who has conscientiously given time to their ascertainment, as it would be for Mr. Faraday to announce in a dubious manner that iron had an affinity of oxygen, and to put it to the vote of his audience whether it had or not (EPA, 31).

Ruskin, then, assumes that chemistry and painting are alike an example of the free activity of the human spirit. According to Collingwood, this analogical method of reasoning is a dangerous weapon to use. But in skilled hands it is a weapon of immense power, clearing the ground of unnecessary argument and accomplishing a vast amount of varied work with the least possible waste of energy (EPA, 32).

Ruskin's belief in the unity of mind leads him to deny that art is a thing by itself, which can thrive in a vacuum, cut off from the general interests of humanity. Art is expression, and it cannot arise until one has something to express. Ruskin opposed the idea of Art for Art's sake, issuing as it did from the analytic or separating tendency in the Victorian mind. He tried to express the idea that for art to be healthy, it must strike its roots deep into the common earth of life, with all its interests, passions and prejudices (EPA, 33–34).

Because of his synthetic view of the human mind, and hence of the connection between art and morality, Ruskin is mystified by the fact that the attainment of perfection in art often seems to herald the downfall of a civilisation, while a high state of moral nobility may coexist with a complete absence of art (EPA, 34). It is for Ruskin 'a dark and terrible mystery that perfection and death should walk hand in hand'. Collingwood's answer is that the perfection of any one artistic style or social ideal

> lays a dilemma before the human spirit: either go on repeating the perfection that has been attained, become merely imitative, or else launch out into the void, feeling for a new style or a new ideal, and acquiescing in the death of the old. Such a death is in every way preferable to the decrepitude which is the only alternative (EPA, 37–38).

For Collingwood, then, 'Ruskin was in philosophy the best–equipped mind of his generation'. In an age that was turning from the ideal of abstract, logical, doctrinaire thinking to an ideal of concrete, historical, imaginative thinking, Ruskin refrained from putting his 'new wine' into the 'old bottles of eighteenth century philosophy' (EPA, 40). Ruskin's philosophy is historical, dialectical and synthetic, and it is not the analytic mind, but the synthetic mind, the mind that sees the unity of things, that is rare (EPA, 41).

According to Johnston, Collingwood, in *Ruskin's Philosophy*, singles out those aspects of Ruskin which most resemble Collingwood himself. The emphasis on seeing things as a whole, on unity of the mind, on willingness to contradict oneself, and on the historical habit of mind are all traits of Collingwood (Johnston, 1967: 64).

Collingwood's concern, then, with the unity of the forms of experience can evidently be placed in the broader context of Romanticism and historicism. The unity of the forms of experience corresponds to what Raymond Williams refers to as the Romantic idea of 'culture'. As Williams points out, according to the English Romantic tradition, 'culture' means 'a whole way of life, material, intellectual and spiritual' (Williams, 1993: xvi). Williams emphasises the importance of art in the conception of a 'whole way of life'. According to Williams,

> An essential hypothesis in the development of the idea of culture is that the art of a period is closely and necessarily related to the generally prevalent 'way of life', and further that, in consequence, aesthetic, moral and social judgements are closely interrelated (Williams, 1993: 130).

This is a product of the intellectual history of the nineteenth century. As an idea, the relation between periods of art and periods of society is to be found earlier, in Europe, in the work of, among others, Vico and Herder and Montesquieu, but the decisive emphasis in England begins in the 1830s. Williams cites Kenneth Clark's *The Gothic Revival*: 'the idea of style as something organically connected with society ... does not occur, as far as I know, in the Eighteenth Century' (Williams, 1993: 130).

The development of Romanticism and the examination of the relations between 'culture' and 'civilization', in Coleridge and Carlyle, had prepared the ground for the influence which first Pugin, and later Ruskin, exerted. According to Williams, Ruskin is a major contributor to the development of the complex ideas of culture. For Ruskin, art criticism and the social criticism are inherently and essentially related because both are applications of his concern with beauty or 'truth' (Williams, 1993: 135). On this view, the function of the artist is to reveal the 'essential truth of things' (Williams, 1993: 137).

According to Ruskin, the artist reveals organic life: his goodness is his 'wholeness', and the goodness of society lies in its creation of the conditions for 'wholeness of being' (Williams, 1993: 138). The 'organic society' and the 'whole way of life' are largely drawn from the study and practice of art. Ruskin's standard by which a society must be judged was 'vital beauty', or 'the felicitous fulfilment of function in living things', and whether in its essential order it created the conditions for such a fulfilment (Williams, 1993: 139).

For Ruskin, the evils of society are to be met by a right understanding of 'what kinds of labour are good for men, raising them, and making them happy' (Williams, 1993: 141). Regarding the division of labour, Ruskin argues:

> It is not, truly speaking, the labour that is divided; but the men — divided into mere segments of men — broken into small fragments and crumbs of life … You must make a tool of the creature, or a man of him. You cannot make both … It is … this degradation of the operative into a machine, which, more than any other evil of the times, is leading the mass of the nations everywhere into vain, incoherent, destructive struggling for a freedom of which they cannot explain the nature to themselves … It is not that men are ill fed, but that they have no pleasure in the work by which they make their bread, and therefore look to wealth as the only means of pleasure. It is not that men are pained by the scorn of the upper classes, but they cannot endure their own; for they feel that the kind of labour to which they are condemned is verily a degrading one, and makes them less than men (cited from Williams, 1993: 141–42).

Hence Ruskin held that a society had to be judged in terms of all the human activities and relationships which the methods of manufacture and consumption brought into existence (cf. Williams, 1993: 144).

Williams' account of the Romantic idea of culture, therefore, not only corresponds with Collingwood's conception of the unity of the forms of experience, but it also illustrates the idea of art as a standpoint for a critique of industrialism. As I will explain in the next chapter, the use of a philosophy of art to criticise industrialism is an important part of Collingwood's proposed antidote to the crisis of Western civilisation.

As examples of the Romantic tradition in the twentieth century, Williams refers to D.H. Lawrence, R.H. Tawney, T.S. Eliot and George Orwell, among others. According to Williams, from the Romantic emphasis on 'a whole way of life', we learn that one element of a complex system cannot be changed without affecting the whole. Also it has given us new illustrations of an alternative way of life, and reassures us that the version of life which industrialism has forced on us is neither universal nor permanent (Williams, 1993: 233).

The Romantic context of Collingwood's concern with the unity of the forms of experience is further revealed by comparisons with both Eliot's and Ortega y Gasset's accounts of culture. 'Culture', Eliot explains, is the way of life of a particular people, as made visible in their arts, in their social system, in their habits and customs, in their religion. Eliot asserts that, unlike machinery, culture is something that must grow and you must wait for it to mature in its due time (Eliot, 1962: 119). There can be no European culture if countries are reduced to an identity: 'We need variety in unity: not the unity of organisation, but the unity of nature' (Eliot, 1962: 120).

In Eliot's view, religion is the dominant force in creating a common culture. The common tradition of Christianity has made Europe what it is, and has brought with it common cultural elements:

> An individual European may not believe that the Christian Faith is true, and yet what he says, and makes, and does, will all spring out of his heritage of Christian culture and depend upon that culture for its meaning. Only a Christian culture could have produced a Voltaire or a Nietzsche ... If Christianity goes, the whole of our culture goes. Then you must start painfully again, and you cannot put on a new culture ready made. You must wait for the grass to grow to feed the sheep to give the wool out of which your coat will be made. You must pass through many centuries of barbarism. We should not live to see the new culture, nor would our great–great–great–grandchildren: and if we did, not one of us would be happy in it (Eliot, 1962: 122).

No political and economic organisation can supply what this cultural unity gives. The unity of culture, in contrast to the unity of political organisation, means a variety of loyalties, not just loyalty to the state or super–state. For example, Eliot argues that universities ought to be independent of the governments of the countries in which they are situated. They should not be institutions for the training of an efficient bureaucracy, and they should stand for the preservation of learning and the pursuit of truth (Eliot, 1962: 123).

The idea of 'culture' as a vital aspect of civilisation and a means to its preservation also strongly features in the thought of José Ortega y Gasset. Whereas Eliot emphasises the importance of art in culture, for Ortega y Gasset 'culture' draws much of its content from science. In *Mission of the University*, Ortega argues that, as well as the teaching of learned professions and scientific research, it is thought that university education ought to impart something called 'general culture', the expression implying that the student ought to be given some kind of ornamental knowledge, which in some way is to educate his or her moral character or intellect (MU, 41–44). However, in the medieval epoch, this was what constituted higher education, proper and entire. According to Ortega,

> It was not an ornament for the mind or a training of the character. It was, on the contrary, the system of ideas, concerning the world and human-

ity, which the man of that time possessed. It was, consequently, the repertory of convictions which became the effective guide of his existence (MU, 43).

Life is a chaos through which a person finds 'roads' or 'ways', in the form of culture. For Ortega, 'Culture is what saves human life from being a mere disaster; it is what enables man to live a life which is something above meaningless tragedy or inward disgrace' (MU, 44). Culture is the vital system of ideas of a period. The contemporary university has developed professional instruction and research, but has abandoned almost entirely the transmission of culture, something which ought to be its basic function.

For Ortega, in order to be a cultured person, one must possess the vital idea of the world which has been created by physics, biology, history and speculative philosophy. Otherwise, all things that one does in the world which transcend the boundaries of one's profession will turn out unfortunately. According to Ortega, regarding the uncultured man,

> His political ideas and actions will be inept; his affairs of the heart, beginning with the type of women he will prefer, will be crude and ridiculous; he will bring to his family life an atmosphere of unreality and cramped narrowness, which will warp the upbringing of his children; and outside, with his friends, he will emit thoughts that are monstrosities, and opinions that are a torrent of drivel and bluff (MU, 47).

Like Collingwood, Ortega argues that professionalism and specialisation have 'smashed the European man in pieces', and the task of the university is to reassemble out of scattered pieces a complete living organism (MU, 48).[5] With instruction in professional matters and the methods of science, there is a fabulous profusion of studies, which the ordinary student cannot master. According to Ortega, 'Instead of teaching what *ought* to be taught, according to some Utopian desire', the university must teach only what can be learned. It was the innovation of Rousseau, Pestalozzi, Froebel, and German idealism to shift the centre of gravity of teaching '... from knowledge and the teacher to the learner, recognizing that it is the learner and his characteristics which alone can guide us in our effort to make something organic of education' (MU, 50).

From the eighteenth century onwards life has assumed a huge complexity, and it is impossible to assimilate the profusion of cultural and technical possessions. Like Collingwood's 'principle of the limited objective' in *The New Leviathan* (31.61), Ortega argues that

---

[5]   In more recent times, Beiner (1983) and Gadamer (1981) have argued against this reliance on the expert.

teaching should be based on the 'principle of economy' in education. The minimum curriculum must include only what is necessary for the life of the student, and what the student can really learn with thoroughness and understanding (MU, 55–57).

Culture, or the vital ideas by which an age conducts its life, is the repertory of our active convictions as to the nature of the world and our fellow creatures: convictions as to the hierarchy of the values of things. The vast majority of these convictions or ideas are received by one's historical environment, and 'in our age, the content of culture comes largely from science'. According to Ortega, 'Culture borrows from science what is vitally necessary for the interpretation of our existence' (MU, 66). Unlike science, culture is always urgent, 'here and now', and '... is required to be, at every instant, a complete, unified, coherent system – the plan of life, the path leading through the forest of existence' (MU, 66). The dispersion and complication of science needs to be counterbalanced by consolidation and synthesising of knowledge. According to Ortega, through culture, and the integration of knowledge, the university becomes an agent for the salvation of science itself (MU, 71–72).

Not only does the university need perpetual contact with science, it also needs contact with public life, and the life of the people needs to have the university participate in its affairs. The university should not be a retreat or an institution exclusively for students. It should intervene in 'the thick of life's urgencies and its passions', and assert itself as a major 'spiritual power', higher than the press, standing for serenity, seriousness and the grasp of intellect (MU, 78).

Ortega's conception of culture, however, is just one part of a philosophy where, like Collingwood's, historical and dialectical thinking are seen as the solution to a crisis of modernity. To sum up, therefore, Collingwood, following the Romantic tradition, saw the unity of the forms of experience as a solution to the crisis of Western civilisation. However, as I have argued, the conception of the unity of the forms of experience and the Romantic idea of culture are interconnected with an emphasis on the importance of artistic expression and historical thinking.

Ruskin's Philosophy and *Speculum Mentis* prefigure some of the central points that Collingwood developed in more detail in his later philosophy. Following *Speculum Mentis*, however, Collingwood came to see both the crisis of civilisation and solutions to the problem in a different way. Collingwood argued that the threat to civilisation came not only from the separation of the forms of experience from one another, but the emergence of one form of experience, natural science, which, through philosophies such as positivism and utilitarianism, threatened to suffocate the rest. Collingwood's solutions to the crisis of civilisation also underwent change. The outline of the five forms of experience that he presented in *Speculum Mentis* came to be seen as inadequate and had to be modified in important ways. In particular, art assumed a role of greater prominence, and history came to be more closely connected with philosophy. This meant that the 'historicist' revolution that he described in *Ruskin's Philosophy* became more developed, and the philosophy of art was improved. A closer *rapprochement* between the forms of experience emerged in Collingwood's philosophy, which as I will demonstrate, corrected some of the inadequacies in his earlier writings.

Following *Speculum Mentis*, Collingwood placed greater emphasis on his philosophies of art and of historical and dialectical thinking, which became related solutions to the crisis of civilisation. As a result, the next three chapters will be dedicated to analysing Collingwood's philosophy of art, and discussion of Collingwood's dialectic and 'historicism' is (mostly) postponed until Part Two.

Chapter Two

Art and Craft

In the unpublished manuscript, 'Realism and Idealism' (1936), Collingwood makes an important point which is particularly pertinent to the order of enquiry in this book. Although a long quotation, it is worth citing at length:

> When new ideas begin to dawn upon the human mind, they generally begin by assuming a poetic or imaginative or sentimental shape; they begin as feeling, not yet able to state themselves in clear theoretical form or justify themselves by argument, but nevertheless strong and definite; and in the course of time they work themselves out in the shape of logical thought and so provide themselves with a scientific organization and justification. Over and over again, in the history of human affairs, you will find that a logically complete and orderly system, whether of science or philosophy or legal or social institutions, has been wrecked, not by cool criticism calling attention to logical flaws in its structure, but by the growth of some blind or shapeless, but enormously powerful, feeling which begins by revolting against it as something stupid and irrelevant; this feeling then proceeds, with no apparent justification in logic, to attack the existing system and destroy it by main force, as it were with dynamite, or else simply withdraws from it and leaves it standing as a picturesque but deserted monument to the ingenuity of a past age, while it begins to build up another more to its liking. (RI, B, VII, sect. 2)

Hence when we are confronted by new movements,

> … it is idle to meet them with criticism derived from thought structures already existing; what we must do is first and foremost to feel by experience the quality of life which these new movements contain, and use our judgement to decide whether it is a genuine life, sincere in its quality and rich in promise of new growth, or either a shallow and frivolous affectation or a mere revival, of something that has already tried and failed.

New movements must be tested not by using our heads, but by using our hearts: 'It is only when they have come to maturity that they learn to use their heads, and it is then that we have to use our heads to appraise their merits' (RI, B, VII, sect. 2).

It is in art, then, that we receive the first intimations of profound change in a civilisation, and it is only later that the details are worked out by thought proper. For Collingwood, it is in art, and the subversion of our artistic life, that we find the first evidence and symptoms of the crisis of modernity, and it is the philosophy of art, rather than other areas of philosophy, that deals most directly with this theme. In a sense, therefore, for the purposes of this book, Collingwood's philosophy of art is logically prior to the other aspects of his philosophy. As a result, I will examine his aesthetics first, before proceeding to a more detailed examination of the theme in his theory of logic and metaphysics, in Part Two, and his theory of society, politics and civilisation in Part Three.

For Collingwood, following the principle of the unity of mind, art is something that affects the whole of life.[1] To some extent, we are all artists. Collingwood argues: 'every utterance and every gesture that each one of us makes is a work of art' (PA, 285). One of the improvements to Collingwood's later philosophy is that art is seen to have a closer union with thought, and the place of emotion in his account of the crisis of civilisation assumes greater importance. The crisis of civilisation, according to his later philosophy, is no longer only due to the fragmentation of the unity of the forms of experience, but is more complex. A particularly important factor is the suppression of emotion. According to Collingwood's philosophy of art, the suppression of emotion in the modern industrial world and the predominance of amusement over art proper are evidence of a profound crisis in contemporary civilisation. The suppression of magic and of the emotional aspects of religion are also contributory factors.

Collingwood's conception of art as a standpoint for a critique of contemporary civilisation and as a solution to its ills depends on a distinction between art proper and craft. His distinction of art from craft supports his contention that art is the truthful expression of emotion. Collingwood's philosophy of art, as it emerges in *The Principles of Art*, takes up and develops the Romantic tradition.

In Book I of *The Principles of Art*, Collingwood argues that craft involves various kinds of distinctions not present in art: a distinction between means and end, a distinction between planning and execution and a distinction between raw material and artefact. Art does not involve the distinction between means and end in that the 'poetic labour' in the artist's mind is not the means for creating a poem in the

---

[1]   As Mink points out, it also rests on the claim made in *An Essay on Philosophical Method* that a philosophical concept 'leaks or escapes' out of any limits imposed on its application, as by the rules of classification (Mink, 1969: 206).

way that the craftsman's tools are a means for making an artefact. Similarly, regarding the distinction between raw material and artefact, the words cannot be seen as the raw material of a poem. Collingwood rejects the idea of art as a craft, and the related doctrine of artistic technique: '… however necessary it may be that a poet should have technical skill, he is a poet only in so far as this skill is not identified with art, but with something used in the service of art' (PA, 27). As Aaron Ridley points out, in Collingwood's distinction between art and craft, his concern is entirely negative: he is not claiming that art, unlike craft, never involves distinctions between means and ends, between planning and execution, between raw material and finished product. He is claiming only that art need not involve these, whereas craft always does (Ridley, 1998: 13). In line with the argument of *An Essay on Philosophical Method*, which I will examine in more detail in Part Two of this book, there is an overlap between art and craft (cf. Donagan, 1962: 111–12).

Also *The Principles of Art*, as Connelly points out, follows the recommendation in *An Essay on Philosophical Method* that

> To define a philosophical concept it is necessary, first, to think of that concept as specifying itself in a form so rudimentary that anything less would fail to embody the concept at all. Later phases modify this minimum definition by adding new determinations, each implied in what went before, but each introducing into it qualitative changes as well as additions and complications. (EPM, 100–1)

Hence, in *The Principles of Art*, Collingwood proceeds from the most rudimentary specification to the most advanced. Book I is provisional and it is only in Book III that the full theory of art is given (Connelly, 2003: 16).

Collingwood argues that, unlike craft, what the artist produces consists of two things: an 'internal' thing and a bodily/perceptible thing. The 'internal' thing is most important: 'There is no such thing as an *objet d'art* in itself; if we call any bodily and perceptible thing by that name or an equivalent we do so only because of the relation in which it stands to the aesthetic experience which is the "work of art proper"' (PA, 37). Also, art is not representative, as representation is a craft. For example, a portrait is a work of representation, and aims to capture a likeness. The portrait painter subordinates his artistic powers to the end of making a portrait. However, a portrait can also be a work of art, when the artistry triumphs over the representation and the portrait is an opportunity to create a work of art (PA, 44–45).

Collingwood argues that the mistaken identification of art with representation is responsible for a modern misinterpretation of

Plato's theory of art. Many modern writers on aesthetics attribute to Plato the view that all art is bad because it is imitative. In fact, Collingwood contends, Socrates in Plato's *Republic* divides poetry into two kinds, one representative and the other not. In Book III of *Republic* Plato banishes from his ideal city the representative artist who creates amusement, but not the representative artist who represents the discourse of a good man. In Book X Plato's opinion has changed. Here all representative poetry is banned because it is representative. However, non-representative poetry is retained. Plato, according to Collingwood, does not regard poetry in general as representative. Tragedy and comedy were kinds of poetry that Plato classified as representative. For Plato in Book X, all drama must go, and he finds himself left with that kind of poetry whose chief representative is Pindar (PA, 46–48). Aristotle's *Poetics* defends amusement art against Plato's attack, arguing that the emotions generated in tragedy, for example, are discharged in the experience of watching tragedy. Plato's analysis, however, is related to the problem of the decadence of the Greek world, which is not appreciated by Aristotle. Plato regards the replacement of an old magico-religious art with a new amusement art as a symptom of this decadence (PA, 50–52).

Collingwood identifies three different levels of representation. Firstly, a naive, almost non-selective representation attempts complete literalness, examples of which can be found in Palaeolithic animal painting and Egyptian portrait-sculpture (PA, 54). Secondly, there is literal representation which emphasises characteristic features and omits all else: for example, a drawing of a dance might leave out the dancers altogether and just trace the pattern. A portrait may depart from literal representation to emotional representation. For example, a portrait of a fearsome wild animal may have its teeth and claws magnified; a person of whom we stand in awe seems to have large and piercing eyes (PA, 54). On the third level, emotional representation abandons literal representation altogether. A Brahms song, for example, may evoke a feeling remarkably similar to that which a person feels on a summer's day (PA, 56).

Representative art, as distinct from art proper, is the subordination of art to a certain end, the end being to induce a certain state of mind or emotion in the audience. Collingwood discusses two kinds of representative art: magic and amusement. Magic, he insists, is not pseudo-science or neurosis. Anthropologists studying 'savage' civilisations were led by their prejudices to compare the magical practices of the savage with the scientific knowledge of civilised man, and concluded that magic is erroneous natural science (PA, 57–61). Similarly, Freud associated magic with neurosis (PA, 63–65). In fact, the purpose of magic is to arouse emotions for the benefit of practical life. For example, a tribe might do a war dance before going to fight its neighbours. This produces warlike emotions, and develops and conserves morale. Unlike in amusement, emotions aroused by magical acts are not discharged by those acts. Instead the emotions are focussed and crystallised and directed upon the conduct of practical life (PA, 66). Collingwood argues that 'Magic is a kind of dynamo supplying the mechanism of practical life with the emotional current that drives it' (PA, 69). Hence it is a necessity for every person and society, and: 'A society which thinks, as our own thinks, that it has outlived the need of magic, is either mistaken in that opinion, or else it is a dying society, perishing for lack of interest in its own maintenance' (PA, 69).

According to Collingwood, magic has flourished unrecognised in modern society, which bases its claim to enlightenment on giving up magic. Examples of magic are: practising a religion, patriotic songs, war memorials, and anything that stimulates loyalty to country, party, class, family or any other social or political unit (PA, 72–73). Other examples of magic include: fox-hunting and amateur football, which are 'part of the religion of being a gentleman', weddings, which create an emotional motive for maintaining the partnership of marriage, the funeral, which is a public undertaking to live in future without the deceased, the dinner-party, which creates and renews friendship, and the dance, which is a courtship-ritual (PA, 73–76). Collingwood points out, however, that magic, in the hands of a true artist, can also be art, if the artistic and magical motives are felt as one motive, as it happened among the Aurignacian and Magdalenian cave-men, the ancient Egyptians, the Greeks, and the medieval Europeans (PA, 77).

Another example of representative art, or art falsely so-called, is amusement. Whereas magic is the arousal of emotions for their practical value, amusement is the arousal and discharge of emotions so that they do not interfere with practical life (PA, 78). For example, the 'thriller' or detective story arouses and discharges emotions of fear, craving for excitement and adventure and delight in power. The earthing of certain emotions, by arousing and discharging them in make-believe situations, makes it less likely that they will discharge themselves in practical life. Similarly, sexual fantasy and pornography are a substitute for sexual passion (PA, 84–86).[2]

Amusement involves the bifurcation of experience into a 'real' part and a 'make-believe' part, and the ill-effects of this are negligible in so far as the emotions aroused in the make-believe part, which is called amusement, are not allowed to overflow into the affairs of 'real life'. Collingwood contends that amusement becomes a danger to practical life when the debt it imposes on our stores of energy is too great to be paid off in the course of ordinary living. When this reaches a point of crisis, practical life has become emotionally bankrupt and a moral disease has set in, whose symptoms are a constant craving for amusement and an inability to take any interest in ordinary affairs of livelihood and social routine. Collingwood compares the modern world to the later Roman Empire, with its unprecedented growth of the amusement trade which is symptomatic of a moral disease, and almost universal agreement that the kinds of work upon which our civilisation depends have become an intolerable drudgery (PA, 96–97).

According to Collingwood, modern Western civilisation suffers from a moral or spiritual disease because art and magic are suppressed and relegated to the status of amusement. He outlines a history of amusement, according to which in the fourteenth century merchants and princes began to change the character of artistic work by diverting it from the Church's use to their own personal service. This provoked violent hostility, which was drawn into the service of the Reformation, and entered into the mainstream of modern civilisation through its inheritance by nonconformist bankers and manufacturers, the dominant class of the modern world, and drove the artistic consciousness into the position of something outcast and persecuted. Having displaced the gentry, the new plutocracy compelled the arts to accept the status of amusements and persuaded themselves to reconcile their enjoyment of these amusements with a religious principle according to which there was no room in life for anything but work. Collingwood asserts:

> The artists, who had struggled from the seventeenth to the early nineteenth century to work out a new conception of art, detaching it from the ideas of amusement and magic alike, and thus liberating themselves from all service, whether of church or of patron, stifled these thoughts, spared themselves the labour of developing their new conception to the

---

[2]   This is compatible with D.H. Lawrence's view, which I discuss in the next chapter.

height of its potentialities, and put on again the servant's liveries they had thrown aside (PA, 100).

This, Collingwood claims, led to a decline in artistic standards during the nineteenth century and also the corruption of the dominant class of merchants and bankers, who got into the habit of retiring into a state of pseudo-gentility on making a fortune, where they had nothing to do but amuse themselves. The merchant class was distinguished from the real gentility by the fact that they had no duties to the community, whether military or administrative or magical, such as occupied the latter. According to Collingwood,

> Until close on the end of the nineteenth century, the rustic population of England had an art of its own, rooted in the distant past but still alive with creative vigour: songs and dances, seasonal feasts and dramas and pageantry, all of magical significance and all organically connected with agricultural work. In a single generation this was wiped out of existence by the operation of two causes: the Education Act of 1870, which, as imposing on the countryman an education modelled on town-dweller's standards, was one stage in the slow destruction of English rural life by the dominant industrial and commercial class; and the 'agricultural depression', to give that vague and non-committal name to the long series of events, partly accidental and partly deliberate, which between 1870 and 1900 wrecked the prosperity of the English agricultural population. A similar process was going on among the poor of the towns. They too had a vital and flourishing folk-art of the same magical type; they too were deprived of it by the organized forces of the law acting as the secular arm of the ruling industrialists' Puritanism. (PA, 101–2)

By 1900 town and country alike had been purged of the magical art known as folklore, and was then replaced by amusement art—football, cinema and wireless. As a result, Collingwood contends, 'Increased production combined with the break-down of economic organization led to the appearance of an unemployed class, forced unwillingly into a parasitic condition, deprived of the magical art in which their grandfathers took their pleasure fifty years ago, left functionless and aimless in the community, living only to accept *panem et circenses*, the dole and the films' (PA, 102). For Collingwood, our civilisation is tracing a path, which is a close parallel to that of the later Roman Empire:

> What we are concerned with is the threatened death of a civilization. That has nothing to do with my death or yours, or the deaths of any people we can shoot before they shoot us. It can be neither arrested nor hastened by violence. Civilizations die and are born not with the waving of flags or the noise of machine-guns in the streets, but in the dark, in a stillness, when no one is aware of it. It never gets into the papers. Long after-

wards a few people, looking back, begin to see that it has happened. (PA, 102–4)

Collingwood's criticism of amusement art and industrialism in *The Principles of Art* is a continuation of similar criticism in earlier essays, 'Art and the Machine' and 'The Place of Art in Education'. In the unpublished manuscript, 'Art and the Machine', thought to have been written around 1926,[3] Collingwood attacks the mechanical reproduction of art: 'The cinema, or mechanized theatre, through the vulgarity and crudeness which are the result of mechanization, is not enjoyed in the sense in which a work of art is enjoyed, at all'. Those who pay for a seat at the cinema, Collingwood asserts, are paying for, not aesthetic enjoyment, but sensuous and emotional stimulation:

> They regard the film not as a work of art but as a form of 'dope'. The ordinary attitude towards dance-music, popular songs and novels is the same. The reason why all these are popular is that everyday life in the present world is so dull and drab that emotional stimulation has become a commodity on sale in the market, and an immense trade has grown up in what may be called pseudo-art, things superficially resembling works of art but in reality having a quite different function and related to genuine art as intoxicating drink is related to nourishment. Whereas the reader of a poem enjoys the poem itself, that is, derives pleasure from the objective contemplation of its structure and effect, the audience at a film enjoys, not the film, but the emotional 'kick' which it gets out of the film. (AM, 8)

Collingwood argues: 'The habit of taking these emotional drugs is not only leading people to rely on them increasingly as part of their daily lives, it is also bringing other forms of art into conformity with these models' (AM, 9). Hence, he argues, modern novels often tend to be forms of 'dope' and not works of art. According to Collingwood, 'A people thus drug-sodden in its mental life, systematically replacing all forms of art by corresponding forms of emotional excitement has naturally lost its power of creating or enjoying art in any form whatever' (AM, 10). This has led to a decline of taste in architecture, furniture and clothing, and 'The great tradition of English poetry has been divided between the despised highbrows and the purveyors of metrical dope' (AM, 10). I think that Collingwood's straightforward identification of cinema (and the use of technology in art) with amusement is questionable, a subject I will return to in Chapter Four. But this does not substantially affect his

---

[3]   This suggestion has been challenged, however, by the editors of *The Philosophy of Enchantment*, who suggest a later date of *c.*1936. 'Art and the Machine' is published in *The Philosophy of Enchantment* (2004: 305-35).

argument that the suppression of art by amusement has serious consequences for civilisation.

In 'Art and the Machine', like in *The Principles of Art*, Collingwood argues that in England the decay of taste roughly corresponds with the decline of agriculture and the predominance of industrial interests. The traditional life of the agricultural population was an aesthetically rich one, in contrast to that of the industrial classes, who dedicated themselves to 'the cult of utility', whose places of worship were bare of architectural grace, and whose housing for workers expressed a repudiation of beauty, giving rise to 'the drab and squalid environment of the English industrial proletariat' (AM, 11). In the industrial world, 'the grimly utilitarian and inartistic character of life was universal' (AM, 12).

Those who attempted to arrest this decline of artistic taste failed, as they overlooked the thriving agricultural life, drew their culture from abroad, and 'rhapsodized' over the heads of their audiences about French cathedrals and Italian paintings, 'thus creating the gulf of misunderstanding that separates the highbrow from the common herd' (AM, 12). The victory of industrial life over agriculture has led to the rejection of art, and the mechanized dope of cinema and wireless' has been brought into every village. For Collingwood,

> This total rejection of art is a thing in which we cannot acquiesce, because ... no mind can be sanely rational without possessing an artistic basis for its rationality. An inartistic civilisation is, to that extent, an insane civilization, melancholy mad (AM, 13).

The pernicious effects of the confusion of art with amusement are also a subject that Collingwood discusses in his 1926 essay, 'The Place of Art in Education'. He rejects the view that 'all art is quite useless', that art is the bare absence of utility:

> Thus art is a relaxation of the practical strain of everyday life, an escape from the all-pervading gloom and squalor of our urban civilization, a side issue, a backwater of the mind, an ornament upon a fabric whose structure is a matter not of art, but of engineering (PAE, 436).

This idea of art as a 'stunt', an 'extra', something luxurious and distanced from real life is based on a 'profoundly vicious philosophy of art'. The truth is that beauty and utility are not the same thing and art is not practical life as such. The error, however, is to define art in terms of this bare negation. Hence:

> ... we are driven to infer that art is nothing real, and to bestow on it a kind or residual or marginal existence, feeding on the crumbs that fall from the table of utility ... Architecture as an art means, in this sense, not the dignity and grace of the naked building, but the prudishness that

> covers this nudity with irrelevant fig leaves; literature means not the expression of meaning but the systematic concealment of meanings behind artificial flowers of speech, and so forth. (PAE, 437–38)

When we revolt against this form of art:

> We want to sweep away the pattern on the wall-paper because we want to see the wall; to get rid of the stencilled roses on the bedroom jug in order to see the jug; to shear away the flowers of speech in order to hear the statement; because the wall and the jug and the statement have each a beauty of its own that cannot be heightened and can only be spoilt by the addition of ornament … The fact is that, though utility and beauty are not the same thing, nothing can be truly useful without thereby acquiring beauty—a peculiar and unique beauty that blossoms, as it were, out of the soil of sound design. (PAE, 438)

According to Collingwood, the superstition that the useful must be ugly and the beautiful useless is a relic of the industrial revolution, which introduced new methods of manufacture necessitating new methods of design, and introduced these new methods so rapidly that the old schools of design failed to keep in touch with them. The old designers retained an out-of-date tradition of manufacture, while the new manufacturers had to create a new tradition of design and did it at first very clumsily. Collingwood explains:

> The artist and the manufacturer, who were identical in the days of Phidias and Leonardo da Vinci, were suddenly torn apart. The artist ceased to be an efficient manufacturer and the manufacturer ceased to be a properly trained artist; and thus artistic design acquired a false association with antiquated methods of production and gimcrack or unseaworthy products, while mechanical efficiency acquired an equally false association with clumsy and repulsive design … If we are to recover the artistic sanity of the Greeks, the Middle Ages and the Renaissance, we must recover the conviction that nothing can be beautifully made unless it is efficiently made, nothing efficiently made unless it is beautifully made (PAE, 438–39).

If something is designed well you will find that it has 'come' beautiful without any decoration, and '… if beauty is the proper object of the aesthetic faculty, everything well designed is a work of art; and the function of art in life is therefore not ornamental, but structural' (PAE, 439). Although, later on, in *The Principles of Art* Collingwood came to reject the association of art with beauty and replace it with the idea of art as the expression of emotion, his argument in this essay emphasises the importance of art as a form of experience and distinguishes it from amusement.

For Collingwood, then, agricultural life is an important aspect of civilisation, and the destruction of the countryside by industrialism is a key feature of the suppression of emotion that afflicts modern life. In 'Man Goes Mad', Collingwood argues that Western civilisation is at bottom an agricultural civilisation, and its vitality or sanity depends on the health of our emotions regarding the land (MGM, 29 and 32).[4] Love of the countryside is neither aesthetic nor political, but 'far deeper and more primitive than that'. It is 'in the deepest sense religious ... And upon the vitality of this religious feeling depends the vitality of civilization as a whole' (MGM, 33). These emotions were strong until the nineteenth century. But, with the rise of industrialisation came the building of cheap and ugly houses for the industrial proletariat, and the defacement of the countryside by railway lines. An antagonism grew up between industry and agriculture as rivals for political patronage, industry gradually gained the ascendancy, and the countryside was economically ruined (MGM, 34).

In the twentieth century the countryside was further damaged by the invasion of town dwellers. If traditional country life had still been intact then the invasion from the towns could have been met by a flood of new buildings in the tradition of country architecture, and they would have become part of the countryside. But the tradition was dead, and 'the architecture of the town, as corrupted by the housing tradition of the industrial revolution' defaced the countryside even further (MGM, 35). In Collingwood's view, we have lost 'that religious sense of loving union' with the soil (MGM, 36). Hence, it is proposed to divide the dead body of our agricultural life into a town-dwellers playground and a museum exhibit. If this is done the emotional foundations of our civilized life will perish. Industry, if it cuts itself off from its roots in agriculture, is a kind of madness with no lasting vitality. According to Collingwood,

> Of this we are beginning to be aware; we know that our civilization has in it a sickness of the mind, a morbid craving for excitement, a hyperaesthesia of emotion, for which it offers no cure. There is a cure, if only we could get it: the deep, primitive, almost unconscious emotion of the man who, wrestling with the earth, sees the labour of his hands and is satisfied (MGM, 37).

Collingwood's reverence for the countryside is obviously Romantic and reminiscent of D.H. Lawrence. It is also influenced by John Ruskin, and was a common theme among liberals in the early part of the twentieth century. In 'Ruskin and the Mountains' Collingwood interpreted Ruskin as primarily a lover of mountains whose inter-

---

[4]   This is published in *The Philosophy of Enchantment* (2004: 305-35).

ests were all connected with this central passion manifesting itself in a sensitivity to town and country relations, and the duties of a tourist both to the landscape and inhabitants of a foreign land (cf. Boucher, 2000: 186). As Connelly points out, Collingwood's emphasis on the importance of the countryside seems prophetic and much of his concerns are at the centre of current discussion in environmental ethics and philosophy (Connelly, 2003: 315).

Collingwood's romanticism is further evident when compared with another member of this tradition, George Orwell. In *The Road to Wigan Pier* Orwell claims: 'We are living in a world in which nobody is free, in which hardly anybody is secure, in which it is almost impossible to be honest and to remain alive' (Orwell, 1989: 158). He refers to '... the frightful debauchery of taste that has already been effected by a century of mechanisation', something that applies to food, furniture, houses, clothes, books, amusements and everything else that makes up our environment (Orwell, 1989: 189–90). According to Orwell,

> The mechanisation of the world could never proceed very far while taste, even the taste-buds of the tongue, remained uncorrupted, because in that case most of the products of the machine would be simply unwanted. In a healthy world there would be no demand for tinned food, aspirins, gramophones, gas-pipe chairs, machine guns, daily newspapers, telephones, motor-cars etc. etc; and on the other hand there would be a constant demand for the things that the machine cannot produce ... But in addition to this there is a tendency for the mechanisation of the world to proceed as it were automatically, whether we want it or not. This is due to the fact that in modern Western man the faculty of mechanical invention has been fed and stimulated till it has reached almost the status of an instinct ... the Western man invents machines as naturally as the Polynesian islander swims. (Orwell, 1989: 190–91)

Although my focus in this chapter is on how Collingwood's conception of the crisis of civilisation relates to his philosophy of art, for Collingwood, the suppression of emotion that impairs Western civilisation also affects religion. In 'Fascism and Nazism', he expresses his conviction that Western civilisation was built on a religious foundation. But, he argues, modernity has stripped religion of its emotional element. Under the influence of 'Illuminism', modern philosophy and science have distilled from Christianity its rational contents, but have discarded the superstitious ideas and magical rituals, in which they were embodied. According to Collingwood,

> Thus in the last two hundred years Christianity has suffered a curious double fate. Whatever in it is capable of logical formulation as a system of first principles has been analysed and codified and has come to func-

tion as the axioms upon which our sciences of nature and history, our practice in liberal economics and free or democratic politics — in short all the things which make up our civilization are built. But whatever is not capable of logical formulation, whatever is in the nature of religious emotion, passion, faith, has been progressively exterminated, partly by ridicule and partly by force, under the names of superstition and magic. (EPP, 188)

Our liberal and democratic principles, then, derive from Christianity. Fascism and Nazism owed their success to the fact that they used pagan pre-Christian religions as a source of emotional energy. They tapped a source unavailable to their opponents, and exhibited a psychological dynamism which liberal democracy lacked. The Nazis, who 'think with their blood', managed to get the better of liberals and democrats who think merely with their brains (EPP, 191–92). Fascism and Nazism, however, aroused emotion at the expense of rational consciousness, and in support of barbarism instead of civilisation. Collingwood, therefore, regards the practice of a religion rich in emotional elements as an indispensable element of a civilisation. Another aspect of the solution to the crisis of civilisation in this respect is awareness of what the fundamental principles of a civilisation are, a subject which Collingwood treats of in his metaphysics, and which I will discuss in Part Two.

According to Collingwood's philosophy of art, therefore, the suppression of emotion has led to a crisis in Western civilisation. The solution to the crisis is a more adequate understanding of art. Art proper, then, is emphatically distinct from amusement and representative art in general, and, for Collingwood, is to play a crucial part in education. In 'Art and the Machine' he claims: 'The only hope is to begin with that part of the people which is not yet sodden with drugs: the children — the problem is an educational one'. He calls for a 'gigantic bonfire' of all mechanised reproductions of art, little editions of Shakespeare and every aid for introducing children to great art (AM, 13). Children ought to be taught that art is not something to be placed on a pedestal and reverently stared at, but an activity by which they become able to speak their minds, and utter themselves clearly and accurately in every medium that they handle. If this is done, children need no longer experience that boredom of school, which is 'the first lesson of a future drug addict'. Collingwood concludes:

> A child so trained will need no dope, for it will be able to do something better with its emotions than stimulate them artificially. It will be able to express them, and so to understand the expressions of other people. Thus its training in art will qualify it to live in a world of reality, facing

> intelligently the facts of its own and other people's lives ... Children so
> trained may or may not turn out great artists: they may or may not turn
> out learned scholars, but they will begin life sane. (AM, 15)

The above lines show that in 'Art and the Machine' the idea of art
as the expression of emotion was already present, something which
Collingwood later developed as a central feature of *The Principles of
Art*. In *The Principles of Art*, Collingwood argues that at first, the artist
is conscious of having an emotion, but not conscious of what this
emotion is. He liberates himself from this oppressed condition by
expressing the emotion. Unlike when emotions are discharged in a
make-believe situation, expression of an emotion is a way of becoming conscious of it (PA, 109–10). Expression is also different from
description. Whereas description generalises, expression individu-
alises (PA, 111–13). Similarly, an artist cannot choose which emotion
to express and which not to express. He does not know the emotion
until he has expressed it (PA, 115–17). That the artist cannot freely
choose which emotion to express is a point that Nietzsche also
makes:

> Every artist knows how far from any feeling of letting himself go his
> "most natural" state is — the free ordering, placing, disposing, giving
> form in the moment of 'inspiration' — and how strictly and subtly he
> obeys thousandfold laws precisely then ... (Nietzsche, 1990: 188).

By expressing his or her emotions, the artist enables the audience
to express theirs. According to Collingwood, 'As Coleridge put it,
we know a man for a poet by the fact that he makes us poets. We
know that he is expressing his emotions by the fact that he is
enabling us to express ours' (PA, 118). Expression does not mean
that the artist should isolate himself from the wider world by being
part of a special clique or ivory tower. In this case the artist neglects
the emotions of the wider world and is mostly manufacturing
amusement art for the members of the ivory tower (PA, 120). Finally,
the expression of emotion is distinguished from betraying the symptoms of emotion and exhibitionism or 'blowing off steam' (PA,
122–23).

As well as the expression of emotion, art involves creation and
imagination. Creation is distinguished from simple making: 'To create something means to make it non-technically, but yet consciously
and voluntarily' (PA, 128). Imagination is distinguished from
make-believe. Make-believe, Collingwood argues, has a motive
which is to provide the audience with fantasies in which their
desires are satisfied, as is the case, for example, with daydreaming,
and Hollywood, which is 'an organized and commercialized devel-

opment of day-dreaming' (PA, 136). Make-believe implies a dissatisfaction with the situation in which one actually stands and a desire for something which we should enjoy if the make-believe were true, whereas imagination is indifferent to desire. Confusion between imagination and make-believe reinforces the confusion between art and amusement (PA, 137–38).

The work of art exists in the imagination of the artist. Music, therefore, is not a collection of noises, but the tune in the musician's head. If the audience listens intelligently to a performance of the music it can reconstruct the tune for itself (PA, 139). Similarly, painting, or viewing a painting, is not just the experience of seeing; we also experience an imaginative sense of distance, space and mass. Collingwood cites the example of Cézanne, who painted 'like a blind man' and proved that painting can never be solely a visual art (PA, 144). What we get from a work of art is the specialised sensuous experience of seeing or hearing, and also the imaginative experience of total activity (PA, 148).

The imaginative experience and the sensuous experience, however, are not two separate things:

> There is no justification for saying that the sensuous part of it is something we find and the imaginary part something we bring, or that the sensuous part is objectively 'there' in the 'work of art', the imaginary part subjective, a mode of consciousness as distinct from a quality of a thing (PA, 150).

Through imagination, Collingwood explains, we find what a picture reveals because the painter has put it there. Similarly, if we see the same colours that the artist saw as he or she painted, that is because of our similar powers of colour-vision (PA, 150).

Art, however, is not just the expression of emotion and an act of creative imagination. In Collingwood's view it is also consciousness of truth. There is in aesthetic experience the beginning of self-awareness and self-knowledge. This will be explained in the next chapter and will illustrate how, for Collingwood, art has a crucial role in overcoming the ills of modernity.

Chapter Three

Art, Consciousness and Truth

As we have seen, in Collingwood's view, in the contemporary Western world there has been a tendency to suppress art proper and replace it with the pseudo-art of amusement, and this has been a primary aspect of the malaise that Western culture now faces. In order to explore this problem more deeply, this chapter will examine what Collingwood regards as the fundamental place occupied by art in human life.

For Collingwood, art is the beginning of the process by which we create the self and the world. The distinctions between the self and the world and between the world as discovered and the world as made only occur at the level of intellect. However, for intellect to function, there must first be art. As Hinz points out, for Collingwood, the world in its most basic and pristine nature is not so much a world that is thought as a world that is felt (Hinz, 1994a: 31). Art, therefore, creates the world by becoming conscious of it. Art also has a transformative effect on a culture. In Collingwood's view, a healthy artistic life will transform a civilisation from one of cultural crisis to one of vigour.

Collingwood's idea of art as self- and world-creation, of art as the revelation of truth, and of art as the antidote to cultural crisis demonstrates that he is part of the same tradition as Ruskin, Nietzsche, Ezra Pound, and D.H. Lawrence. Like all of them, Collingwood saw the role of the artist as crucial in maintaining the standards of civilisation.

According to Collingwood in 'The Place of Art in Education', the art of literature is the art of speaking one's mind, which is the same thing as making up one's mind. The thought that before utterance lies obscured and unrealised in the dark places of the soul comes into living existence in the act of expressing it:

> ... a person who has not, somehow and in some kind of language, said what he means, strictly cannot be said to have a meaning. Thus the act of imagining, which is the act of uttering language, is not an embroidering of a pre-existent thought; it is the birth of thought itself. Speaking or writing is, therefore, at once practising the art of literature and bringing into actuality the thought of one's mind (PAE, 440).

Collingwood argues that education is in essence aesthetic or imaginative. Art is divided into poetry and prose, where poetry is pure imagination, and prose is imagination controlled by and consciously expressive of thought. Poetry precedes prose. The false view is that prose comes first, and poetry decorates this pre-existent object. He argues:

> The consciousness that first expresses itself in poetry, in fantasy and myth, afterwards clarifies out and sobers down into prose, into science and philosophy. The progress of thought is a perpetual passage from poetry to prose and a perpetual birth of new thought in the form of poetry (PAE, 442).

Hence education sets imaginary problems and solves them according to arbitrary rules, thereby enabling the pupil to solve the problems of real life. In real life imagination is awake and active, but working under the control of thought. For Collingwood, then, 'a right training in art is the absolute bedrock of all sane human life' (PAE, 448).

However, with the development of Collingwood's philosophy, a change takes place. Collingwood's theory of art as the expression of emotion, put forward in *The Principles of Art*, was the result of a change from his earlier philosophy of art. According to the 'phenomenology of mind' in earlier works such as *Speculum Mentis* and *Outlines of a Philosophy of Art*, art is the first of five forms of experience, which constitute a scale of forms, where the more advanced both contain and correct the more primitive. Art, as the most primitive of the five, is purely imaginative. The value of art lies outside itself, and therefore it is transcended by the more adequate forms of experience: religion, science, history and philosophy (cf. Donagan, 1964: x–xi).

The consequence of this position, as Donagan points out in his Introduction to *Essays in the Philosophy of Art*, was that artists as artists are unaware of what their work means. In order to resolve this problem, in Collingwood's later philosophy art assumes a role of greater prominence and is seen as having a more intimate relation with thought. As Donagan argues,

> Whereas in the Outlines he had held that art, or imagination, always exists "in the closest union with thought", which transcends it, in The Principles of Art he recognizes that imagination is a necessary element in every act of thought. To think is not to transcend imagination, but to put imagination to work in a specific way (Donagan, 1964: xii).

According to Collingwood in *The Principles of Art*, there are two types of feeling: sensation and emotion. Every sensation carries an emotional charge, and sensation and emotion, thus related, are twin elements in every experience of feeling. Feeling has the character of a foundation upon which the superstructure of our thought is built (PA, 162–64). Collingwood proposes that imagination occupies an intermediate position between sensation and thought: freer than sensation and less free than thought (PA, 197–98). Through imagination the colours, sounds, and so forth that we perceive through sensation are retained before the mind, anticipated and recalled, although the same colours and sounds, in their capacity as sensa, have ceased to be seen or heard (PA, 202). Collingwood explains that it was in order to distinguish imagination from sensation that Hume distinguished impressions from ideas, and it is imagination, not sensation, to which appeal is made when empiricists appeal to 'experience' (PA, 203).

According to Collingwood, before we classify and detect resemblances between sensa, we must attend to them, distinguish each as a thing by itself, and appreciate its qualities. Attention divides sensa present to the mind between the conscious part that we pay attention to and the unconscious part that we remove from the focus of attention (PA, 204). Seeing and hearing are species of sensation; looking and listening are species of attention:

> The principle of this analysis depends on the fact that attention (or, as we may now indifferently call it, consciousness or awareness) has a double object where sentience has a single. What we hear, for example, is merely sound. What we attend to is two things at once: a sound, and our act of hearing it (PA, 206).

Attention chooses what sensation or feeling to place in the focus of consciousness. The self dominates the feeling, making it conform to a certain structure. It takes and retains a feeling from the flux of sensation, and converts it from impression to idea (PA, 210). The work of determining the relations between sensa depends on having these things held before the mind so that we can compare them with one another. What consciousness, or attention, produces out of sensation, Collingwood asserts, is imagination. Imagination, therefore, (or ideas, as distinct from impressions) is sensations that we have become conscious of and not yet interpreted by thought (PA, 213).

According to Collingwood, consciousness is a kind of thought, but not yet intellect. It is thought in its fundamental and original shape. Therefore, it has the bi-polarity of thought: what it thinks may be true or false. As consciousness gives attention to certain feelings and leaves others unattended, a true consciousness, Collingwood argues, is a confession to ourselves of our feelings. A false consciousness disowns them thinking: 'That feeling is not mine' (PA, 216). Consciousness, therefore, is 'corrupt' when it rejects a feeling it has already focused attention on because it is alarmed at the idea that the impression is being converted into.

Ridley claims that the corruption of consciousness is a failure at the level of ideas: a failure to get our ideas clear rather than a failure in converting an impression into an idea (Ridley, 1998: 5–6). But, I think that Ridley is mistaken.[1] For Collingwood, there is no distinction between converting impressions into ideas and getting ideas clear, and he is emphatic that the corruption of consciousness is a failure in the process of conversion. A corrupt consciousness, then, means that the whole picture of imagination now has vital omissions (PA, 218).

As psychologists describe it, the disowning of experience is called repression, the ascription of these to other persons, projection, their consolidation into a mass of experience, homogeneous in itself, dissociation, and the building up of a sham experience which we admit to be our own, fantasy-building (PA, 218–19). Collingwood defines the corrupt consciousness as 'evil'. It is evil as yet undifferentiated into evil done and evil suffered. The attempt by psychoanalysts to rescue those in whom this evil has advanced has 'won a great place in the history of man's warfare with the powers of darkness' (PA, 220–21).

According to Collingwood, language comes into existence at the level of consciousness and is an imaginative activity whose function is to express emotion. Intellectualised language is language modified to express thought. The difference between language in its original form and intellectualised language is the difference between

---

[1]   As Ridley (1998: 4) remarks, Collingwood's use of Hume's terminology may have been unhelpful: a point also mentioned by Lund (1998: 3).

language and symbolism. Language, in its original form, is prior to symbolism. Contrary to traditional language theory, Collingwood argues that a symbol is something whose meaning is arrived at by agreement, and this presupposes the existence of an original language out of which agreement can be arrived at (PA, 225). He rejects the idea of taking the language we use for expressing our thoughts as the fundamental character of language: '... beneath all the machinery of word and sentence lies the primitive language of mere utterance, the controlled act in which we express our emotions' (PA, 236).

Unlike psychical expression, which occurs prior to consciousness and consists of involuntary and often unconscious bodily acts which relate to the emotions they are said to express, at the level of consciousness our emotions no longer arise in us as brute facts, but are dominated in such a way that we can summon them, suppress them or alter them. According to Collingwood, the difference between psychical expression and language (in its primitive form) is illustrated by the difference between a small child's uncontrolled cry of emotion and a self-conscious cry to call attention to its needs. With the second cry, language is born, and its articulation into fully developed speech is only a matter of detail (PA, 236).

Collingwood contends that language is any controlled and expressive bodily activity. Speech is a system of gestures, where each gesture produces a characteristic sound. Every kind of language, he argues, is a specialised form of bodily gesture: hence 'the dance is the mother of all languages' (PA, 244). The predominance of the language of the vocal chords is explained by the fact that the habit of going heavily clothed cramps the expressiveness of all bodily parts except the face. The cosmopolitan civilisation of Europe and North America, with its tendency towards rigidly uniform dress has limited our expressive activities almost entirely to the voice (PA, 244–45). Different kinds of language, then, cannot express the same feeling. The English language expresses different emotions from French, and music expresses different emotions to speech. Every kind of language is an offshoot of an 'original' language of total bodily gesture. This means that whenever we express ourselves, we do so with our whole bodies — and rigidity is a gesture no less than movement (PA, 246).

Because, in language, our bodily activity is raised from the psychical level to the conscious level and is converted from object of sensation to object of imagination, language, Collingwood asserts, is identical with art (PA, 247). According to Collingwood, consciousness begins as consciousness of our own existence and, simultaneously, consciousness of the existence of others. The discovery of myself as speaker and hearer is also the discovery of speakers and hearers other than myself (PA, 248). As we have seen, by being conscious of an emotion we convert it from impression into idea. The expression of an idea is inseparably linked to having the idea, and this is important for Collingwood's claim that art is apprehension of truth.[2] Collingwood argues: '... it is only because we know what we feel that we can express it in words; it is only because we express them in words that we know what our emotions are' (PA, 249–50).

The person to whom speech is addressed is conscious of the other's personality as correlative to his own. He takes what he hears exactly as if it were speech of his own, and thus constructs in himself the idea which these words express. There is no absolute assurance for the hearer or speaker that one has understood the other, but if they understand each other well enough to go on talking, that is as much understanding as they need (PA, 251).

A second stage in the development of language, where it undergoes modification to serve the purposes of the intellect, is the grammatical analysis of language. Language is seen as a product or 'thing', 'speech' or 'discourse'. This 'thing' is cut up into parts and, through lexicography, rules of syntax and so forth, relations between the parts are devised. However, the rules only hold 'for the most part' (PA, 257). According to Collingwood,

> Language as it lives and grows no more consists of verbs, nouns and so forth than animals as they live and grow consist of forehands, gammons, rump-steaks and other joints. The grammarian's real function ... is not to understand language, but to alter it: to convert it from a state (its original and native state) in which it expresses emotion in to a secondary state in which it can express thought (PA, 257).

---

[2]   Louis Mink denies that we can know an emotion simply by expressing it. He argues that '... an artist may know completely what he has created (as an imaginative object) without knowing in any other way what he has expressed' (Mink, 1969: 226). For Mink, if emotions become objects of consciousness in the same way that impressions become ideas, the products of imagination would all be objects of consciousness and would all be describable, and there would be no necessity for any theory of expression (Mink, 1969: 235). However, Mink assumes that for objects of consciousness to be knowledge they must be describable. For Collingwood, expression is also knowledge, at a primitive level. I think that Mink is making too strong a distinction between expression and consciousness, and that Collingwood's effective identification of expression and consciousness is coherent. It seems that Mink denies Collingwood's claim that art is knowledge because he has an overly rationalistic conception of knowledge.

This function is fulfilled, but only in a limited and qualified way, as language resists the grammarian's efforts and retains a measure of its original vitality and expressiveness. Logic, Collingwood explains, is a further development in this adaptation of language to the expression of thought. But the logician's modification of language, like the grammarian's, can never be carried out entirely. Language only retains its function as language in so far as this process of intellectualisation is incomplete. Every attempt to state truths retains an element of emotional expressiveness (PA, 264).

Collingwood argues that an emotion is always the emotional charge upon some activity. For every different kind of activity there is a different kind of emotion and a different kind of expression. As the emotions of consciousness are expressed by language in its original form, intellect also has its emotions, which are expressed by language in its intellectualised form. Archimedes' cry of 'Eureka' expressed the excitement of a man who had just solved a specific scientific problem (PA, 267). The expression of thought is not direct or immediate expression. It is mediated through the peculiar emotion which is the emotional charge on the thought. The speaker expresses to the hearer the particular emotion with which he or she thinks the thought, and the hearer thinks out this emotion for himself or herself and rediscovers the thought whose peculiar emotional tone the speaker has expressed.[3] The progressive intellectualisation of language means acquiring new emotions (PA, 267–69).

For Collingwood, then, art is identified with language. Art does not use a 'ready-made language', but creates language as it goes along. This is because language is '… not a utilizable thing but a pure activity' (PA, 275). However, 'the by-products of this creative activity, ready-made words and phrases, types of pictorial and sculptural forms, turns of musical idiom, and so forth, can be used as means to ends' (PA, 276). Craft, therefore, or art falsely so-called, makes use of, not language, but clichés from language. Collingwood compares the difference between art and craft to the difference between a live man and a dead man, and the difference between good art and bad art to the difference between two living men, one good and the other bad (PA, 277).

A work of art is good or bad depending on the extent of the artist's corruption of consciousness. Good art means successful expression. Bad art means a failure in expression, a failure to become conscious

---

[3]　This implies that Collingwood's theory of historical re-enactment can include the re-enactment of emotion as well as thought.

of a given emotion. Corruption of consciousness, however, is always only partial. Nobody's consciousness can be wholly corrupt. The failure of expression will not be recognised as good art by the artist. The artist will have expressed himself or herself successfully on other occasions, and through comparison of these with the occasion of failure in expression, he or she can recognise bad art (PA, 284). According to Collingwood,

> Art is not a luxury, and bad art not a thing we can afford to tolerate. To know ourselves is the foundation of all life that develops beyond the merely psychical level of experience. Unless consciousness does its work successfully, the facts which it offers to intellect, the only things upon which intellect can build its fabric of thought, are false from the beginning. A truthful consciousness gives intellect a firm foundation upon which to build; a corrupt consciousness forces the intellect to build on quicksand. The falsehoods which an untruthful consciousness imposes on the intellect are falsehoods which intellect can never correct for itself. In so far as consciousness is corrupted, the very wells of truth are poisoned. Intellect can build nothing firm. Moral ideals are castles in the air. Political and economic systems are mere cobwebs. Even common sanity and bodily health are no longer secure. But corruption of consciousness is the same thing as bad art (PA, 284–85).

For Collingwood, therefore, art is essentially the pursuit of truth, truthfulness about one's emotions. However, it is truth of consciousness, as distinct from truth of intellect. Intellect, unlike consciousness, is concerned with the 'relations between things', and because the truth of intellect is a relational truth it apprehends it through arguing or inferring (PA, 287). Collingwood argues:

> A poet will say at one time that his lady is a paragon of all the virtues; at another time that she has a heart as black as hell. At one time he will say that the world is a fine place; at another that it is a dust-heap and a dunghill and a pestilent conglomeration of vapours. To the intellect these are inconsistencies … on the poet's behalf it may be replied, to some one who argues that a lady cannot be both adorably virtuous and repellently vicious, or that the world cannot be both a paradise and a dust-heap, that the arguer seems to know more about logic than he does about ladies, or about the world (PA, 287–88).

Collingwood explains this point as follows:

> Art is not indifferent to truth; it is essentially the pursuit of truth. But the truth it pursues is not the truth of relation, it is a truth of individual fact. The truths art discovers are those single and self-contained individualities which from the intellectual point of view become the 'terms' between which it is the business of intellect to establish or apprehend relations. Each of these individualities, as art discovers it, is a perfectly concrete individual, one from which nothing has yet been abstracted by

the work of intellect. Each is an experience in which the distinction between what is due to myself and what is due to my world has not yet been made (PA, 288).

Art, then, is knowledge of the individual. In art, distinctions between theory and practice, thought and action, and subject and object have not yet arisen (PA, 290). Aesthetic experience is a knowing of oneself and of one's world. It is also a making of oneself and of one's world. The self which was psyche is remade in the shape of consciousness and language (PA, 292).

Also, the emotions that art expresses are not taken solely from the psychical level. Thought also has emotions which we are not conscious of and which can be expressed in art. Collingwood gives the example of 'Romeo and Juliet', which expresses the intellectual apprehension of how sexual passion can break across socio-political divides (PA, 294). Similarly, T.S. Eliot in the one great English poem of this century, has expressed his idea (not his alone) of the decay of our civilization, manifested outwardly as a break-down of social structures and inwardly as a drying-up of the emotional springs of life'(PA, 295). For Collingwood, therefore, it seems that poetry and philosophy overlap one another:

> Good philosophy and good poetry are not two different kinds of writing, but one; each is simply good writing. In so far as each is good, each converges, as regards style and literary form, with the other; and in the limiting case where each was as good as it ought to be, the distinction would disappear (PA, 298).

As Mink explains, art, in Collingwood's thought, is the dynamic power which spurs the mind to further adventures. Every mental activity is accompanied by its own characteristic emotion, which remains unexpressed at that level, and this unexpressed significance lies on the mind as a burden, challenging one to find some way of uttering it. According to Mink, 'What drives the mind to a higher level is not the thirst for knowledge or novelty, but the need to express the emotion attendant on thinking at the lower' (Mink, 1969: 237). The expression of emotion is a source of energy for all rational enquiry, and the truths we seek must not only satisfy the logical criteria of knowledge but also express the emotions which well up through the levels of consciousness (Mink, 1969: 238).

Mink's account emphasises the connection between Collingwood's philosophy of art and the dialectic of mind. Collingwood's philosophy of art, Mink points out, identifies in the aesthetic transformation of first-level consciousness the origin of all those modes of thought and action which culminate in the historical consciousness. As we have seen, whereas in *Speculum Mentis* art is a primitive stage which is superseded by thought, in *The Principles of Art* this view is transformed. Art is now the process where feeling is converted into self-conscious emotions capable of being expressed, and conscious activity at every level has its attendant emotions of which we may become fully conscious by successfully expressing them (Mink, 1969: 197–98). But the activity of expressing an emotion not only consists in becoming conscious of that emotion but is accompanied by a new emotion. As Mink argues, 'At every level of consciousness (above the first) it is necessary to distinguish between the emotion expressed and the emotion attending the activity of expressing. The activity of expressing makes us conscious of the former, and simultaneously brings the latter into being as something of which we may become conscious only in a further expressive act' (Mink, 1969: 203).

As Collingwood argues, a higher level of consciousness differs from the lower in having a new principle of organisation. It does not supersede the old but is superimposed on it. Each level of experience must organise itself on its own principles before a transition can be made to the next. Emotions of consciousness must be formally or linguistically expressed before a transition can be made from the level of consciousness to the level of intellect (PA, 233–34).

To sum up, then, for Collingwood, aesthetic activity is the crucial initial stage where we both create and apprehend ourselves and the world. A truthful consciousness is an integral and indispensable part of this. The corruption of consciousness, if it is sufficiently widespread, means the corruption of civilisation.

Collingwood's conception of art as a solution to the crisis of Western civilisation, therefore, ought to be seen in the context of the Romantic idea of art as truth. Collingwood's later philosophy provides a more detailed and nuanced account of how this is so, improving on his Ruskin-inspired early work. Nevertheless, the notion of art as the apprehension of truth, as we have seen in Chapter One, has an important place in the work of Ruskin. For example, in 'Traffic', Ruskin argues:

> … a nation cannot be affected by any vice, or weakness, without expressing it, legibly, and for ever, either in bad art, or by want of art; and … there is no national virtue, small or great, which is not manifestly expressed in all the art which circumstances enable the people possessing that virtue to produce (Ruskin, 1908: 55).

For Ruskin, a nation's art reflected the state of its spirit or inner being, and no nation could produce great art without corresponding greatness of spirit (cf. Johnston, 1967: 21).

The idea of aesthetic activity as a vehicle for rescuing European civilisation from decadence is important in the Romantic tradition, and especially for Nietzsche. Nietzsche's thinking contributed to what might be called the Ruskin tradition,[4] especially as it manifested itself in the work of D.H. Lawrence and the modernist writers, Yeats and Pound. Like Collingwood, Nietzsche regards art as having a potentially transforming effect on Western culture.

For both thinkers, as Hinz demonstrates, the world in its most basic and pristine nature is not so much a world that is thought as it is a world that is felt. Art is the creation of a world, or centre of feeling (Hinz, 1994a: 31). Nietzsche asserts, in *Thus Spoke Zarathustra*, that 'all life is dispute over taste and tasting! Taste: that is at the same time weight and scales and weigher; and woe to all living creatures that want to live without weight and scales and weigher!' (Nietzsche, 1969: 139–40). In *The Will to Power*, Nietzsche argues:

> The aesthetic state possesses a superabundance of means of communication, together with an extreme receptivity for stimuli and signs. It constitutes the high point of communication and transmission between living creatures — it is the source of languages. This is where languages originate: the languages of tone as well as the language of gestures and glances. The more complete phenomenon is always the beginning: our faculties are subtilized out of more complete faculties. But even today one hears with one's muscles, one even reads with one's muscles (Nietzsche, 1968: 809, pp. 427–28).

Nietzsche's view of the primacy of art and its transformative effect is evident in his account of artistic inspiration:

> Has anyone at the end of the nineteenth century a distinct conception of what poets of strong ages called inspiration? If not, I will describe it. — If one had the slightest residue of superstition left in one, one would hardly be able to set aside the idea that one is merely incarnation, merely mouthpiece, merely medium of overwhelming forces. The concept of revelation, in the sense that something suddenly, with unspeakable certainty and subtlety, becomes visible, audible, something that shakes and

---

[4] According to Thatcher, 'The aesthetics of Pater tended to assume an inevitable opposition between art and the way society was organized. Nietzsche, working in the tradition of Arnold, Ruskin and Morris, broadened aesthetic enquiry, releasing it from the oppressively narrow confines which Pater, and later Wilde, had imposed on it. Although Nietzsche granted art its own autonomy, he also stressed the vital relationship of art to life and society as a whole. He stood for civilization as opposed to aestheticism, and also … to socialism' (Thatcher, 1970: 273-74).

overturns one to the depths, simply describes the fact. One hears, one does not seek; one takes, one does not ask who gives; a thought flashes up like lightning, with necessity, unfalteringly formed – I never had any choice. An ecstasy whose tremendous tension sometimes discharges itself in a flood of tears, while one's steps now involuntarily rush along, now involuntarily lag ... a depth of happiness in which the most painful and gloomy things appear, not as antithesis, but as conditioned, demanded, as a necessary colour within such a superfluity of light ... Everything is in the highest degree involuntary but takes place as in a tempest of a feeling of freedom, of absoluteness, of power, of divinity. The involuntary nature of image, of metaphor is the most remarkable thing of all; one no longer has any idea what is image, what metaphor, everything presents itself as the readiest, the truest, the simplest means of expression. It really does seem, to allude to an expression of Zarathustra's, as if the things themselves approached and offered themselves as metaphors ... This is my experience of inspiration; I do not doubt that one has to go back thousands of years to find anyone who could say to me 'it is mine also' (Nietzsche, 1969: 22–23).

For both Collingwood and Nietzsche, as Hinz argues, artistic activity is the fundamental activity which creates self and world. The self-creative process is a development, and genuine self-creation can only be an ongoing practical accomplishment, independent of any external *telos* or ideal. For both Collingwood and Nietzsche, 'the self *becomes* what it is' (Hinz, 1994a: 51–52).

However, Nietzsche's understanding of the role of art is different from Collingwood's. The artistic process, for Collingwood, is a process of knowing, where knowing is a kind of making of self and world. For Nietzsche, the artistic process is a process of self-overcoming. Whereas for Collingwood the assertion of the self is an act of self-awareness, for Nietzsche the assertion or domination of the self is an act of self-transfiguration. According to Nietzsche, the self dominates its situation and imposes a kind of harmony on feelings through language and art. Hence one 'gives style' to one's character (see Hinz, 1994a: 38–41). However, Nietzsche regards conscious activity as not essential to art.

According to Nietzsche, as Hinz explains, the self-creative process of imposing order and form on a situation may fail due to a lack of vitality of the self or because of the recalcitrance of the situation. In the first case the self is 'sick' or decadent, and the decadent person has to fight his instincts. The second case is a case of weakness. The attempt to overcome a situation is directed back on the self, through a process of internalisation, and leading to 'bad conscience'. The other effect of internalisation is *ressentiment*, which means retaliation against the situation (Hinz, 1994a: 46–47).

For Nietzsche, consciousness is a development of instinctive activity, and therefore its primary function cannot be the pursuit of knowledge. Reason is no more than a reflection of irrational drives and is a vehicle for untruth (cf. Hinz, 1994a: 74–75). Nietzsche's different conception of rational consciousness from Collingwood's, as we will see in subsequent chapters, leads to a quite different view of the role of philosophy in combating the decadence of Western civilisation.

Ezra Pound was influenced by both Ruskin and Nietzsche, but it seems that Pound's emphasis on the importance of art in regenerating civilisation is more akin to Ruskin and Collingwood than Nietzsche.[5] Like Ruskin and Collingwood, Pound understands art as the apprehension of truth. Pound separates art from entertainment. He intemperately rejected the idea of poetry as entertainment, remarking: '… it flatters the mob to tell them that their importance is so great that the solace of lonely men, and the lordliest of the arts, was created for their amusement' (Pound, 1954: 64–65). According to Pound,

> The arts, literature, poesy, are a science, just as chemistry is a science. Their subject is man, mankind and the individual … The arts give us a great percentage of the lasting and unassailable data regarding the nature of man, of immaterial man, of man considered as a thinking and sentient creature (Pound, 1954: 42).

Therefore:

> Bad art is inaccurate art. It is art that makes false reports … Yet it takes a good deal of talking to convince a layman that bad art is 'immoral'. And that good art however 'immoral' it is, is wholly a thing of virtue. Purely and simply that good art can *not* be immoral. By good art I mean art that bears true witness, I mean the art that is most precise … The serious artist is scientific in that he presents the image of his desire, of his hate, of his indifference as precisely that, as precisely as the image of his own desire, hate or indifference. The more precise his record the more lasting and unassailable his work of art (Pound, 1954: 44–46).

---

[5]   Coyle points out the influence of Nietzsche and Ruskin on Pound: 'Pound indisputably absorbed a good deal of Nietzsche, but he did so through the mediation of A.R. Orage and such of his circle as J.M. Kennedy … [This] meant that the "Nietzsche" he picked up came already mixed with a stiff dose of Ruskinian cultural organicism' (Coyle, 1995: 6). According to Coyle, Pound attempted to perpetuate the Carlylean or Ruskinian tradition of treating cultural endeavour in all its aspects as an organic whole: 'In his historicist equation of artistic with economic production, his belief that discussion of the work "may almost require a discussion of its where and amid what", we can locate the fundamentally Ruskinian underpinnings of Pound's critical practice' (Coyle, 1995: 29).

For Pound,

> 'Artists are the antennae of the race.' If this statement is incomprehensible and if its corollaries need any explanation, let me put it that a nation's writers are the voltometres and steam-gauges of that nation's intellectual life. They are the registering instruments, and if they falsify their reports there is no measure to the harm that they do (Pound, 1954: 58).

The idea of art as apprehension of truth and as a means of regenerating a decadent civilisation is also proposed by D.H. Lawrence.[6] Lawrence separates art which has sexual content from pornography. The right sort of sexual stimulus is invaluable to human life, in contrast to pornography, which you can recognise '… by the insult it offers, invariably, to sex, and to the human spirit' (Lawrence, 1955: 37). According to Lawrence, it is a catastrophe for our civilisation that the deep instincts have gone dead, and sex is identified with dirt. Wagner and Charlotte Bronte are nearer pornography than Boccaccio because they were both in a state where the strongest instincts have collapsed, and sex has become something slightly obscene (Lawrence, 1955: 39). For Lawrence, there is an emphatic difference between what he calls

> the sneaking masturbation pornography of the press, the film and present-day popular literature, and then the creative portrayals of the sexual impulse that we have in Boccaccio or the Greek vase-paintings or some Pompeian art, and which are necessary for the fulfilment of our consciousness (Lawrence, 1955: 51).

The purpose of this chapter has been to highlight Collingwood's view of the crucial role of art in generating a solution to the crisis of Western civilisation. As we have seen, in Collingwood's view, becoming conscious of our emotions by expressing them is the fundamental first step in self-understanding and self-creation. It also rescues us from the 'darkness' of the corruption of consciousness. In this respect, Collingwood is working in the tradition of such writers as Ruskin, Nietzsche, Pound and Lawrence. For Collingwood, like Ruskin, Pound and Lawrence, art is the revelation of truth. Nietzsche, as I have pointed out, takes a different view.

Collingwood draws together various strands of Romantic and modernist ideas about art into a systematic and comprehensive philosophy, and this philosophy is an improvement on the Romantic cultural wholeness argument of *Speculum Mentis*. He also extends

---

[6]   Williams points out that, for Lawrence, competitive acquisitiveness and 'sheer mechanical materialism' leads to the ugliness of industrial society. Lawrence argues that 'The human soul needs actual beauty even more than bread' (cited from Williams, 1993: 201).

the Romantic philosophy of art by connecting it, as we will see in Part Two, with the idea of historical process in a systematic way. Art provides the truths, or 'self-contained individualities' (PA, 288), of individual works of art. But through these individual truths it is also constructing a world. The nature of this world (and hence the nature of the crisis of civilisation and its solution) is only fully revealed by a theory of logic and metaphysics. As I will show in Part Two, in logic and metaphysics Collingwood replaces a 'realist' conception of truth with a dialectical one.

Through aesthetic activity we first become conscious of the symptoms of the crisis of modernity, and this activity provides the first steps towards a solution. But the kind of solution that is unfolding in the activity of art becomes clearer when we look at another important aspect of this activity: the interaction between artist and community. The interaction between artist and community provides another standard for truth in art, supplementing the idea of the truthful consciousness, which I have discussed in this chapter. But it also indicates the kind of solution that Collingwood provides in his theory of logic and metaphysics for the crisis of civilisation.

Chapter Four

Artist and Community

The idea of art as a solution to the crisis of Western civilisation culminates in the notion of interaction between artist and audience, or community. For Collingwood, as this chapter will explain, art is the community's 'medicine' for the corruption of consciousness. In Part Two, I will demonstrate that the world that is constructed out of the 'self-contained individualities' of art is a dialectical one. However, this dialectical world is already implicit in the activity of art itself, as is particularly evident in his account of the interaction between artist and community. This interaction or collaboration between artist and community also supplements the idea of the truthful consciousness in art that I examined in the previous chapter.

Collingwood rejects the idea of the artist as some kind of transcendent genius, separated from common humanity. Interaction with an audience is necessary for an artist. Collingwood contends:

> The man who has something to say is not only willing to say it in public: he craves to say it in public, and feels that until it has been thus said it has not been said at all. The public is always, no doubt, a circumscribed one: it may consist only of a few friends, and at most it includes only people who can buy or borrow a book or get hold of a theatre ticket; but every artist knows that publication of some kind is a necessity to him (PA, 313).

Every artist attaches some importance to the reception he or she gets from the public. The reaction of the audience affects the artist's judgement as to the soundness of the work that he or she has done. Unless the audience agrees that the work is good, the artist wonders whether it really is good or not, and whether he or she was suffering from a corruption of consciousness. In spite of all disclaimers, Collingwood argues, artists do look upon their audiences as collaborators with themselves in the attempt to answer the question: is this a genuine work of art or not? (PA, 314)

Artistic labour, then, is undertaken not as something individual and private, but on behalf of the community to which the artist belongs. Furthermore, it is a labour in which the artist invites the community to participate. The artist will feel this

> … not only after his work is completed, but from its inception and throughout its composition. The audience is perpetually present to him as a factor in his artistic labour; not as an anti-aesthetic factor, corrupting the sincerity of his work by considerations of reputation and reward, but as an aesthetic factor, defining what the problem is which as an artist he is trying to solve — what emotions he is to express — and what constitutes a solution of it. The audience which the artist thus feels as collaborating with himself may be a large one or a small one, but it is never absent (PA, 315).

As the artist needs an audience, the audience also needs the artist. In so far as he or she feels at one with the audience, the artist will express not private emotions, but shared emotions. The artist will conceive himself or herself as the audience's spokesperson, saying for it things it wants to say, but cannot say unaided (PA, 312).

For Collingwood, the bodily or perceptible 'work of art' plays an important role in the communication between artist and audience. As we have seen, the work of art is not a bodily or perceptible thing, but an activity of the artist's consciousness. But, in order to communicate his or her experience to other people, the artist uses a bodily and perceptible thing: for example, a painted canvas, a carved stone or a written paper (PA, 300). Taking the example of painting, Collingwood argues that the aesthetic experience and the painting of a subject are bound up together. One paints a thing in order to see it. 'Seeing' here means awareness, noticing what you see. It also includes awareness of solid shapes of things, relative distances, warmth, coolness, stillness and noise. This is 'a total imaginative experience'. He argues:

> There are two experiences, an inward or imaginative one called seeing and an outward or bodily one called painting, which in the painter's life are inseparable, and form one single indivisible experience which may be described as painting imaginatively (PA, 304–5).

Every imaginative experience, Collingwood explains, is a sensuous experience raised to the imaginative level by an act of consciousness. Thus, the aesthetic experience presupposes a corresponding sensuous experience. This sensuous experience may come into being at the same time as consciousness so that it no sooner comes into being than it is transmuted into imagination. The sensuous experience in this example is the psycho-physical activity of painting, and out of this consciousness generates the aesthetic experience. The person who looks at the subject without painting it has a sensuous experience which is scantier, poorer and less highly organised than that of the artist (PA, 306–8).

A picture produces in the viewer a sensuous-emotional or psychical experience which is transmuted by consciousness into a total imaginative experience that is, in principle, identical with that of the painter. Of course there is no assurance that the imaginative experience of the spectator is identical with that of the artist, just as there is no assurance of mutual understanding between speaker and hearer in ordinary language. Our imaginative experience may often be partial and imperfect. But with a good work of art (Collingwood gives the examples of Dante's *Inferno* and Eliot's *Sweeney Among the Nightingales*), a determined and intelligent audience will always penetrate far enough to get something of value (PA, 309–11).

For Collingwood, then, the work of art properly so-called is the imaginative experience, shared by artist and audience. However, appreciation of a work of art cannot be accomplished without a physical medium, although this physical medium is not part of what is defined as art. Collingwood's emphasis on the physical medium involves a modification of his earlier claim in *The Principles of Art* that the work of art exists in the artist's head, which I mentioned in Chapter Three, and that, referring to music, 'the tune is already complete and perfect when it exists merely as a tune in the artist's head, that is, an imaginary tune' (PA, 139). Collingwood modifies his view when he comes to discuss the relation between artist and audience. Art is no longer complete in the 'head' (i.e. imagination) of the artist, but in the shared imagination of artist and audience. As a result, the physical medium, although it is not itself identified with art, becomes indispensable.

There is some controversy among commentators on this point (see Ridley, 1998; Dilworth, 1999; and Winchester, 2004). According to Collingwood's theory, a work of art is not complete until it involves interaction with an audience. Because of this, Ridley is correct in his view that works of art are not complete without being worked on in a physical medium (Ridley, 1998: 20).[1]

---

[1] However, Ridley's argument that, rather than seeing works of art as existing solely in people's heads, Collingwood thought that everything exists in people's heads, because he was a global ideal theorist (Ridley, 1998: 21) is mistaken. In

Collingwood sees it as important for the future of art and aesthetic theory that we understand the audience's function as collaborator and reject the individualistic view of art. Traditionally we think of the artist as a self-contained personality and of his or her work as 'self-expression'. In fact, Collingwood argues, everything the artist does is done in relation to others like himself or herself. Artists only become artists by learning from others. They become poets, painters or musicians by living in a society where these languages are current.[2] Self-awareness is constantly being reinforced, developed and applied in new ways through communication with others (PA 316–17).

The artist, therefore, should not become isolated from the wider world by being part of a special clique or ivory tower. Collingwood claims:

> ... it was the call of practical life that rescued Yeats from the sham world of his youthful Celtic twilight, forced him into the clear air of real Celtic life, and made him a great poet (PA, 120).

All artists have modelled their style upon that of others, used subjects that others have used and treated them as others have treated them already. In the history of art, Collingwood contends, so-called 'plagiarism' has always been the rule. The idea of plagiarism as a crime he associates with artistic barrenness and mediocrity, and a concern more with reputation than the intrinsic value of artistic work. Artists are urged to 'steal with both hands whatever they can use, wherever they can find it' (PA, 318–20). Similarly, for the dramatist and musician, there should be collaboration between author and performer. What the author puts on paper is merely the rough outline of a performance, and the performers must fill in the details. Performers should not accept their texts as fool-proof (PA, 320–21).

Collingwood takes theatre as an example of collaboration between artist and audience. In a rehearsal for a play, the performers go through the motions of acting a play, but no play is being acted. It only becomes a play when the audience is present. The play is an activity in which the audience is partner. The audience is not pas-

---

the interests of using ordinary language and avoiding metaphysical controversy, Collingwood explicitly puts to one side the idea that 'the things we describe as being in our minds are thereby as real as anything else' (PA, 131).

[2]   John Ruskin elaborates on this point in *The Political Economy of Art* (1907). As Johnson argues, in Collingwood's close connection between art and the community, '... we hear a powerful echo of those Ruskinian ideas with which he had been familiar since youth' (Johnson, 1998: 93).

sively receptive of the performance, but determines by its reception how the performance is to be carried on (PA, 322).

Collingwood therefore puts forward a series of recommendations to encourage the various kinds of artistic collaboration. He recommends getting rid of the concept of artistic ownership, and the law of copyright, as it has a detrimental effect on art:

> If he [the artist] could take what he wants wherever he could find it, as Euripides and Dante and Michelangelo and Shakespeare and Bach were free, his larder would always be full, and his cookery might be worth tasting (PA, 325).

In theatre and music, he criticises the heavy use of stage directions, as they indicate the author's distrust of the performer. Authors must become willing to let performers into their counsel, and performers must take an intelligent and instructed interest in the problems of authorship (PA, 327–28). Similarly, the audience should feel itself a partner in the work of artistic creation. This would require small and stable audiences, like that of a theatrical or musical club, where the audience feel themselves involved in the aims and projects of the group (PA, 329–30).

However, a problem arises over the place of technology in the collaboration between artist and audience. It is a weakness of printed literature, Collingwood argues, that the reciprocity between reader and writer is difficult to maintain. The relationship between artist and audience is weakened by every new mechanisation in art. Gramophone music, wireless and cinema take away the collaborative role of the audience. According to Collingwood,

> The consequence is that the gramophone, the cinema, and the wireless are perfectly serviceable as vehicles of amusement or of propaganda, for here the audience's function is merely receptive and not concreative; but as vehicles of art they are subject to all the defects of the printing-press in an aggravated form (PA, 323).

Hence, the modern popular entertainment of the cinema, unlike the Renaissance popular entertainment of the theatre, cannot produce a new form of great art because the Renaissance theatre collaboration between author, actors and audience is lacking in cinema.

But Collingwood's view is questionable here. He does not tell us why the mechanisation of art *necessarily* makes the audience's role merely receptive and not also collaborative. Collingwood rightly recognises the importance of maintaining the distinction between art proper and craft, but in his anxiety to do so he makes the mistake of identifying craft, or pseudo-art, with the use of technology as such.

Earlier, as we have seen, Collingwood held the view that the reception of a work of art cannot be separated from, and is an integral part of, the audience's collaboration with the artist in the artistic process. The audience, he claimed, is perpetually present to the artist as a factor in artistic labour (PA, 314–15). The question therefore arises: can collaboration between artist and audience take place despite the use of mechanisation in art? Or, to put it differently, can there be art proper that makes use of modern technology? Collingwood does not give us convincing reasons to the contrary.

Instead, Collingwood's distinction between art proper and craft (which resembles the distinction between 'high art' and 'mass culture') is clumsily applied, so photography and cinema are excluded from the category of art proper, along with almost everything except some painting, theatre, literature, dance and classical music. Contrary to Collingwood, it could plausibly be argued that cinema and photography, for example, can become for the artist vehicles for expressing emotion, and not only means of creating amusement or magic, can accommodate collaboration between artist and audience, and consequently can be transformed into art.

However, Collingwood seems to change his view (slightly) a few pages later, as he thinks that in art forms such as painting and literature, there can be some degree of collaboration between the artist and the wider community. Despite a note of pessimism: 'The promiscuous dissemination of books and paintings by the press and public exhibition creates a shapeless and anonymous audience whose collaborative function it is impossible to exploit' (PA, 330), he argues that with the arts of painting and non-dramatic writing (which, of course, makes use of the technology of the printing press), critics, reviewers, and literary and aesthetic journals ought to work at establishing contact between a writer or painter and the kind of audience he or she needs.

It is possible, then, Collingwood seems to say, for art proper and collaboration between artist and audience to take place in spite of mechanisation, although there are difficulties to be overcome. (At least, it is possible with writing/publishing, and if this is the case then why not also with cinema and photography?) Non-dramatic literature and painting, Collingwood argues, can be rescued by bringing them back into contact with their audience. In the case of literature, this can be done by writing on subjects about which people want to read. The artist, he suggests, can spontaneously share the interest which people around him or her feel in certain subjects, and let that determine what he or she writes about. It is necessary to leave behind the blind alley of nineteenth century individualism, and adopt a new path where the artist is the spokesperson of his or her audience (PA, 331–33).

Collingwood selects T.S. Eliot for praise on this point. Eliot took as his theme 'a subject that interests everyone, the decay of civilization' (PA, 333). Eliot's early work is seen as a series of sketches and studies leading up to *The Waste Land*. Collingwood comments:

> The poem depicts a world where the wholesome water of emotion, which alone fertilizes all human activity has dried up. Passions that once ran so strongly as to threaten the defeat of prudence, the destruction of human individuality, the wreck of men's little ships, are shrunk to nothing. No one gives; no one will risk himself by sympathizing; no one has anything to control. We are imprisoned in ourselves, becalmed in a windless selfishness. The only emotion left us is fear: fear of emotion itself, fear of death by drowning in it, fear in a handful of dust. (PA, 335)

The poem is not amusement, for example, an entertaining description of vices, or magic, for example, an incitement to political virtue. It forgoes both entertainment value and magical value and draws a subject matter from the audience themselves. Art proper is prophetic, in that it tells the audience the secrets of their own hearts and the community needs the artist because no community altogether knows its own heart. According to Collingwood, 'Art is the community's medicine for the worst disease of the mind, the corruption of consciousness' (PA, 336).[3]

The implications of the terms 'audience' and 'community', as Collingwood uses them, are beguilingly complex. It is possible to distinguish two different aspects to the dialogical relation between the artist and the 'audience' or 'community', or two senses to the term 'audience' or 'community'. Firstly, in Collingwood's description of artist and community, there is a dialogue between the artist and his or her immediate audience, perhaps a cultured and sympathetic few. But, secondly, there is a dialogue between this artistic elite and the community as a whole.

This is something that is misunderstood by Donald Taylor, who criticises Collingwood for regarding the reception of a work of art as

[3] Although Collingwood uses the word 'medicine', it is important to note that art is not to be understood instrumentally. Some commentators (Ridley, 1998; Johnson, 1998; Lewis, 1995) have found difficulties with this point. But, as Ridley argues, if art as expression is the proper business of consciousness, then art is the remedy for the corruption of consciousness, since it simply is the successful execution of the task that the corrupt consciousness fails to perform: 'Expression is not a means to the end of solving the problem posed by corruption, since it just is the solution to that problem' (Ridley, 1998: 40).

part of the collaborative activity of the audience. Taylor argues that if the artist tells the audience painful truths he or she may not receive such a favourable response, as was the case with *Madame Bovary* and *Ulysses*, among other examples of the ignorant or trivialising reception of major works of art (Taylor, 2000: 38–39). But, contrary to Taylor, great works of art, by definition, always receive a favourable reception, even if it is only from a cultured minority or from an audience in later generations: they are great works of art only in so far as they 'speak' to an audience. Nietzsche and Pound, for example, address themselves to audiences composed of the discerning few and future audiences which, at the time of writing, can only be imagined.[4]

In order to further elucidate Collingwood's account of the artist and the community, I will now compare Collingwood with Ortega y Gasset and T.S. Eliot. The role of a cultured minority in the dialogue between artist and community is highlighted by Ortega y Gasset. In *The Dehumanization of Art*, Ortega argues that whereas the art of the nineteenth century was popular with the masses, modern art is essentially unpopular. It divides the public into two groups: one very small who are favourably inclined towards it, and another very large – the hostile majority, who do not understand it (DA, 5–6). Modern art is unpopular, according to Ortega, because it distinguishes 'the illustrious' minority from 'the vulgar' masses, and undermines the assumption that all men are equal (DA, 7).

Ordinary people's view of art involves an emphasis on individuals and emotional arousal. A man likes a play when in the human drama presented to him the emotions move his heart as though it were happening in real life:

> And he calls a work 'good' if it succeeds in creating the illusion necessary to make the imaginary personages appear like living persons. In poetry he seeks the passion and pain of the man behind the poet. Paintings attract him if he finds on them figures of men and women whom it would be interesting to meet. A landscape is pronounced 'pretty' if the country it represents deserves for its loveliness or its grandeur to be visited on a trip (DA, 9).

Ortega contends: 'Not only is grieving and rejoicing at such human destinies as a work of art presents or narrates a very different thing from true artistic pleasure, but preoccupation with the human content of the work is in principle incompatible with aesthetic enjoyment proper' (DA, 9–10). A work of art 'vanishes from sight for a

---

[4]   The dedication in Nietzsche's *Thus Spoke Zarathustra*, for example, is 'A book for everyone and no one'.

beholder who seeks in it nothing but the moving fate of John and Mary or Tristan and Isolde and adjusts his vision to this' (DA, 10).

> But [according to Ortega] not many people are capable of adjusting their perceptive apparatus to the pane and the transparency that is the work of art. Instead they look right through it and revel in the human reality with which the work deals. When they are invited to let go of this prey and to direct their attention to the work of art itself they will say that they cannot see such a thing, which indeed they cannot, because it is all artistic transparency and without substance (DA, 11).

For Ortega, nineteenth century art, which he refers to as 'Romanticism', reduced the strictly aesthetic elements to a minimum and let the work consist almost entirely in a fiction of human realities. Hence they were realistic, and Romanticism and naturalism have common realistic roots. Accordingly, modern art 'divides the public into two classes, those who understand it and those who do not understand it — that is to say, those who are artists and those who are not. The new art is an artistic art' (DA, 12).

The new artists found that they had no use for traditional art; and their way of feeling represents the inevitable and fruitful result of all previous artistic achievement. The alternative to developing a new art is to obstinately remain shut up in old forms (DA, 13). The most general and characteristic feature of the new artistic sensibility, modern artistic production, is the tendency to dehumanise art. But, as Ortega explains:

> This new sensibility is a gift not only of the artist proper but also of his audience. When I said above that the new art is an art for artists I understood by 'artists' not only those who produce this art but also those who are capable of perceiving purely artistic values (DA, 20n).

Whereas nineteenth century art tended to reflect reality, the modern artist, in contrast, sets out to deform it and dehumanise it. The sentiments and passions of the new art belong to something other than primary human life. Rather they evoke secondary passions, specifically aesthetic sentiments (DA, 22). But it is not simply a matter retreating from reality: 'to construct something that is not a copy of "nature" and yet has a structure of its own is a feat which presupposes nothing less than genius' (DA, 23). Ortega contends that the realism of the nineteenth century was a 'freak in aesthetic evolution', and that 'All great periods of art have been careful not to let the work revolve about human contents' (DA, 25). Thus the new inspiration on one point is a return to the road of art, which is called the 'will to style'. To stylize is to deform reality and to dehumanise (DA, 25).

Consequently, modern art aims to distinguish between delight and titillation. Art must not proceed by 'psychic contagion', as in Romanticism:

> … art ought to be full clarity, high noon of the intellect. Tears and laughter are, aesthetically, frauds. The gesture of beauty never passes beyond smiles, melancholy or delighted. If it can do without them, better still (DA, 27).

As Ortega argues, seeing requires distance. Art removes and transfigures its objects, and without this derealisation, there is perplexity:

> The new sensibility, it seems to me, is dominated by a distaste for human elements in art very similar to the feelings cultured people have always experienced at Madame Tussaud's, while the mob has always been delighted by that gruesome waxen hoax (DA, 29).

In the new art metaphoric expression is one of the instruments of dehumanisation:

> Before, reality was overlaid with metaphors by way of ornamentation; now the tendency is to eliminate the extrapoetical, or real, prop and to "realize" the metaphor, to make it the *res poetica* (DA, 36–37).

According to Ortega, a distance separates the idea from the thing. Yet, with the natural attitude, our yearning for reality leads to an idealisation of reality. If we take ideas for what they are and realise them, we do not move from the mind to the world. Rather, we 'worldify' the immanent (DA, 38). Ortega's explanation of this point resembles Collingwood's distinction between art and traditional portrait painting:

> A traditional painter painting a portrait claims to have got hold of the real person when, in truth and at best, he has set down on the canvas a schematic selection, arbitrarily decided on by his mind, from the innumerable traits that make a living person. What if the painter changed his mind and decided to paint not the real person but his own idea, his pattern, of the person? Indeed, in that case the portrait would be the truth and nothing but the truth, and failure would no longer be inevitable. In foregoing to emulate reality the painting becomes what is authentically is: an image, an unreality (DA, 38).

For Ortega, then, modern art has grown out of a conscious antagonism to traditional style. An ever-growing mass of traditional styles hampers the direct and original communication between the nascent artist and the world around him. In this case one of two things may happen. Either tradition stifles all creative power, or the new art, step by step, breaks free of the old which threatened to smother it. 'The latter', Ortega claims, 'is typical of Europe whose futuristic instinct, predominant throughout its history, stands in marked contrast to the irremediable traditionalism of the Orient' (DA, 44). The dehumanisation of art is inspired by just such an aversion against the traditional interpretation of realities.

Ortega argues that the tendency in modern art to attack all previous art betrays a hatred of Western civilisation up until the present time. Hence cubism, for example, makes fun of itself as art, and the new art ridicules art itself. Curiously, Ortega's argument culminates in the assertion that art has become a thing of no transcending importance (DA, 49). Art no longer undertakes to save mankind, as it did in the nineteenth century. Instead it has changed its position in the hierarchy of human activities and interests. Art has now moved to 'the outer rings' and become a minor issue. The trend towards pure art is a sign of modesty (DA, 52).

Nevertheless, it seems that art retains much of its importance for Ortega, as he regards changes in art as symptomatic of changes in civilisation. For Ortega, it is in art and pure science, precisely because they are the freest activities and least dependent on social conditions, that the first signs of any changes in collective sensibility become noticeable:

> A fundamental revision of man's attitude towards life is apt to find its first expression in artistic creation and scientific theory. The fine texture of both these matters renders them susceptible to the slightest breeze of the spiritual trade-winds. As in the country, opening the window of a morning, we examine the smoke rising from the chimney-stacks in order to determine the wind that will rule the day, thus we can, with a similar meteorological purpose, study the art and science of the young generation (DA, 42).

There are interesting similarities between Ortega's account of the transcending of realism with a purer and more dehumanised art and Collingwood's account of the gradual distinction of art proper from amusement and magic. But there are important differences. Unlike Ortega, for Collingwood, as we have seen, art is not something distinct from reality and the effect of art is not to distance one from reality; rather art uncovers the truth about human emotions, and creates reality anew. And this different conception of art leads to a different view of the role of the audience and wider community. Like Ortega, Collingwood recognises that the audience which an artist addresses himself or herself to is often a cultivated minority. But whereas Ortega draws a distinction between art and life, for Collingwood art is co-extensive with the whole of human experience. We are all artists in our everyday lives because every utterance and gesture that we make is a work of art (PA, 285). The implication of Collingwood's philosophy of art is that the barrier between 'the masses' and those who understand art is permeable and flexible. For Collingwood, unlike Ortega, people are not essentially incapable of adjusting their perspective in order to appreciate art proper. If they are incapable at a given time, this is something that can change with education and experience. In this sense, Collingwood takes a more democratic and 'dialectical' view than Ortega.

Collingwood's view is that, although the 'community' or audience that the artist primarily appeals to may be only a select few, everybody is, nevertheless, to some degree a part of this community or audience. In this Collingwood resembles T.S. Eliot. Eliot held the view that, in the interaction between the artist and the wider community, it is to the benefit of art that the community should be as broad as possible. He argues that art tends to flourish when it has a wide variety of cultural influences, and that the development of art in individual European countries owes much to a common European culture. On the subject of poetry, he contends that no one nation or language would have achieved what it has if the same art had not been cultivated in neighbouring countries and in different languages. When several countries of Europe are cut off from each other, literature and poetry in every country must deteriorate (Eliot, 1962: 112–13).

According to Eliot, literary review journals are an important part of the transmission of ideas which 'fertilises and renovates' literature in individual European countries, and the failure of his own literary review, *The Criterion*, was due to a 'closing of the mental frontiers of Europe' in the 1930s (Eliot, 1962: 116). Also, literature of that period suffered from a divisive obsession with politics, which 'tends to destroy the cultural unity of Europe' (Eliot, 1962: 117). *The Criterion*, on the other hand, had 'a common concern for the highest standards both of thought and of expression', and

> … a common curiosity and openness of mind to new ideas. The ideas with which you did not agree, the opinions which you could not accept, were as important to you as those which you found immediately acceptable. You examined them without hostility, and with the assurance that you could learn from them (Eliot, 1962: 117–18).

This stress that Eliot places on cultural openness and transmission of ideas resembles Collingwood's account of 'historicism', in *Ruskin's Philosophy*, as fundamentally tolerant, and of his later distinction between dialectical discussion and eristical discussion in *The New Leviathan* (NL, 24.58–59). Hence Eliot's conception of cultural dialogue points to a connection between Collingwood's dialogical view of the interaction between artist and community and his historicist and dialectical view of philosophy in general. Collingwood's response to the crisis of civilisation is only fully evident when we move beyond his philosophy of art to his theory of logic and metaphysics, which I examine in Part Two. But his dialectical logic and metaphysics, with its emphasis on dialogue, is implicit in his account of the artist and the community. Unlike Eliot, however, Collingwood does provide a systematic and comprehensive dialectical logic and metaphysics, and, as I will demonstrate in Part Three, this is the conceptual framework for a liberal politics.

For Eliot, like Ortega, the artist interacts not only with his or her community but with a tradition. According to Eliot in *Tradition and the Individual Talent*, the value of a work of art is only to be judged against the background of the entire literary tradition, and poetry is 'not the expression of personality, but an escape from personality' (cited from Vanheeswijck, 1996: 80). Eliot argues that tradition is a living, conscious power, and the artist writes '... not merely with his own generation in his bones, but with a feeling that the whole literature of his own country has a simultaneous existence and composes a simultaneous order' (cited from Vanheeswijck, 1996: 85). I contend that there is implicit in Collingwood's account of the creative process as a dialogue between artist and community an interaction between innovation and tradition. Ortega places more emphasis on the innovative side of this interaction, and Eliot on the traditional. Collingwood's philosophy of art, then, is consistent with a historicist view of philosophy. The interaction between innovation and tradition described here also corresponds with Larmore's account of Romanticism. Larmore's description of irony, or 'the disquiet of never feeling fully at home' (1996: 70), coincides with the Ortegean emphasis on innovation.

Collingwood's view of the relation between artist and community is not outrightly elitist, in the sense that is often attributed to Nietzsche and the modernist writers of the early twentieth century, such as Pound, Lawrence, Yeats and Eliot. In Collingwood's philosophy of art elitism has a positive role to play. An artistic elite may provide the dynamic impetus to extend our boundaries, explore new ground, and escape from the stifling weight of what is already accepted as tradition in any particular community. However, this is complemented by the dialogical view that the 'community' which an artist interacts with is open-ended and unlimited.

The elitism of Nietzsche and the modernists is sometimes seen as responsible for their toying with illiberal, and, in the case of Pound, fascist, political views.[5] It may be the case, therefore, that these illiberal political views stem from a failure in their philosophies to provide an account of the dialogical relation between artist and community. Alternatively, where their philosophies are sound, the political anti-liberalism of the modernists may be due to a failure to apply them coherently and consistently to politics.

As I have argued in the previous chapter, Collingwood's later philosophy improved and modified the view of art that he held in *Speculum Mentis*. Whereas in the latter art was an inadequate form of experience, transcended by thought, in *The Principles of Art* Collingwood recognised that imagination (or art) is an integral part of thought.

Similarly, in *The Principles of Art*, the idea of artist and community that Collingwood appeals to improves on his view in *Speculum Mentis*. As Taylor demonstrates, Collingwood's understanding of the role of the audience gradually changed in the development of his philosophy of art. In *Speculum Mentis* and *Outlines of a Philosophy of Art*, the audience to a work of art is seen as having a merely passive or receptive role. But by the time of *The Principles of Art*, the audience is seen as having a more important role, involving a close partnership with artists (Taylor, 2000: 32–34). The collaborative role of the audience, outlined in *The Principles of Art*, is an improvement on Collingwood's attempt to find a solution to the crisis of civilisation through a union of the forms of experience in *Speculum Mentis*, as it demonstrates to a greater degree that art can have a regenerative effect for people who are not professional artists.

However, this more historicised view of art, and the dialogical account of interaction between artist and community, was already implicit in Collingwood's early philosophy. As we have seen, in *Ruskin's Philosophy* he discussed Ruskin's confusion as to how greatness in art often seems to herald the downfall of a civilisation, while a high state of moral nobility may coexist with a complete absence of art. In response, Collingwood argued that the perfection of any one style leads to a dilemma between becoming imitative or launching out into the void in search of a new style or a new ideal (EPA, 37–38).

---

[5]   John Carey provides an interesting account of the elitism of Nietzsche and the modernists, albeit a somewhat polemical and lop-sided one, in *The Intellectuals and the Masses* (1992). For a more sober analysis of Pound's fascism, see Redman's *Ezra Pound and Italian Fascism* (1991).

According to Donagan, working out this more historicised conception of art compelled Collingwood to change from explaining art as the apprehension of beauty to conceiving art as the expression of emotion. In Donagan's view, the earlier definition of art as imagination referred only to its cognitive side. Collingwood needed to answer the question of what we are trying to achieve by imagining, and of what does an artist try to become aware. To do this, he had to go from Ruskin to Croce. Croce solved the problem by arguing that art is the expression of emotion, and emotion strives towards expression. Collingwood gradually assimilated this solution, and had wholly done so by the time he came to write *The Principles of Art* (Donagan, 1964: xvii–xix). Here he argues that 'aesthetic theory is the theory not of beauty but of art' (PA, 41). Collingwood, then, moves beyond Ruskin's more static conception of art to provide a thoroughly historicised account of art as an ever-continuing process.

Collingwood's conception of 'art proper' in *The Principles of Art*, however, has been criticised as being Platonist by T.J. Diffey, who argues that, unlike in the earlier *Outlines of a Philosophy of Art*, Collingwood fails to discuss the history of art (Diffey, 1995a: 242). According to Diffey, Collingwood drops his idea of 'art proper' on top of his cultural narrative without offering any historical explanation for its entrance. Despite Collingwood's attempts to reconcile history and metaphysics, Diffey claims:

> ... 'art proper' as a metaphysical notion, must seem securely immune to and above any historical change or development which might, and indeed does, actually occur in the arts. 'Art proper' remains a Platonic standard outside historical developments in art which some particular works of art will approximate to more than others (Diffey, 1995a: 241).

However, in the Introduction to *The Principles of Art*, Collingwood does indicate that the word 'art' has a history and gives an, albeit very brief, outline of this history. Collingwood points out that the Greeks and the Romans had no conception of what we call art as something different from craft. He argues:

> It was not until the seventeenth century that the problems of aesthetic began to be disentangled from those of technic or the philosophy of craft. In the late eighteenth century the disentanglement had gone so far as to establish a distinction between the fine arts and the useful arts; where 'fine' arts meant, not delicate or highly skilled arts, but 'beautiful' arts (les beaux arts, le belle arti, die schöne Kunst). In the nineteenth century this phrase, abbreviated by leaving out the epithet and generalized by substituting the singular for the distributive plural, became 'art'. (PA, 6)

It seems that Collingwood would concur with Raymond Williams who also argues that the idea of 'art', as distinct from craft, is the outcome of an historical process. According to Williams, in the late eighteenth century and early nineteenth century, a number of words came for the first time into common English use, or, where they had already been generally used in the language, acquired new and important meanings. In this context are five key words: 'industry', 'democracy', 'class', 'art' and 'culture' (Williams, 1993: xiii). The word 'art' changed around this time from its original sense of a human attribute, a 'skill', to a particular group of skills, the 'imaginative' or 'creative' arts. A separation grew up between 'artist' and 'craftsman' (Williams, 1993: xv–xvi).

Collingwood, then, should not be seen as Platonist or essentialist in his conception of art. As Diffey observes, if there is an essentialist fallacy, Collingwood does not commit it because Collingwood's view is that 'art proper' names not a property which works of art share, but rather 'art proper' designates that complex and corporate activity undertaken by artists and audiences in a reciprocal relationship described at length in *The Principles of Art* (Diffey, 1995b: 76). Collingwood's theory of meaning is different from that of the Wittgensteinians in being both broader and normative (cf. Diffey, 1995b: 74):

> The proper meaning of a word … is never something upon which the word sits perched like a gull on a stone; it is something over which the word hovers like a gull over a ship's stern. Trying to fix the proper meaning in our minds is like coaxing the gull to settle in the rigging, with the rule that the gull must be alive when it settles: one must not shoot it and tie it there. The way to discover the proper meaning is to ask not 'what do we mean?' but, 'what are we trying to mean?' And this involves the question 'What is preventing us from meaning what we are trying to mean?' These impediments, the improper meanings which distract our minds from the proper one, are of three kinds. I shall call them obsolete meanings, analogical meanings, and courtesy meanings (PA, 7).

As Alan Donagan rightly points out, whether art properly so called is definable cannot be settled *a priori*. You must examine the aesthetic usage of the word, and Collingwood's aim was to define the actual usage of the word 'art' in the modern European critical tradition (Donagan, 1962: 122 and 104). According to Donagan, Collingwood appeals to and his definition is roughly true of the critical tradition in literature of Coleridge, Croce and T.S. Eliot, which condemns every work that is in any degree inexpressive (Donagan, 1962: 123 and 126), and which I refer to as 'Romanticism'.

Collingwood's philosophy of art belongs to a tradition, but it also explains and develops that tradition. Collingwood also adds to what I have called the Romantic tradition, as I will demonstrate in Part Two, by working out a dialectical conception of logic and metaphysics as a solution to the crisis of civilisation, something which I have argued is implicit in his philosophy of art.

Peters argues that Collingwood's philosophy of art failed to rectify the problem of subjectivism. Collingwood's attempt to develop the idea of art as language, to identify error with the corruption of consciousness, and to view art as a communal activity failed to provide a solution to this problem, Peters claims, asserting that 'counting heads is not a measure for objectivity' (Peters, 1995: 124). According to Peters, Collingwood only overcame subjectivism by basing the dialectic of subjective mind on historical inter-subjectivity in his work on logic, metaphysics and theory of civilisation, something which was incomplete because of ill health and premature death (Peters, 1995: 125).

However, contrary to Peters, the idea of historical inter-subjectivity is present in Collingwood's philosophy of art. Collingwood, as we have seen, argues that the corruption of consciousness will be recognised through comparison with other occasions of successful and failed expression (PA, 281–84). Truthfulness in art is measured not simply by the 'counting of heads', but by taking into account the history of the artist's and the community's previous expressions. The expressive labour of the artist is normative, or 'criteriological' (to use the term that Collingwood employs in *An Essay on Metaphysics*).

We move, therefore, from considering the importance of Collingwood's philosophy of art (as a critique of the crisis of civilisation) to outlining the importance of his theory of dialectic not, as Peters seems to argue, because of a flaw in Collingwood's philosophy of art which is corrected by his theory of civilisation and dialectic, but because from the truths which art expresses, the details are worked out by thought proper. The crisis of civilisation becomes more fully revealed in his account of logic and metaphysics.

Part Two

Logic and Metaphysics

Chapter Five

A Revolution in Logic

Part One demonstrated the importance of Collingwood's philosophy of art as a critique of contemporary civilisation. I first outlined Collingwood's conception of the crisis of civilisation in terms of the separation of the forms of experience from one another and then in terms of a suppression of emotion, the symptoms of which are industrialisation and the predominance of amusement art in contemporary culture. As a solution, Collingwood advocates the Romantic idea of 'unity of mind', and stresses the importance of art. Art, as we have seen, is the expression of emotion and consciousness of truth, and involves collaboration between artist and audience.

For Collingwood, we first apprehend and create the world through aesthetic activity, but it is only through thought proper that the nature of the world is fully revealed to us. Hence, Collingwood's philosophy of art provides the first steps towards recognising the symptoms of the crisis of modernity and finding a solution, but the nature of this crisis and its solutions are only fully understood by examining his theory of logic and metaphysics.

Part Two will explain how Collingwood's reformulation of traditional logic and metaphysics in a dialectical and historicist manner provides a diagnosis and a solution to the crisis of Western civilisation. It will become apparent that, for Collingwood, the essence of the problems facing contemporary Western civilisation is an over-reliance on abstract forms of thought connected with natural science and a failure to think historically and dialectically. The solution, then, is dialectical thinking.

As Mink comments, Collingwood's philosophy is informed by a conceptual system that is '*dialectical*, in a complex and original way' (Mink, 1972: 155), and 'the key to understanding Collingwood's thought is an appreciation of how fundamentally and pervasively dialectical it is' (Mink, 1972: 168). Peters also points out that 'Collingwood's philosophy is thoroughly dialectical', and that Collingwood's logic of question and answer should be interpreted as an original reform of the Hegelian dialectic (Peters, 1995: 107-8).

A convenient place to begin an examination of Collingwood's account of the transitions that Western civilisation has undergone and the difficulties it faces is his unpublished manuscript, 'A Foot-note to Future History', written in 1919. In this manuscript Collingwood argues that 'The history of civilisation is known to us as the history of Platonism. The modern world first becomes coherent in Greece, and Plato is the expression of the Greek idea' (FFH, 1). Platonism was the philosophy of the Greco-Roman world and of the Middle Ages: '… the Middle Ages are Platonism become incarnate: and no other philosophy has ever achieved this fullness of self-determination' (FFH, 2).

But, according to Collingwood, the Platonism of the Middle Ages has been gradually drawing to a close ever since Descartes pointed the road to a new philosophy—subjective, idealistic, concrete, where Platonism is objective, realistic, and abstract. The seeds of change, Collingwood asserts, lay in Platonism itself. Plato's ethics are idealistic and subjective, and therefore in open conflict with his metaphysics: 'Idealism was always ready to raise its head in the heart of the Platonic system' (FFH, 3).

The new philosophy struggled to birth with Descartes, Locke, Berkeley and Kant, but 'It remained for Hegel to go to the root of the matter, to deny the axioms of Aristotle's logic and to assert the unity of the real and the phenomenal, in the synthetic concept of history. The new philosophy foreshadowed by Descartes, was thus at last expressed. It is the absolute antithesis of Platonism—a dialectical antithesis: in fact a synthesis of Platonism with the philosophical nihilism against which Plato fought' (FFH, 4). Since Descartes, Collingwood argues, idealism and Platonism have been at war with one another:

> In this century live Hegelism is struggling with the dead matter of the corpse of Platonism. There can be no doubt which will win: and as Platonism was the philosophy on which all human life was built up to the present time, so Hegelism is that of the next age. But Hegelism does not yet exist. It has had its Plato: it may yet find its Aristotle: in order to become the philosophy of all mankind it must pass through all the stages through which Platonism passed, till a new Age of Faith systematises it into a concrete civilization founded on Hegel as the Middle Ages were founded on Plato. (FFH, 2)

According to Collingwood,

> Hegelism today is the property of the learned: the common people are Platonists. We speak of the 'plain man's realism'; but the plain man learnt his realism and his logic at the feet of Aquinas and Duns Scotus, in the Sorbonne and the Great Hall of the University of Oxford. He must learn idealism and the philosophy of contradiction in the unfounded universities of the future—after he has unlearnt his realism. (FFH, 7)

For Collingwood, then, Platonism needs to be replaced by a new philosophy and this involves what he later referred to in *An Autobiography* as a 'revolution' in logic (A, 52). The different aspects of the crisis or decadence that Collingwood draws attention to are manifestations of a failure by Western civilisation to fully adapt itself to this new philosophy. Collingwood's first attempts to work out his contribution to the revolution in logic came in the unpublished manuscripts *Truth and Contradiction*, written in 1917, and *Libellus de Generatione*, of 1920. Because of their importance in providing a detailed account of Collingwood's dialectical logic, I will make extensive reference to both.

In *Truth and Contradiction*, Collingwood re-evaluates the coherence theory of truth. According to the coherence theory of truth, non-contradiction, consistency with itself, is the mark of truth, and a collection of true statements will cohere with one another. This view is summed up in the three 'laws of thought' of traditional Aristotelian logic, according to which firstly A is A, secondly A cannot also be B, and thirdly any given thing must be either A or not A. These are the three laws of identity, contradiction and excluded middle (TC, 1).

However, unless a false statement contains in itself the truth which it contradicts, it is coherent and as such true. It may be replied that there is a body of true opinions, whether we can distinguish them from false ones or not, and their nature is to cohere with themselves and with each other (TC, 4). 'Thus', Collingwood points out,

> the last word of the coherence theory seems to be an appeal from the world of judgements as we know them to a transcendent world of absolutely true judgements; a world in which error is entirely absent and truth has taken on a final form incapable of improvement. Metaphysically this seems to be Platonism, the erection of an ideal world over against the phenomenal world, of a world from which the recalcitrant elements of our own are forcibly banished. (TC, 5)

However, this does not explain error, development and change. The transcendent world of the coherence theory does not explain the way in which truths are attained and stated in the real world of our own experience. The formula 'A is A', Collingwood argues, is the formula of tautology, but the element of tautology is present as a kind of substratum in every judgement. The formula 'A is A' has a certain value, but it acquires this value when we recognise as its complement the formula 'A is B' (TC, 6). The law of identity only becomes true when it is interpreted as the law of identity as difference, and of difference as identity.

The coherence theory of truth assumes that in the case of a discussion between contradictory views, one view must be right and the other wrong; and the debate would be devoted to discovering which was right and which was wrong. Collingwood explains: 'The debate described in these terms is what Plato would call not dialectic but eristic; it aims not at truth but at victory' (TC, 8). However, the real reason for debate, Collingwood contends, is to increase the comprehension of each by the inclusion in one's own view of that which seemed to contradict it:

> There can be no more real advance in knowledge than the discovery that your opponent's diabolical heresy is your own dearest truth in disguise. The advance lies not merely in the satisfaction at having won an ally, or in the removal of the helpless feeling of despair that anyone should be so perverse in his opinions; but in a real growth of one's own view, which gains strength, vitality and truth by comprehending and including its opponent. (TC, 8)

For Collingwood, then, 'That truth is greatest or truest which expresses most, which includes most successfully within itself a number of diverse and by themselves conflicting points of view. The victories by which a truth lives are not the annihilation but the conquest and absorption of its opponents. It is no use proving to a man that he is mistaken; your task is to show him why he went wrong, and how his real meaning is provided for and safeguarded by the view which he was attempting to resist' (TC, 8–9).

Thought, therefore, cannot be split up into unitary judgements, which are true or false: 'Truth and falsehood are attributes not of single isolated judgements but of systems of thought, systems in which every judgement is coloured by all the others' (TC, 12a). A single judgement may be true, but '… true not by being isolated from others, but by absorbing into itself and acquiring in the process its significance; by becoming the concentrated vehicle of a whole system of thought' (TC, 12b).

Furthermore, truth and falsehood are not merely matters of degree. A theory which supersedes another is different not merely in degree, but in kind. One theory may express fully the truth of another and at the same time supersede it by reconciling to it the contradictory which previously had proved recalcitrant (TC, 14). Hence Collingwood argues:

> We seem forced to the conclusion that the truth of a judgement is shown, not by its power of resisting contradiction and of preserving itself unchanged in the face of opposition, but precisely by the ease with which it accepts contradiction and undergoes modification in order to include points of view which once it excluded. Not self-preservation but self-criticism is the mark of a truth; and the enjoyment of truth is not an achievement but an activity. It is an activity, because every statement must have a contradictory. (TC, 14b–14c)

Collingwood rejects the notion of absolute truth, outside of which nothing can fall, which human thought can attain. The absolute is an abstraction, and to imagine it '… is only to express our weariness of the labour involved in continual thinking; to attain it would be not the consummation but the negation of life' (TC, 14c). The activity of thought is its own end, and '… its own value is only shown by the readiness with which it will decompose in the soil of a future crop. Truth is not a possession, but an activity' (TC, 15).

However, the view that no truth is truer than it's contradictory also applies to our own theory of truth (TC, 16). Collingwood's dialectical account of logic is true only in so far as it includes within itself and transcends traditional Aristotelian logic. Boucher is correct therefore in his view that Collingwood's theory can be seen as an 'extension and elaboration' of coherence theory (Boucher, 1985: 66). Collingwood's theory does 'absorb' coherence theory, but nevertheless it also transcends it.

In disputing with an antagonist we do not rely on mere refutation. Collingwood sums up the dialectical account of truth in the following way:

> We do not simply aim at showing him that he is wrong, and thereby drive him to adopt our view as the only alternative. We aim rather at understanding his view and sympathising with it; we admit freely that within limits it is true and sound; and only when that is accomplished do we go on to show that it falls short of being as satisfactory as it might be, and that it is capable of certain more or less definable improvements. (TC, 20)

Error, therefore, is incomplete truth: truth that fails to be quite satisfactory because it is not sufficiently comprehensive, and because it has left outside itself unassimilated contradictions. Equally, no truth is final, and every truth is partial error. There is a 'union of truth and falsehood in every judgement'. (TC, 20)

Henry Jones, in his reader's report on *Truth and Contradiction*, appreciated the dialectical nature of Collingwood's account of thought:

> I do not know any writer more frank. He cares not one whit to what extent he exposes his flanks to his critics, and makes statements which, taken by themselves, look either purely absurd or preposterously untrue. But that is only one side: on the other is the fact that these statements are *stages* or *steps* in the development of his main argument, half truths or sheer errors in which it is not possible to rest and which just compel a movement onwards to a wider truth. And this is precisely what he means, and rightly means, by 'dialectic', the way in which 'the development of thought' takes place (EPP, 230).

According to Jones, 'All the time he is showing the true nature of Philosophy, and finding that *movement, activity, process* is the living soul of all thinking and of all objects of thought' (EPP, 231).

Collingwood's revolution in logic became further developed in his unpublished manuscript of 1920, *Libellus de Generatione*. This manuscript also presents a clearer account of how the revolution in logic is a solution to a crisis in Western civilisation. According to Collingwood,

> My fundamental doctrine is that reality is becoming, that is to say reality not so much is as happens, which implies that the reality of mind is the process of its experience, its life, and nothing else. Nor do I admit any dualism between mind and its object such that while mind is wholly process its object can be conceived as a static whole outside it. The object is process too, and these are not two processes but one process (Collingwood, 1920a: 1).

Since Plato, Collingwood explains, all philosophy has revolved around the concept of being, and the general epistemology of being, with its clear-cut distinction between knower and known, 'subject' and 'object', has even commended itself to

> ... the man in the street and the man behind the plough ... It seems to us, today, a philosophy natural to the human condition: we forget the vast process of education by which our world has assimilated it, and we do not realise that it was definitely created by the Greeks, imposed upon humanity by the commanding prestige of their authority, and liable, like other human inventions, to reach its term of life and yield place to a successor (Collingwood, 1920a: 4).

When subject and object are regarded as separate entities with a knowledge-relation between them, it emerges that each is indifferently the other: the subject is defined in terms of the object and vice versa. A mind is nothing but its being conscious of something and has no character of its own in distinction from the object. Similarly the object becomes defined in terms of what I know about it and has no content except the content of the subject (Collingwood, 1920a: 6–8).

There are therefore two forms of realism, that is, of the philosophy which conceives the subject and the object as independent existences united by a relation. Firstly, there is objectivism, whereby the mind simply is the object. But it fails to explain why there should be such a thing in the world as somebody's process of thinking about something. On its assumption this process ought not to exist (Collingwood, 1920a: 12). A second possibility is subjectivism, whereby the subject is complete at every moment. It can have no defect of anything; it has nothing to aim at, because any goal is already within itself. All problems and difficulties are exorcised by the formula 'that which is, is' (Collingwood, 1920a: 15). Objectivism and subjectivism are opposites whose conclusions turn out to be indistinguishable: 'Each alike denies space, time and change, because each begins from a formula which excludes these and gives a static account of thought' (Collingwood, 1920a: 16).

Realism, then, leads to a rigid static monism, as has been discussed by the *Parmenides* of Plato. Subjectivism and Objectivism are both names for the same fundamental position: that opposites are indifferently identical (Collingwood, 1920a: 19). According to Collingwood, 'This *coincidentia oppositorium* is the necessary outcome, though at the same time the flat contradictory of the realist or materialist logic, and here realism expires by its own hand' (Collingwood, 1920a: 35). In following out the implications of this logic, therefore, we arrive at the conclusion that opposites coincide: a discovery indicated by Plato and a commonplace of Christian mysticism. The whole world of being, the whole philosophical tradition that we inherit from Plato and Aristotle, crumbles into dust at the sight of this principle. According to Collingwood,

> The whole of that Greco-medieval world upon whose foundations our own is for the most part still standing was a world constructed on the logic of abstract identity, and its life depended on its success in silencing that principle of *coincidentia oppositorum* which was yet its own necessary consequence … The world of realistic logic has never been free from bad dreams. Far more than the natural sorrows and pains of life it has suffered from the awful brooding shadow of nothingness, the shadow of that gulf which to the question 'to be or not to be?' answers 'being is itself nothing'. To a world living under that shadow, it seemed reasonable enough that people who pointed to the shadow would be burnt alive (Collingwood, 1920a: 37).

Like Nietzsche, therefore, Collingwood regards Western civilisation as reaching a point of crisis because of the contradictions inherent in the Platonic ontology of being. The different aspects of the crisis of civilisation that Collingwood draws attention to throughout his philosophy can be seen as manifestations or symptoms of the struggle to overcome realism, or Platonism, and to develop a dialectical logic as a solution.

Nietzsche similarly argued that Western culture was confronted by 'nihilism' because of the dominance of decadent modes of valuation based on *ressentiment*. For Nietzsche, nihilism is the culminating condition of Western culture because of contradictions within its dominant modes of valuation (cf. Hinz, 1994a: 161–65). Parallels with both Nietzsche and Ortega y Gasset help to illuminate our understanding of Collingwood's conception of the decadence of the West, but these parallels will be examined in more detail further on in Chapter Seven.

In finding a solution to the crisis of civilisation, Collingwood explains in *Libellus de Generatione*, any attempt to develop a philosophy antithetical to that which we have analysed would be futile. An idealist or spiritualist or monist philosophy '… will only prove identical with its opposite and lead to the same result, the destruction of itself and its world in the gulf of undifferentiated identity' (Collingwood, 1920a: 37).

But, in the cycle of realism from its rise to its final collapse something was all the time going on which was not its own opposite: namely the march of argument, the process of thought. This is the world of becoming or process, and '… it neither contains nor rests upon nor presupposes a world of being' (Collingwood, 1920a: 45). Collingwood argues:

> In the world of becoming distinctions are real just because they are not pure: A is A not by rejecting Bness, but by admitting it, by being B: it achieves identity just by undergoing diversity, asserts itself as itself by negating itself and becoming something else. This means that if we take any pair of opposites we shall never find either in a 'pure' state, excluding its other: we shall invariably find both together in a synthesis where the presence of each depends on the presence of the other (Collingwood, 1920a: 47).

Hence we must reinterpret the category of identity and difference, and 'here we arrive at the fundamental principle of the world of becoming, namely the synthesis of opposites' (Collingwood, 1920a: 48–49). Identity means that the past phase of a process is preserved in the present phase. However reality is no more change than it is permanence: 'The world is not divided into two parts, that which changes and that which remains permanent: it changes through and through, down to its very bones. And in this incessant change it remains unalterably the same' (Collingwood, 1920a: 56).

To regard the two moments of becoming, change and permanence, as embodied in separate worlds is the error of a philosophy of being. Collingwood remarks:

> These are fashions of speech borrowed by Christianity from Platonism, and ill-suited to her own peculiar genius. Indeed, Christianity has long been straitened in this tabernacle of Platonism and it may be that in a philosophy of becoming she has a house to her liking at last (Collingwood, 1920a: 57).

As Massimo Iiritano points out, Collingwood re-interprets Hegel's dialectic, retaining the moment of opposition, although in tension with a synthesis, which consequently is no longer conceived as a third moment of the process, beyond the contradiction. The synthesis of opposites is an ever-becoming process, in which there is no third term. The actual opposition between the two terms, Iiritano explains, is never eliminated, precisely because it is a real and not an ideal opposition (Iiritano, 2002: 53). In 'Notes on Hegel's Logic', a manuscript written in 1920, Collingwood recognises a residue of Platonism in Hegel's *Logic*. For Collingwood, as Iiritano demonstrates, Hegel's idea of the Absolute is a 'realistic' residue: it shuts him up in a conception of totality which is still a 'world of Being' (Iiritano, 2002: 54).

Hence in *Libellus de Generatione*, like in *Truth and Contradiction*, Collingwood rejects the Absolute. There is a synthesis of wholeness and partness. According to Collingwood, 'There is no Whole. Becoming is not a series that can be summed to any number of terms, nor yet to infinity' (Collingwood, 1920a: 61). Each phase is a whole in that it is all that exists: it is the one permanent and eternal reality. But at the same time each phase is a part in that it is only a phase, destined to give way to another (Collingwood, 1920a: 61–62). As Iiritano puts it, 'In the world of becoming there is no logical conception of totality, but only the endless open becoming of a process ...' (Iiritano, 2002: 54).[1]

---

[1] According to Collingwood in 'Notes on Hegel's Logic', Hegel posits a dualism between thought and sense: 'Hegel has no idea of an a priori synthesis between the symbol and meaning. He thinks, like Plato, that we philosophise by getting out of our senses, instead of deepening them' (Collingwood, 1920b: 1). In his dualism Hegel risks '... weakening completely the ontological fertility of the dialectical principle' (Iiritano, 2002: 55).

The relation between the world of becoming and the world of being is not a relation of opposites. To conceive them as opposites would be to fall back into the mistake we are trying to condemn (Collingwood, 1920a: 66). To conceive truth and error existentially as concrete realities is to convert abstract moments into concrete determinations, and to reassert the world of being. As Collingwood points out, 'In the world of becoming there is no such thing as error: there is only the moment of falsity correspondent to the moment of truth in this or that concrete phase of thought' (Collingwood, 1920a: 67). Plato's realism, then, has its merits and its defects. Collingwood argues:

> If we understand the synthesis of opposites we shall see that no truth can exist at all except in a particularised form, which is the same thing as being conditioned by error. All truth is truth only so long as the error which it negates has not yet been effectively negated; once the error is definitely abandoned the truth becomes tautology and therefore untrue (Collingwood, 1920a: 68).

The same point can be made regarding the antitheses of subject and object, thought and action, and history and philosophy. The cardinal mistake to avoid is the existentialism of the opposing categories. Subjectivity and objectivity are synthetically present in every moment of reality (Collingwood, 1920a: 71). As Iiritano explains, 'In the category of becoming, subject and object put themselves ontologically as moments of the same *process*, phases of the same *activity*, which constitute them' (Iiritano, 2002: 60). Similarly, history and philosophy '... are opposite moments which never exist apart, of which all real thinking is a concrete synthesis' (Collingwood, 1920a: 78).

As an alternative to the Platonic ontology of being, therefore, Collingwood seeks to link the movement of thinking with the movement of reality. According to Collingwood in *Draft of an opening chapter to a 'Prolegomena to Logic'*, (written in 1920–21):

> If there were a science of thought, we should expect it to fulfil the task of showing why, if reality is changeless and stable, our thoughts about reality change, develop, ebb and flow, so conspicuously lack just this quality of immobility (Collingwood, 1920–21: 37).

The philosophy of being, or realism, leads to a denial of a science of thought capable of being at the same time a science of thinking. Realism

> ... means drawing a distinction between real thought, thus conceived as a timeless intuition, and the process which we generally call thinking,

i.e. the process of asking, searching, inquiring, doubting (Collingwood, 1920–21: 40).

Hence Collingwood, as Iiritano points out, characterises thinking in terms of what he later refer to as the 'logic of question and answer' (Iiritano, 2002: 64). The process of so-called thinking had been quietly set aside by traditional logicians, who concentrated their analyses on, not thinking, but thought, regarded as a quiescent state of apprehension (Collingwood, 1920–21: 41).[2]

In Collingwood's mature philosophy, he expounded his dialectical logic in *An Essay on Philosophical Method*. In this book there is less explicit reference to a crisis in European civilisation. However, Collingwood does remark that despite two great constructive movements in philosophy since the Middle Ages, the Cartesian and the Kantian, now is a time of crisis and chaos in philosophy, and this can be remedied by agreeing upon principles of method (EPM, 6). Many of Collingwood's books, however, employ a different terminology and Collingwood varied his terminology according to the context of publication and his intended audience. In *An Essay on Philosophical Method* he does not explicitly refer to his method as dialectical. Instead he uses the term 'scale of forms'. However, Collingwood remarks that the method he has been outlining has been used by Socrates, Aristotle and Kant, and that Hegel 'used this method throughout his philosophical works' (EPM, 103).[3]

According to Collingwood, in *An Essay on Philosophical Method*, philosophy never reaches its ultimate goal and it is characterised by being an activity or process (EPM, 3). In a philosophical inquiry

> … what we are trying to do is not to discover something of which until now we have been ignorant, but to know better something which in some sense we knew already; not to know it better in the sense of coming to know more about it, but to know it better in the sense of coming to

---

[2] For Collingwood, the dialectical logic of becoming is however confronted with a dilemma regarding the beginning of thinking: 'If the mind has no knowledge already of the nature of reality, the process of thinking in order to acquire such knowledge cannot begin: if it has knowledge, the process is obviously not necessary … We should perhaps try to evade this difficulty by saying either (i) the process of thinking begins with knowledge and leads to knowledge, but the knowledge on which it is based is not the same as that to which it leads, or (ii) the process is based not on knowledge at all, but on *faith, guesswork or instinct*' (Collingwood, 1920–21: 48–9). Collingwood's answer is to suggest that there has never been a beginning and that thought has always been underway. Iiritano points out that the question has been deferred to a more penetrating analysis later in Collingwood's career (Iiritano, 2002: 66).

[3] Connelly argues that *An Essay on Philosophical Method* is a restatement of Hegelian dialectic in non-Hegelian language (Connelly, 2003: 74).

know it in a different and better way — actually instead of potentially, or explicitly instead of implicitly, or in whatever terms the theory of knowledge chooses to express the difference ... (EPM, 11).

Collingwood rejects the principle that 'when a generic concept is divided into its species there is a corresponding division of its instances into mutually exclusive classes' (EPM, 49). This principle may be true in natural science, but is false in philosophy. Therefore the traditional philosophical theory of classification and division must be modified. The classes of a philosophical genus overlap, rather than exclude, one another. Some concepts have a philosophical and a non-philosophical phase (EPM, 31–33). For Collingwood,

> ... when a concept has a dual significance, philosophical and non-philosophical, in its non-philosophical phase it qualifies a limited part of reality, whereas in its philosophical it leaks or escapes out of these limits and invades the neighbouring regions, tending at last to colour our thought of reality as a whole. As a non-philosophical concept it observes the rules of classification, its instances forming a class separate from other classes; as a philosophical concept it breaks these rules, and the class of its instances overlaps those of its co-ordinate species (EPM, 35).

In logic and in ethics the traditionally recognised concepts are specified into overlapping classes. As Modood argues, species of a philosophical concept can be said to 'overlap', because no one species of such a concept can make its contribution to human understanding without calling upon and being qualified by other species of that concept (Modood, 1995: 42). We cannot fully understand expediency or self-advantage without reference to duty, as Plato's *Gorgias* and *Republic* demonstrate. To claim that the good is self-advantage raises questions about who or what the self is, about how we can be sure what is to its advantage, and about the relations between one self and another. For Collingwood, Modood points out, we must expect from cultural life both a greater variety and a more integrated unity than is to be found within a narrowly scientific or intellectualistic framework (Modood, 1995: 43).

Collingwood argues that a failure to appreciate the overlap of classes in philosophy leads to the 'fallacy of precarious margins' (EPM, 48). This means ignoring ambiguous instances and confining our attention to the part of the subject-matter in which the overlap seems to be absent:

> It consists in assuming that the overlap which has already affected a certain area of the class in question can be trusted not to spread, and that beyond it lies a marginal area in which the instances exhibit only one of the specific forms, uncontaminated by the presence of the other (EPM, 48).

In avoiding this fallacy one might fall into the opposite error. Once it is recognised that the overlap is in principle unlimited, one might think that two concepts are identical, for example, identifying duty and happiness. This is the 'fallacy of identified coincidents' (EPM, 49).

Besides overlap or interdependence, Collingwood explains, hierarchy is a feature of philosophy. The philosophical concept includes differences of degree combined with differences in kind: a system Collingwood calls a scale of forms (EPM, 57), and text book logic is to be modified in the light of the scale of forms (EPM, 63). Not only is there a logical relation of overlap between different species or aspects of a genus, but the genus is differently related to each of the species that constitute it. Temperance, fortitude, and wisdom, for example, as species of virtue are different kinds of virtue (EPM, 56). Yet, at the same time, they also differ in degree: they are not equally examples of virtue but form a scale in which the higher embodies more of the generic essence than the lower examples (cf. Modood, 1995: 43). Because the specifications of a philosophical concept are differences at once in degree and in kind (differences of degree are fused with differences of kind), they cannot be measured, for measurement applies only to pure differences of degree (EPM, 73).

Similarly, the kind of opposition which is found among philosophical terms is at once opposition and distinction (EPM, 75). In a scale of forms the variable is identical with the generic essence and therefore the zero end forms no part of the scale; for in it the generic essence is altogether absent. The lower end of the scale lies not at zero, but at unity, or the minimum realisation of the generic essence (EPM, 81). As Modood puts it, the two sets of criteria, the minimal and the maximal, those necessary for identifying mere instances and those necessary for identifying instances of excellence, form a unified concept (Modood, 1995: 47). The goodness or badness of expediency cannot be judged by expediency itself but by another species of the same genus as expediency, by one which as a species is truer to the generic essence, to the fullness of the genus. Knowledge of expediency presents us with an awareness of its goodness but not of its badness unless we have a superior awareness of goodness than is available in the notion of expediency. Thus, expediency is — not just morally but logically — an inferior species of good than, say, right or duty (Modood, 1995: 49–50).

The same relation which exists between the lowest member of the scale and the next above it reappears between any two adjacent forms. Each is good in itself, but bad in relation to the one above

(EPM, 84). The higher term in a scale of forms possesses not only that kind of goodness which belongs to it in its own right, but also the kind which originally or in itself belonged to its neighbour: 'It not only surpasses its neighbour in degree of goodness, but beats it, so to speak, on its own ground' (EPM, 87). The lower professes to exhibit a certain kind of goodness, but can only do so in an approximate and inadequate manner. As Collingwood argues,

> The higher thus negates the lower, and at the same time reaffirms it: negates it as a false embodiment of the generic essence, and reaffirms its content, that specific form of the essence, as part and parcel of itself (EPM, 88).

Each term in the scale sums up the whole scale to that point. Infinity as well as zero can be struck out of the scale because the specific form at which we stand is the generic concept itself, so far as thought yet conceives it (EPM, 89).

Conceiving philosophy in terms of scales of forms means that in the case of philosophical statements the relation between affirmation and negation is peculiarly intimate. In philosophy every negation implies an affirmation, and every affirmation a negation: something Collingwood refers to as the principle of concrete negation and the principle of concrete affirmation (which I briefly discussed in the Introduction). An affirmative non-philosophical judgement denies indiscriminately all the judgements incompatible with it. But where the generic concept is philosophical, specified in a scale of forms of which the judgement is intended to affirm the highest, its denial of all the inferior forms is summarised in one denial, namely that of the proximate form; since each summarises the whole scale up to that point, and the denial of that involves the denial of all that it summarises (EPM, 108).[4]

According to Collingwood's dialectical conception of philosophy in *An Essay on Philosophical Method*, therefore, there is a continuity between experience and theory. The 'conclusions' of philosophical thinking and the 'experience' on which they are based are names for any two successive stages in the scale of forms of philosophical knowledge. What is called experience is relatively crude and irrational as compared with the next stage above it, in which its philosophical elements are more fully developed. The higher stage explains the lower (EPM, 172). The task of explaining a body of experience by

---

[4]   This point is also made in Collingwood's 1927 manuscript, 'The Idea of a Philosophy of Something, and in particular, a Philosophy of History', published in the revised edition of *The Idea of History* (IH, 337–38).

constructing a theory of it is nothing but the same experience raised to a higher level of rationality. Whatever positive doctrine has been propounded, the next step for philosophy is to demolish it as a theory and leave it standing only as an experience. That experience is explained by reference to new principles implied in the critical process itself (EPM, 173–74). The scale of forms, then, posits an overlap and dynamic tension between theory and practice, something which Collingwood later referred to in *An Autobiography* as a rapprochement between theory and practice (A, 147; cf. Modood, 1995: 57).

For Collingwood, in the history of thought

> ... all the philosophies of the past are telescoped into the present, and constitute a scale of forms, never beginning and never ending, which are different both in degree and in kind, distinct from each other and opposed to each other (EPM, 195)

and every particular philosophical system is 'nothing but an interim report on the progress of thought down to the time of making it' (EPM, 198).

Collingwood's philosophical method, then, is self-conscious and self-corrective (cf. Mink, 1969: 77). In philosophy '... the whole body of knowledge must be remade from the foundations at every step in advance' (EPM, 180). As in his earlier manuscripts, Collingwood abandons Hegel's Absolute, but retains dialectic. Philosophy does not culminate in a single final Truth, and the development of mind is contingent and reversible. As Modood indicates, for Collingwood, like Gadamer on this point, we can always imagine further dialogue and inquiry, criticism and counter-criticism (Modood, 1995: 55-56).

For Collingwood, therefore, Western civilisation was confronted by a crisis or decadence because of the unsustainable nature of its philosophical foundations. His development of dialectical logic was intended as a solution to this problem. However, his dialectical logic is paralleled by a reform of metaphysics. This is because the dialectical logic outlined here presupposes an ontological claim about the nature of reality. Collingwood expounds his reform of metaphysics in *An Essay on Metaphysics*.

In both *An Essay on Metaphysics* and *An Autobiography* Collingwood also returned to the subject of dialectical logic, characterising it now as the logic of question and answer. The next chapter will provide an account of how Collingwood's metaphysics responded to the crisis of the West and of its relation with the logic of question and answer.

Chapter Six

Metaphysics and the Logic of Question and Answer

As we have seen in the preceding chapter, for Collingwood, the Platonic ontology of being had given rise to a decadence and crisis in Western civilisation because it placed all value in a transcendent world and failed to give an account of the actual processes of reality and becoming. Collingwood's dialectical logic is inextricably linked with an ontological claim that reality is dialectical. Therefore, his promotion of dialectical logic as a solution to the ailments of Western civilisation is paralleled by a reconstruction, or reform, of metaphysics.

Traditionally understood as the study of static and eternal truths, and as the 'science of pure being', metaphysics now becomes a historical science: historical in terms of both its methodology and its object. We move, then, from the world of being to the world of becoming. Metaphysics is a study of the nature of reality. However, for Collingwood, an account of reality cannot be separated from an account of the processes by which we both apprehend and create reality. (These processes, according to the argument of *Speculum Mentis*, are art, religion, natural science, history and philosophy.) What Collingwood referred to in *An Autobiography* as a *rapprochement* between philosophy and history (A, 77) becomes in this context a *rapprochement* between logic and metaphysics.

Collingwood argues in *An Essay on Metaphysics* that metaphysics is a science. However:

> The word 'science', in its original sense, which is still its proper sense not in the English language alone but in the international language of European civilization, means a body of systematic or orderly thinking about a determinate subject-matter. This is the sense and the only sense in which I shall use it. There is also the slang sense of the word, unobjectionable (like all slang) on its lawful occasions, parallel to the slang use of the word 'hall' for a music hall or the word 'drink' for alcoholic drink, in which it stands for natural science (EM, 4).

According to Collingwood, the science of metaphysics is logically prior to the particular sciences, and the principles of metaphysics are presupposed by the particular sciences. All science is universal or abstract in that it ignores differences between particular things and focuses on what they have in common. There is a hierarchical relationship between the sciences: the subject matter of a science can be divided into sub-forms, which are less abstract and universal, logically generating subordinate sciences (EM, 12).

Collingwood asserts that Aristotle was wrong in the claim that metaphysics is the science of pure being. The 'science of pure being' is not a science as it does not have any definite subject matter. It goes beyond the limits of abstraction. Abstraction means taking out differences and studying what is common between things. In this case, abstraction has gone so far that there is nothing left for science to investigate. Collingwood argues that this was implied by Berkeley, who attacked 'abstract general ideas', by Hume, who agreed with Berkeley's attack, by Kant, who argued that 'being is not a predicate', and by Hegel, who said that pure being is the same as nothing (EM, 15).

Having rejected Aristotle's proposition that metaphysics is the science of pure being, Collingwood extracts another proposition from Aristotle which describes the true nature of metaphysics: metaphysics is the science which studies presuppositions. Collingwood explains that when a person expresses a thought in words, there are also presuppositions of that thought in his or her mind. For example, to point at a piece of string and say 'that is a clothes-line' is to make a presupposition: that the line was put there for a purpose. The presupposition has logical priority, but not priority in time (EM, 21).

There is a difference between '... the desultory and casual thinking of our unscientific consciousness and the orderly and systematic thinking we call science':

> In unscientific thinking our thoughts are coagulated into knots and tangles; we fish up a thought out of our minds like an anchor foul of its own cable, hanging upside-down and draped in seaweed with shellfish sticking to it, and dump the whole thing on deck quite pleased with ourselves for having got it up at all. Thinking scientifically means disentangling all this mess, and reducing a knot of thoughts in which everything sticks together anyhow to a system or series of thoughts in which thinking the thoughts is at the same time thinking the connexions between them (EM, 22–3).

For Collingwood, logic must give an account of the activity of metaphysicians:

> Logicians have paid a great deal of attention to some kinds of connexion between thoughts, but to other kinds not so much. The theory of presuppositions they have tended to neglect … I will try to state so much of this theory as seems necessary for my present purpose (EM, 23).

According to Collingwood's 'theory of presuppositions', then, every statement is made in answer to a question. The question is logically prior to the answer. Every question involves a presupposition. Directly, it involves only one presupposition, but this immediate presupposition may in turn have other presuppositions. For a question to be asked, this one immediate presupposition has to be made. Otherwise, the question 'does not arise'. To say that a question does not arise means that it involves a presupposition which is not in fact being made. The fact that something causes a certain question to arise he calls the 'logical efficacy' of that thing (EM, 27). The logical efficacy of a supposition does not depend on the truth of what is supposed, or even on it being thought true, but only on its being supposed. In scientific thinking, for example, one may often argue from suppositions known to be false, or concerning which we have neither knowledge nor belief as to whether they are false or true (EM, 28).

According to Collingwood, a presupposition is either relative or absolute. A relative presupposition is one which stands relatively to one question as its presupposition, and relatively to another question as its answer. That certain presuppositions are questionable is not disproved by the fact that someone who makes them fails to see that they are questionable. Collingwood explains:

> To question a presupposition is to demand that it should be 'verified'; that is, to demand that a question should be asked to which the affirmative answer would be that presupposition itself, now in the form of a proposition (EM, 30).

To speak of verifying a presupposition is to suppose that it is a relative presupposition.

An absolute presupposition is one which stands, relatively to all questions to which it is related, as a presupposition, never as an answer. For example, an absolute presupposition of medicine is that every event has a cause. Absolute presuppositions are not verifiable, and the idea of verification does not apply to them. Their use in science is their logical efficacy, and the logical efficacy of a supposition does not depend on its being verifiable: it depends only on its being supposed. Absolute presuppositions are not propositions, as they are never answers to questions. Absolute presuppositions, therefore, are not true or false, this distinction being peculiar to propositions. To put the same point differently: absolute presuppositions are not propounded, but only presupposed (EM, 32–3).

According to Collingwood, unscientific thought, at its lowest level, has a deceptive appearance of immediacy about it: it appears that things just are as we intuit them to be. Realism is the belief that this is all that knowledge is (EM, 34–5). At this level of thinking, we are unaware that every thought is an answer to a question, and that each question arises from a presupposition. This low-grade thinking cannot give rise to metaphysics. Collingwood asserts that man has created himself and civilisation through high-grade or scientific thinking, by thinking energetically instead of idly: 'Everything that we call specifically human is due to man's power of thinking hard' (EM, 37).

High-grade thinking means an increase of mental effort and skill in the direction of that effort. An increase of mental effort means asking questions, and skill in the direction of mental effort means asking questions scientifically. This means disentangling and arranging questions. Collingwood chooses as an example the (politically incorrect) question: 'have you left off beating your wife yet?' This can be disentangled into four questions and arranged in their logical order: (1) have you a wife? (2) Were you ever in the habit of beating her? (3) Do you intend to manage in future without doing so? (4) Have you begun carrying out that intention? (EM, 38) For Collingwood, therefore,

> The analysis which detects absolute presuppositions I call metaphysical analysis; but as regards procedure and the qualifications necessary to carry it out there is no difference whatever between metaphysical analysis and analysis pure and simple ... In either case the question is being constantly asked, 'Is this presupposition relative or absolute?' and the *modus operandi* is the same, whichever answer is given. As regards its *modus operandi*, then, all analysis is metaphysical analysis; and, since

analysis is what gives its scientific character to science, science and metaphysics are inextricably united, and stand or fall together (EM, 40–1).

It might seem that it should be easy to distinguish between relative and absolute presuppositions, but, Collingwood contends, people have a motive to deceive themselves because absolute presuppositions are unfashionable. The conventional view is that all presuppositions are relative (EM, 42–3). In our less scientific moments, absolute presuppositions '… are doing their work in the darkness, the light of consciousness never falling on them' (EM, 43). To discover absolute presuppositions takes skilful analysis.

In analysis, ordinary science focuses on relative presuppositions, in order to justify them, whereas metaphysics focuses on absolute presuppositions, in order scientifically to describe them. Collingwood describes absolute presuppositions as 'superstition', as 'uncanny' and as inspiring terror.

> This mattered less at a period of history when people had their well-established methods (magic, we call them) of dissipating the terror and enabling them to face the things that inspired it. Ours is an age when people pride themselves on having abolished magic and pretend that they have no superstitions. But they have as many as ever. The difference is that they have lost the art, which must always be a magical art, of conquering them. So it is a special characteristic of modern European civilization that metaphysics is habitually frowned upon and the existence of absolute presuppositions denied … If this neurosis ever achieves its ostensible object, the eradication of metaphysics from the European mind, the eradication of science and civilization will be accomplished at the same time (EM, 46).

The aim of metaphysics, therefore, according to Collingwood, is to find out what absolute presuppositions have been made by certain people, on certain occasions, in the course of certain pieces of thinking. It will then consider whether these absolute presuppositions are made singly or in groups, and so on. Pseudo-metaphysics treats absolute presuppositions as relative presuppositions, and asks questions of them with regard to truth or falsehood, evidence, and demonstration (EM, 47).

Collingwood argues that metaphysical questions either are, or resolve themselves into, historical questions. For example, in Newtonian physics every event either has a cause or alternatively operates according to a law. Nineteenth-century physics, or Kantian physics, claimed that all events have causes. In modern physics the notion of causes has disappeared, and every event happens according to laws (EM, 50). Pseudo-metaphysics would treat this as a problem of three different schools of thought, and endeavour to say which one is the true absolute presupposition. Science, however, does not depend on the truth of its absolute presuppositions, only on their being supposed. The business of the scientist is to presuppose certain absolute presuppositions for his scientific work. The business of the metaphysician is to find out what absolute presuppositions are in fact being made. The metaphysician, then, asks historical questions, and the rubric for metaphysics is: '*in such-and-such a phase of scientific thought, it is (or was) absolutely presupposed that* ...' (EM, 55). The rubric is left out because the reader already assumes it, or because of ignorance about metaphysics. As Collingwood argues, it is a mistake to take the characteristics of a certain historical milieu for characteristics of mankind at large (EM, 57).

Metaphysics, therefore, is an historical science. Unlike the 'scissors-and-paste' method, where the historian repeats statements about the past made by authorities, modern historical method means that the historian makes statements on his or her own authority, according to the evidence. The evidence is analysed with a certain question in mind, and '... absolutely cogent inferences about the past are drawn from interpretation of the evidence it has left behind' (EM, 58). Metaphysics, Collingwood contends, must proceed according to this method in finding absolute presuppositions (EM, 60).

Hence, for Collingwood, the reform of metaphysics is an important part of the solution to the crisis that confronts Western culture. Aristotle's idea of a science of pure being has led to the suggestion that metaphysics should consist in groping blindly for non-existent truths and is inadequate as an attempt to provide an account of reality. Instead metaphysics, Collingwood argues, must use historical methods and uncover facts. As a science, however, metaphysics has its own presuppositions: it shares the presuppositions of history (EM, 63).

Metaphysical facts, like historical facts, Collingwood explains, are independent of one another, but exist in constellations of facts.

> I speak of a set of absolute presuppositions, because if metaphysics is an historical science the things which it studies, namely absolute presuppositions, are historical facts; and anyone who is reasonably well acquainted with historical work knows that there is no such thing as an historical fact which is not at the same time a complex of historical facts. Such a complex of historical facts I call a 'constellation'. If every historical fact is a constellation, the answer to the question 'What is it that such and such a person was absolutely presupposing in such and such a piece of thinking?' can never be given by reference to one single absolute pre-

supposition, it must always be given by reference to a constellation of them (EM, 66).

Each absolute presupposition in a constellation must be *consupponible* with all the others: this means that it must be logically possible, when supposing one of them, to suppose all the rest (EM, 66). However, in supposing one of them, one cannot be logically committed to supposing any of the others. If this were the case the first would be a presupposition of the second, and therefore the second would not be an absolute presupposition. Accordingly, metaphysics is not a deductive or quasi-mathematical science. A so-called metaphysical 'doctrine', Collingwood argues, is really a metaphysician's description of absolute presuppositions. For example, Spinoza states an historical fact about the religious foundation of seventeenth-century natural science, that nature is the same as God (EM, 68–9).

Because metaphysics is an historical science, its scope can be enlarged beyond the present or recent past and encompass the past in its entirety. Metaphysics will show that different sets of absolute presuppositions correspond with differences in the fabric of civilisation, and discover on what occasions and by what processes one constellation of absolute presuppositions has changed into another. According to Collingwood,

> This is the only legitimate (that is, historical) way in which he, or anybody else, can answer the question 'Why did such and such a people at such and such a time make such and such absolute presuppositions?' (EM, 73).

One phase in history, Collingwood explains, changes into another because its fabric was not at rest; it was always under strain. The historian and metaphysician must analyse these internal strains and the effect they have on historical facts. Hence, Collingwood criticises Gibbon and Spengler for not being sensitive enough to the internal strains of what they wrote about, and praises Hegel and Marx. Collingwood argues:

> Where there is no strain there is no history. A civilization does not work out its own details by a kind of static logic in which every detail exemplifies in its own way one and the same formula. It works itself out by a dynamic logic in which different and at first sight incompatible formula somehow contrive a precarious coexistence; one dominant here, another there; the recessive formula never ceasing to operate ... The historian in his study can perhaps afford to neglect these strains, because he does not really care about being a good historian; but the man of action cannot afford to neglect them. His life may depend on his ability to see where they are and to judge their strength. It was not by gunpowder alone that

> Cortez destroyed Montezuma; it was by using gunpowder to reinforce the strains which already tended to break up Montezuma's power (EM, 76).

For Collingwood, not only is metaphysics to reform itself by becoming an historical science, but the extent to which metaphysics has already been a science in the past is governed by the extent to which it has already been history (EM, 77).

In Collingwood's view, therefore, logic and metaphysics are inextricably linked and his reform, or revolution, in logic is closely related to his reform of metaphysics. Logic and metaphysics provide an account of the world of becoming and thereby provide a remedy to the crisis of Western civilisation, which is brought about by the inadequacy of the Platonic and Aristotelian philosophy of being.

In *An Autobiography* Collingwood asserted: 'For a logic of propositions I wanted to substitute what I called a logic of question and answer' (A, 36–7). Truth

> ... was something that belonged not to any single proposition, nor even, as the coherence-theorists maintained, to a complex of propositions taken together; but to a complex consisting of questions and answers ... Each question and each answer in a given complex had to be relevant or appropriate, had to 'belong' both to the whole and to the place it occupied in the whole (A, 37).

Each question had to 'arise', and each answer must be 'the right' answer to the question it professes to answer. Collingwood distinguishes 'right' from 'true':

> The 'right' answer to a question is the answer which enables us to get ahead with the process of questioning and answering. Cases are quite common in which the 'right' answer to a question is 'false'; for example, cases in which a thinker is following a false scent, either inadvertently or in order to construct a *reductio ad absurdum*. Thus, when Socrates asks (Plato, *Republic*, 333 B) whether as your partner in a game of draughts you would prefer to have a just man or a man who knows how to play draughts, the answer which Polemarchus gives – 'a man who knows how to play draughts' – is the right answer. It is 'false', because it presupposes that justice and ability to play draughts are comparable, each of them being a 'craft', or specialized form of skill. But it is 'right', because it constitutes a link, and a sound one, in the chain of questions and answers by which the falseness of that presupposition is made manifest.
>
> What is ordinarily meant when a proposition is called 'true', I thought, was this: (a) the proposition belongs to a question-and-answer complex which as a whole is 'true' in the proper sense of the word; (b) within this complex it is an answer to a certain question; (c) the question is what we call a sensible or intelligent question, not a silly one, or in my

terminology it 'arises'; (d) the proposition is the 'right' answer to that question. (A, 38)

Collingwood points out that the question 'to what question did So-and-so intend this proposition for an answer?' is an historical one, and cannot be settled except by historical methods (A, 39).

What Collingwood referred to, therefore, in *An Autobiography* and *An Essay on Metaphysics*, as the logic of question and answer is a continuation and refinement of the dialectical logic that he developed from the early manuscripts to *An Essay on Philosophical Method*, which I outlined in the previous chapter. Peters points out that Collingwood's 'revolution' (A, 52) in logic ought to be seen as part of a wider movement, including British Idealists and pragmatists, which tried to replace formal logic with a theory of inquiry. However, whereas the reforms of these philosophers were orientated towards science, Collingwood's reform was orientated towards history, and in this, he was at one with the Italian Idealists (Peters, 1999: 6).

Peters also indicates a correlation between Collingwood's theory of dialectic and his theory of art. As Peters explains, Collingwood rejected Croce's identity of intuition and expression in his aesthetics, by pointing out that an artist does not express himself in a single blow, but begins with a primitive expression which he gradually develops into a fuller expression. Similarly, in contrast with Croce's view that philosophical concepts are formed simultaneously with the historical judgement, Collingwood defended a theory which accounts for the gradual development of concepts in a question and answer process (Peters, 1999: 9). This, Peters argues, is why Collingwood saw his life's work not in Croce's terms of an identity of philosophy and history, but in terms of a *rapprochement* between philosophy and history. Thus truth does not come in a single blow, but develops gradually in a question and answer process, beginning from vaguer truths leading to more precise truths (Peters, 1999: 10).[1]

Collingwood's autobiographical account of his meditations on the Albert Memorial demonstrates that the only way to explain the co-existence of beauty and ugliness in a work of art was to regard it

---

[1]   Peters points out that, similarly, in *Religion and Philosophy*, Collingwood argues that every truth takes its form by correcting some error (RP, 138). Truth and error cannot co-exist in relation with one another, because if they are brought into contact the error is abolished by truth. But this process is never completed because the life of the world, like the life of man, consists in perpetual activity (RP, 141; Peters, 1999: 12).

as a product of a process of attempts and failures, or problems and solutions (Peters, 1999: 14).[2] Peters explains:

> On this basis Collingwood would further modify Croce's account of the question and answer process. Croce had always sharply distinguished that question and answer process from the process of intuitions and expressions of art. Meditating on the ugliness of the Albert Memorial, Collingwood began to understand that such a distinction is untenable, and that what is required is a description of a continuous process, or 'overlap', beginning from the intuition in art and ending with the formation of concepts in philosophy. Not surprisingly this is exactly the theory that Collingwood expounded in *Speculum Mentis* (SM, 76–80) and elaborated in *The Principles of Art*. (Peters, 1999: 15)

According to Peters, the close relation between art and logic also yielded Collingwood's 'principle of correlativity' (A, 32): every answer is distinct and yet inseparable from the question which leads to it. The principle of correlativity meant that Collingwood could reject the principle of contradiction: the idea that two propositions in themselves can contradict each other. Collingwood held that two propositions can only contradict each other if they are answers to the same question (A, 33; Peters, 1999: 16).

For Collingwood,

> Meaning, agreement, and contradiction, truth and falsehood, none of these belonged to propositions in their own right, propositions by themselves, they belonged only to propositions as answers to questions: each proposition answering a question strictly correlative to itself (A, 33).

As we have seen, then, Collingwood argued that truth and falsehood do not belong to propositions as such, but to the entire complex of questions and answers of which these propositions belong. The true unit of thought is not the proposition, but the entire question and answer complex (A, 37; cf. Peters, 1999: 17).

The logic of question and answer that Collingwood presents in *An Autobiography* and *An Essay on Metaphysics*, therefore, is a re-presentation and fine-tuning of the logic that Collingwood first outlined in *Truth and Contradiction*. It follows from Collingwood's claim in *Truth*

---

[2]   Peters indicates that, for Collingwood, both the Idealist coherence-theory of truth and the Realist correspondence-theory of truth wrongly assume the 'propositional principle'. The propositional principle means the assumption that truth is a quality of one proposition, regardless of the context of other propositions (A, 36; Peters, 1995: 110). According to Collingwood in *The Principles of Art*, the propositional assumption presupposes a clean distinction between feelings and emotions on the one side and thought on the other side (PA, 259–61). Collingwood points out against all logicians that propositions are never purely logical entities, but also linguistic entities. Logicians should always take the development of the meaning of concepts into account (Peters, 1995: 110).

and Contradiction that whereas coherence-theorists of truth tend to 'dissect' theories into true and false statements, 'Truth and falsehood are attributes not of single isolated judgements but of systems of thought, systems in which every judgement is coloured by all the others' (TC, 11).

As we have seen, it is through the use of the logic of question and answer that the metaphysician uncovers absolute presuppositions. Rex Martin, however, denies that there is any essential connection between Collingwood's logic of question and answer and the theory of absolute presuppositions. Martin in his Introduction to the revised edition of *An Essay on Metaphysics* argues that absolute presuppositions would have no meaning if seen as a part of the logic of question and answer—because, he argues, 'meaningfulness for statements is grounded in the very same way as truth values in a question-and-answer complex (see A, 33)' (Martin, 1998a: xxiii).[3].

Martin indicates that, in terms of the development of Collingwood's theory of metaphysics, Collingwood's essay, the 'Function of Metaphysics in Civilization',[4] which was written in 1938, like the later *Essay on Metaphysics*, and unlike his 1934 lecture, 'The Nature of Metaphysical Study', denies that the governing principles of natural science can be described as true, or proven true or false (Martin, 1998a: lxxiv; cf. EM, 393–409). However, Martin asserts, unlike *An Essay on Metaphysics*, the logic of question and answer does not appear in the 1938 lecture: there is no explicit claim here that truth values are essentially and internally related to the linked questions, to which various statements stand as answers (Martin, 1998a: lxxv). Also missing from the 1938 essay is any mention of *absolute* presuppositions (Martin, 1998a: lxxvi). This means, according to Martin, that we have reason to challenge the alleged *essential* relationship between fundamental presuppositions and the logic of question and answer.[5]

---

[3]   Martin also discusses this point in 'Collingwood's Logic of Question and Answer, its Relation to Absolute Presuppositions: a Brief History' (1998: 124).

[4]   This essay is published in the revised edition of *An Essay on Metaphysics*, pp. 379–421.

[5]   Martin also argues that in 'Notes for an Essay on Logic' (written in 1939, after Collingwood had completed Parts I and II of *An Essay on Metaphysics*, and incorporated in the revised edition of *An Essay on Metaphysics*, pp. 422–27) Collingwood's discussion of suppositions is not accompanied by a *logic* of question and answer. Martin claims that, although Collingwood argues that supposing, questioning and asserting go on concurrently, there is no flat-out claim that either the meaning or the truth of an assertion is logically dependent on the question it is said to be answering (Martin, 1998a: lxxx–lxxxi). But, contrary to

Martin claims that the *logic* of question and answer, properly speaking, was not present in Collingwood's earlier work and was only developed in *An Autobiography*. He also argues that fundamental presuppositions existed as features of Collingwood's thought before he developed his logic of question and answer, and were expressed and understood independently of that logic. Collingwood's use of the logic of question and answer to explain absolute presuppositions in Part I of *An Essay on Metaphysics*, Martin argues, was not a happy device, for that explication, in removing truth value from these presuppositions, also removed meaning from them (Martin, 1998a: lxxvii).

Contrary to Martin, however, Collingwood's claim about meaning being dependent on a prior question does not apply to absolute presuppositions. It applies to 'statements' and propositions: Collingwood uses the words 'statements' and 'propositions' interchangeably (for Collingwood, in *An Autobiography*, a 'statement' is a proposition). On p. 33 of *An Autobiography*, Collingwood argues that '... you cannot tell what a *proposition* means unless you know what question it was meant to answer ...' (italics added). On p. 31 Collingwood makes the same claim about 'statements':

> ... you cannot find out what a man means by simply studying his spoken or written statements ... In order to find out his meaning you must also know what the question was ... to which the thing he has said or written was meant as an answer.

Collingwood quickly changes terms from 'statements' to propositions, and continues thus:

> It must be understood that question and answer, as I conceived them, were strictly correlative. A proposition was not an answer, or at any rate could not be the right answer, to any question which might have been answered otherwise. A highly detailed and particularized proposition must be the answer, not to a vague and generalized question, but to a question as detailed and particularized as itself (A, 31–2).

Collingwood describes his 'revolt' against the current logical theories of the time, comparing it to the revolt against scholastic logic by Bacon and Descartes in the late sixteenth and early seventeenth centuries.

> The *Novum Organum* and the *Discours de la Méthode* began to have a new significance for me. They were the classical expressions of a principle in logic which I found it necessary to restate: the principle that a body of knowledge consists not of 'propositions', 'statements', 'judgements', or

Martin, Collingwood does actually claim that 'Every P is an answer to a Q', where Q is question and P is proposition (EM, 425).

whatever name logicians use in order to designate assertive acts of thought (or what in those acts is asserted: for 'knowledge' means both the activity of knowing and what is known), but of these together with the questions they are meant to answer; and that a logic in which the answers are attended to and the questions neglected is a false logic (A, 30–1).

Collingwood, however, does not say or imply that the meaning of an *absolute presupposition* is dependent on it being an answer to a question. Unlike 'statements', or propositions, absolute presuppositions cannot be asserted and do not have truth-value. Nevertheless absolute presuppositions do have meaning. Their meaning, I suggest, is their 'logical efficacy'. Also, the meaning of a set of absolute presuppositions is only fully realised in the context of the questions and answers that it actually gives rise to. As Peters argues, Martin's claim that the logic of question and answer makes absolute presuppositions meaningless is based on the unwarranted assumption that there is only one kind of meaning, namely the meaning of propositions as answers to questions, whereas Collingwood distinguishes many kinds of meaning, ranging from the meaning of artistic expressions,[6] to the meaning of presuppositions (Peters, 1999: 3).

Martin's claim that the logic of question and answer was only developed in *An Autobiography* is untenable. As I have argued, Collingwood's logic, from his early manuscripts to the *Autobiography*, can be seen as part of a unitary development.[7] The idea of absolute presuppositions also has a long history. The idea of 'a solid ring of thought' in *Ruskin's Philosophy* (EPA, 10) has often been interpreted as a first statement of the notion of absolute presuppositions, and, as Peters indicates, the term appears with almost the same connotations in Bradley's *Presuppositions of Critical History* of 1874 (Peters, 1999: 23). Absolute presuppositions and the logic of question

---

[6]   Collingwood changes his position on the question of whether or not artistic expressions have meaning. In *The Principles of Art*, as we have seen, he equates art with language at its most primitive level. Art or language is primitive utterance. 'Meaning' and the rules of grammar, syntax, and logic, are something imposed on language afterwards. On the other hand, in *The New Leviathan*, as we will see in Part Three, Collingwood argues that language at its most basic level is the expression of meaning (NL, 6.1).

[7]   According to Peters, Collingwood developed his logic of question and answer in *Truth and Contradiction*, translations of two books by de Ruggiero, *Libellus de Generatione*, half a dozen manuscripts on logic, his Moral Philosophy Lectures and *Speculum Mentis*. Contrary to Martin, Peters indicates that *Speculum Mentis* does contain a logic of question and answer, and that Collingwood continued to refine this logic in later works. Peters cites p.78 of *Speculum Mentis*: 'People who are acquainted with knowledge at first hand have always known that assertions are only answers to questions' (Peters, 1999: 22).

and answer, therefore, are evidently inter-connected. Also absolute presuppositions derive their meaning from their function as presuppositions of an entire question and answer complex of a given science (cf. Peters, 1999: 25).

As I have argued, then, Collingwood's dialectical logic has an ontological aspect. As Peters puts it, it is a form of noetic logic: it is both a study of the structure and development of our thought and a metaphysics or a theory of reality. According to Peters,

> In Collingwood's mature thought experience, logic and metaphysics are united in one single logic of question and answer which elucidates the problematic character of reality. The logic of question and answer enters in the tradition of dialectical Idealist logic which was founded by Hegel (Peters, 1995: 108).

Collingwood criticised Bradley because he had bequeathed to his successors the following dilemma.

> Either reality is the immediate flow of subjective life, in which case it is subjective and not objective, it is enjoyed but cannot be known, or else reality is that which we know, in which case it is objective and not subjective, it is a world of real things outside the subjective life of the mind and outside each other (IH, 141).

As Peters argues,

> In Collingwood's view Bradley accepted the first horn of the dilemma by holding that all experience was the immediate flow of subjective life. The Realists accepted the second horn of the dilemma and holding 'that what mind knows is something other than itself, and that mind itself, the activity of knowing, is immediate experience and therefore unknowable' (IH, 141–2). In Collingwood's view both Bradley and the Realists thus agree, in a strange *coincidentia oppositorum*, on the concept of mind as a mere immediate flow of feeling and sensation, devoid of all reflection and self-knowledge. Feeling and thought are thus completely separated by Bradley and the Realists. (Peters, 1995: 109)

Peters indicates that in response to this problem, and to the subjectivism of Gentile, Collingwood used Hegel's Ontological Argument (Peters, 1995: 113). Collingwood, however, thought that Hegel had not applied the Ontological Argument thoroughly enough and that Hegel's philosophy contained residues of Platonism.[8]

---

[8]   Peters argues: Hegel's failure to apply the Ontological Argument to particular objects of thought caused an enormous tension within his philosophy. For Collingwood, this tension set the problem for the whole post-Hegelian development of philosophy and would determine his own philosophical career: an insight expressed in 'A Footnote to Future History' (Peters, 1995: 114). Collingwood criticises Hegel for separating experience from thought, and this is the beginning of his reform of the Hegelian dialectic (Peters, 1995: 116). For

Collingwood had emphasised the ontological dimension of philosophy in his treatment of the Ontological Proof in *An Essay on Philosophical Method*. Collingwood argues that, whereas the judgements of mathematics and empirical science are hypothetical, philosophy consists of judgements about a subject matter conceived as real, or categorical judgements. The Ontological Proof is a recognition of this principle. Following Plato, Anselm argued that when we really think we must be thinking of a real object. His argument applied not to thought in general, but only to thought about one unique object, the absolute of Neo-Platonic metaphysics. In the special case of metaphysical thinking the distinction between conceiving something and thinking it to exist is a distinction without a difference (EPM, 124–5).

According to Collingwood,

> Descartes, the acknowledged father of modern philosophy made it the mainspring of his system; it was the Ontological Proof that gave him the power to move from the pin-point of momentary subjective consciousness to the infinite process of objective knowledge (EPM, 126).

It was criticised by Kant, but rescued by Hegel. The Ontological Proof, Collingwood asserts, proves that essence involves existence, not always, but in one special case, the case of God in the metaphysical sense: the object of metaphysical thought. However, metaphysics among the philosophical sciences is not unique in its objective reference or in its logical structure:

> … all philosophical thought is of the same kind, and every philosophical science partakes of the nature of metaphysics, which is not a separate philosophical science but a special study of the existential aspect of that same subject matter whose aspect as truth is studied by logic, and its aspect as goodness by ethics (EPM, 127).

According to Collingwood, philosophy is a form of thought in which essence and existence are inseparable. Thus, logic and ethics stand committed to the Ontological Proof. Logic not only discusses, but contains reasoning. Its subject matter cannot be conceived except

---

Collingwood, we can no longer say that two propositions contradict each other absolutely, but we must say that they contradict each other from a certain point of view. For this reason Collingwood held that Hegel's dialectic was mono-perspectival. Hegel assumed that the meaning of concepts had not changed and only by abstracting from the development of meaning Hegel could write his logic. For Peters, the attempt to improve on Hegel's dialectic and overcome subjectivism is the key point of Collingwood's philosophy, something which was incomplete because of ill health and premature death (Peters, 1995: 121–5).

as actual. Also, moral philosophy is both normative and descriptive (EPM, 127–133). For Collingwood,

> The hypothetical judgments of science, as we have seen, involve various kinds of categorical judgments as accessories or conditions of their substantive being; and conversely if the body of philosophical knowledge consists of categorical judgments it must at least be surrounded, as it were, by a scaffolding of hypotheticals; I mean that, in order to decide that a certain theory is true, our affirmation of this theory must be supported by considering what the consequences would have been, had any of the alternative theories been true (EPM, 133).

There is an overlap, however, between the hypothetical and the categorical:

> Even in science, therefore, the overlap exists; and this I have already recognized by showing that the purely hypothetical propositions forming the body of science involve certain categorical elements which are necessary to their being but form no part of their essence *quo* science; these are, as it were, a solid structure of facts and truths upon which the pliant body of scientific hypothesis leads a parasitic life. But in the case of philosophical judgments the overlap becomes particularly intimate; the categorical element is no longer something external to the hypothetical, even if necessary to it; both elements alike are the essence of philosophy as such. As before, what we find here is a peculiar fusion of logical elements which elsewhere are found either separate or united in a relatively loose and external way (EPM, 135).

Accordingly, there is in Collingwood's philosophy what might be called a *rapprochement* between logic and metaphysics. The logic of process and becoming that Collingwood puts forward as a solution to the ailments of Western culture is paralleled by a metaphysics of becoming. Metaphysics, as a study of reality, is necessarily a study of the processes by which we construct and apprehend reality through 'scientific' (that is, 'systematic or orderly') thinking.

There is, however, some controversy surrounding the view that I am defending here. Some commentators deny that Collingwood's logic and metaphysics imply an ontological claim about the nature of reality. Because Collingwood's logic of question and answer supplements but does not replace formal logic, Mink argues that it is not a theory of logic at all, in the ordinary sense of that term, but a hermeneutics (Mink, 1969: 131).[9] Similarly, Oldfield contends that the logic

---

[9]   According to Mink, the logic of question and answer might more properly be called the dialectic of question and answer. This would make clear that the relation between question and answer must be understood as occurring in processes which are prospectively open but retrospectively determinate (Mink, 1969: 132). Mink emends Collingwood's theory to argue that the logical efficacy

of question and answer is not really a logic, but a method of enquiry (Oldfield, 1995: 186).

However, as Stein Helgeby argues, Collingwood's logic of question and answer can be understood as logic in the sense of a theory of thought, where thought, like everything else in the world, is seen as a process emerging from less complex structures and processes. Collingwood's logic must be consistent with his broad ontology of process and action. Helgeby argues:

> Despite sounding chiefly hermeneutical, the logic of question and answer cannot be simply about interpretation; it must also be about a kind of organisation already implicit in the organisation of the world, particularly the psyche (Helgeby, 1994: 97).

Collingwood's logic has clear ontological foundations: 'In so far as hermeneutics is a theory of interpretation, applicable to the human sphere, the logic of question and answer includes hermeneutics but goes well beyond its confines' (Helgeby, 1994: 98). As Helgeby explains,

> ... the logic of question and answer is logic come to terms with the process and activity of history in a world that is entirely process. The logic of question and answer unravels the historical process, but it also presupposes that the world is in process (Helgeby, 1994: 102).[10]

It has also been denied that Collingwood's metaphysics involves the apprehension of reality. Modood, for example, regards Collingwood's use of the term 'metaphysics' as inappropriate, and argues that what Collingwood calls metaphysics is merely a 'history of ideas' (Modood, 1989: 117). Giuseppina D'Oro argues that Collingwood wished to distinguish between epistemological issues, or issues pertaining to the order of knowledge, and ontological issues, or issues pertaining to the order of existence. According to D'Oro, Collingwood, like Kant, saw metaphysics not as a study of reality, but as an enquiry into the a priori element within knowledge, which explains how knowledge or experience is possible (D'Oro, 1999: 31).

---

of a presupposition is not a force which causes a question to arise, just as the existence of a problem is not a sufficient cause of its solution. It is rather a property which accrues to presuppositions in retrospective reconstruction. This would make the logic of question and answer closely analogous to the structure of the scale of forms. In the scale of forms each lower level or earlier stage is a necessary condition of the next, does not necessitate the emergence of the next level, but is seen from the standpoint of that level as leading to it and incorporated in it (Mink, 1969: 134–5).

[10] Helgeby's views are presented in more detail in *Action as History: The Historical Thought of R.G. Collingwood* (2004).

For D'Oro, Collingwood's metaphysics of absolute presuppositions provides a purely conceptual map of reality.[11] D'Oro contends
that the doctrine of the overlap of classes illustrates the purely
epistemological nature of the principles which lie at the basis of
experience and that the subdivision of experience into religious,
artistic, scientific, historical, does not cut nature at the joints because
such a subdivision serves a merely epistemological purpose (D'Oro,
1999: 33). According to D'Oro, if the distinction between the presuppositions which govern say, the natural sciences and history was not
purely conceptual, there could be no overlap in the class of objects
studied by natural scientists and the class of objects studied by historians (D'Oro, 1999: 34). The artist, the scientist, and the historian disclose the world in different but complementary ways (D'Oro, 1999:
39).

Accordingly, D'Oro interprets Collingwood's use of the Ontological argument as 'innocent of ontological implications' (D'Oro, 2000:
183). In D'Oro's view, Collingwood's use of the ontological argument preserves only the kernel of truth that certain logical forms are
necessarily expressed by the kind of statements that are
paradigmatically made by historians and natural scientists:

> The ontological proof applies to the object of philosophical thought only
> in the rather weak sense that the logical forms which structure a given
> domain of enquiry and which are the object of philosophical study are
> implicit in the statements of historians and natural scientists (D'Oro,
> 2000: 178).[12]

Contrary to D'Oro, however, for Collingwood, art, religion, science, history, and philosophy are nevertheless real experiences. The
artist, the scientist, and the historian not only disclose the world in
different ways, but they also disclose different worlds, or different
realities, albeit worlds which complement one another. I suggest
that D'Oro's distinction between epistemological issues and ontological issues in Collingwood's philosophy is mistaken.
Collingwood's metaphysics attempts to overcome the distinction
between thought and reality, and his rejection of metaphysics as the
science of pure being does not entail a rejection of metaphysics as a
study of the nature of reality. As we have seen, in *Truth and Contradiction* and *Libellus de Generatione*, Collingwood had rejected the dis-

---

[11]   D'Oro also discusses this point in 'On Collingwood's Rehabilitation of the On-
       tological Argument' (2000: 182).
[12]   D'Oro's interpretation of Collingwood is more fully elaborated upon in
       Collingwood and the Metaphysics of Experience (2002).

tinction between a phenomenal world and an ideal transcendent world as unsustainable and ultimately nihilistic.

The ontological dimension to Collingwood's metaphysics is evident in 'The Nature of Metaphysical Study'[13] of 1934:

> The distinction between processes that we can discover in the object, and processes which we can discover in our minds when we reflect on our thought about the object, is a distinction that we have no right to make here, because, as we learnt in reflecting upon the idea of nothing, we are here in a realm of thought in which there is no object, and in which therefore whatever necessarily happens in our minds when we think about a given concept is a process necessarily ascribed to the concept itself (NMS, 12–13).

Collingwood argues that the principles of science are not

> … mere fictions of the scientific mind, having no basis in reality, for that would make them mere appearances, and there are no mere appearances. It is for the metaphysician of today to work out a general conception of reality into which all these findings of modern science will dovetail naturally, to the mutual comfort and confirmation of metaphysics and science (NMS, 31; EM, 375).

Our time is a time of 'intellectual crisis' and the task of metaphysicians is to lay 'the foundations of a new age' (NMS, 31; EM, 375).[14]

In an unpublished manuscript of 1935, 'Method and Metaphysics',[15] Collingwood wrote: 'The enterprise which goes by the name of metaphysics may be described as an attempt to find out what we can about the general nature of reality' (MM, 1; cf. Vanheeswijck, 1997: 166). The kind of reality that metaphysics describes is a reality of, not pure being, but becoming.[16] Collingwood argues that you simply cannot think about pure abstract being, or that if you do think about

---

[13] Part of this manuscript is published in the revised edition of *An Essay on Metaphysics*, pp. 356–78.

[14] Here I am drawing upon Guido Vanheeswijck, 'Collingwood's Metaphysics: Not a Science of Pure Being, but Still a Science of Being' (1997: 161).

[15] This is published in the revised edition of *An Essay on Philosophical Method* (2005: 327–55).

[16] Vanheeswijck points out that Collingwood's understanding of metaphysics as the study of reality complements his rejection of the idea of metaphysics as ontology in *An Essay on Metaphysics*, as ontology was his name for the study of pure being (Vanheeswijck, 1997: 165). Collingwood was responding to A.J. Ayer's *Language, Truth and Logic*, published in 1936, whose first chapter is devoted to the destruction of the possibility of metaphysical knowledge. For Collingwood, Ayer's attack on metaphysics is an attack not on metaphysics but on pseudo-metaphysics (EM, 163). In Collingwood's idiosyncratic terminology pseudo-metaphysics means 'metaphysics as ontology', or metaphysics as the study of pure being. But, this does not imply a rejection of the study of the nature of reality (Vanheeswijck, 1997: 166).

it you find that it won't stay pure (NMS, 10). Being is never devoid of peculiarities:

> Pure being *becomes* its own determinations, or *develops* them, for becoming or development is a process of change initiated from within ... The idea of metaphysics in general cannot be grasped in abstraction by a purely formal definition unless we allow this abstract idea to sprout determinations of its own in the shape of particular metaphysical problems (NMS, 11–13; cf. Vanheeswijck, 1997: 163).

A theory of metaphysics, then, provides an account of how we both apprehend and create the world through absolute presuppositions and thought. For Collingwood, as we have seen, metaphysics disentangles our thoughts, separating absolute presuppositions from relative presuppositions. We are ordinarily unaware of the connections between our thoughts, something which becomes apparent only through scientific thinking. Thought is ordinarily 'unconscious'.

Collingwood introduced the notion of 'unconscious thought' while explaining how a civilisation came to hold the absolute presuppositions it does and how these came, in the course of time, to be rejected in favour of others.

> People are not ordinarily aware of their absolute presuppositions, and are not, therefore, thus aware of changes in them: such a change, therefore, cannot be a matter of choice. Nor is there anything superficial or frivolous about it. It is the most radical change a man can undergo, and entails the abandonment of all his most firmly established habits and standards for thought and action. Why, asks my friend, do such changes happen? Briefly, because the absolute presuppositions of any given society, at any given phase of its history, form a structure which is subject to 'strains' of greater or less intensity, which are 'taken up' in various ways, but never annihilated. If the strains are too great, the structure collapses and is replaced by another, which will be a modification of the old with the destructive strain removed; a modification not consciously devised but created by a process of unconscious thought (EM, 48n).

Through converting 'unconscious' thought into conscious thought, the metaphysician distinguishes relative from absolute presuppositions. In this respect, metaphysics plays a similar role to art in Collingwood's philosophy. As we have seen, for Collingwood, art also provides a foundation for thought by bringing into the light of consciousness what was previously unconscious.

As Vanheeswijck explains, the notion of 'unconscious thought' is a central concept in Collingwood's thought. According to Vanheeswijck, spread over Collingwood's entire works the same idea is expressed by means of three different images: the conceptual contrast implicit/explicit, the 'light-darkness' metaphor, and the motto 'credo ut intelligam', borrowed from patristic philosophy. In *Religion and Philosophy*, *Ruskin's Philosophy*, and *Speculum Mentis*, Collingwood defines philosophy in terms of implicit and explicit. The 'light-darkness' metaphor is used, for the first time, in *Ruskin's Philosophy*, and it reappears in all his major philosophical writings as an indication of the specificity of the philosophical activity, and as an indication of the main task of the metaphysician (Vanheeswijck, 1994: 115). With the publication of 'Reason is Faith Cultivating Itself' and *Faith and Reason* in 1927, Collingwood introduced a motto illustrating the philosopher's task of making explicit what we implicitly know: 'credo ut intelligam' (Vanheeswijck, 1994: 116).

In *An Essay on Philosophical Method* (as we have already seen) Collingwood characterises philosophical inquiry as the elaboration of the so-called Socratic principle that in a philosophical inquiry what we are trying to do is to know better something which in some sense we always knew: to know it '... actually instead of potentially, or explicitly instead of implicitly ...' (EPM, 11). Hence, for Vanheeswijck, '... the notion 'unconscious thought' is no marginal datum at all, but functions precisely as a hermeneutic key to unlock the quintessence of Collingwood's thought' (Vanheeswijck, 1994: 116).

Vanheeswijck demonstrates that Collingwood developed the function of 'unconscious thought' and illustrated the ontological dimension of his metaphysics in two manuscripts, 'Method and Metaphysics' (1935) and 'Realism and Idealism' (1936). In the manuscript 'Method and Metaphysics' Collingwood distinguishes three kinds of reality: abstract entities, minds, and bodies. Abstract entities are mere potentialities, logically preceding both material reality and human thought, which are actualised only in minds and bodies (Vanheeswijck, 1994: 117, and 1997: 167).[17]

In the manuscript 'Realism and Idealism', Collingwood links the future of metaphysics with what he calls 'objective idealism'. For Collingwood, unlike subjective (Kantian) idealism,

---

[17] According to Collingwood, abstract entities are actualised in the world of bodies and minds in a different way. Vanheeswijck indicates: 'In the world of bodies, what has once happened has forever disappeared. In the world of minds, the past can be called up again. Hence, a distinction can be made between cosmology (i.e. the study of material changes) and history proper (i.e. the study of human thinking). Metaphysics, then, is primarily the study of the general characteristics of reality by means of an enquiry into the changing absolute presuppositions of human thought, of which cosmology is an important part' (Vanheeswijck, 1997: 168).

> Objective idealism is epistemologically realistic; it believes we know the object itself as it really is … Thus it conceives the world of nature as something derived from and dependent upon something logical prior to itself, a world of immaterial ideas; but this is not a mental world, a world of mental activities or of things dependent on mental activity, although it is an intelligible world or a world in which mind, when mind comes into existence, finds itself completely at home (RI, B, IX, sect. 1).

As Vanheeswijck points out, implicitly, these abstract entities, or a priori concepts, are always present as the condition of potentiality of all the forms of actual reality. In the historical evolution of the absolute presuppositions of human thought they are time and again made explicit (Vanheeswijck, 1994: 117).[18]

Between 1933 and 1936, therefore, Collingwood wrote that metaphysics is an attempt to find out about the general nature of reality. After 1936, he defined metaphysics as the historical study of absolute presuppositions. Despite what might seem to be a contradiction, these two views are consistent with one another. As Vanheeswijck explains, before 1936 Collingwood's aim is to describe what *a priori* ideas are, and to construct a metaphysical theory, in particular the theory of objective idealism. After 1936, (responding to Ayer and the logical positivists) Collingwood describes the way in which we know *a priori* ideas. This means identifying metaphysics with the historical study of changing absolute presuppositions (Vanheeswijck, 1997: 169).

------

[18]   Vanheeswijck indicates that, from 1927 onwards, Collingwood states that religion implicitly contains all the intellectual content philosophy could know throughout its evolution. This thesis that each form of knowledge and action presupposes a religious belief is not contradicted by the fact of the historical evolution of religious belief: as is demonstrated by Collingwood's account in *An Essay on Metaphysics* of how religious faith has evolved from natural religion through polytheism to monotheism.

Showing the interrelations between religion and the presuppositions of successive forms of scientific thought is, for Collingwood, a primordial task of the metaphysician. Specifically, Collingwood shows in *An Essay on Metaphysics* how the presuppositions of *modern* science are interrelated to the *Christian* interpretation of religious belief (EM, 213–27; Vanheeswijck, 1994: 118). In *An Essay on Metaphysics* Collingwood argues: '… if science is 'experience' interpreted in the light of our general convictions as to the nature of the world, religion is what expresses these convictions in themselves and for their own sake and hands them on from generation to generation. And it does this irrespectively of whether we know by means of metaphysical analysis what these convictions are' (EM, 198). Thus, Vanheeswijck argues, the title Collingwood gave to his 1927 article, 'Reason is Faith Cultivating Itself', could also be applied to *An Essay on Philosophical Method* and *An Essay on Metaphysics* (Vanheeswijck, 1994: 119).

Collingwood, however, aims to overcome the distinction between how we know the world and what the world is. According to Collingwood, in 'Realism and Idealism',

> It is a speculation at least worth considering, that a world which had no mind to know it would be an immature, seedling or embryonic world, having many of its potentialities as yet undeveloped; and that the appearance, in such a world, of minds able to know it would bring some of these potentialities into actuality, and thus, so far from falsifying the object, would realise the object or make it more fully and truly itself (RI, A, VII, sect. 14).

The world we perceive does really and truly exist just as we perceive it, but it exists *as* we perceive it only *because* we perceive it. The addition of new qualities that a thing receives through our act of perception is a realisation of its own inner potentialities (RI, A, XII, sect. 1). The key to difficult problems in modern metaphysics, Collingwood contends, consists in the discovery that the subjective and objective worlds are not mutually exclusive: 'Modern idealism and modern realism in some of the more familiar senses of those terms simply consists in alternative ways of breaking down the distinction' (RI, B, IV, sect. 9). For Collingwood, following Hegel,

> The mistake of subjective idealism, he proclaimed, was to think that ideas could only exist in our heads ... The mistake of the materialist is to think that ideas could exist only as embodied in matter (RI, B, VIII, sect. 3).

Collingwood's view of metaphysics as the study of reality, according to Vanheeswijck, complements Collingwood's conclusion to 'The Function of Metaphysics in Civilization' (an unpublished manuscript from 1938): 'We must start again at the beginning and construct a new metaphysical theory which will face the facts revealed by history. This work has never yet been done' (EM, 420). But, as Vanheeswijck indicates, Collingwood did not undertake this task in *An Essay on Metaphysics*. In his preface to *An Essay on Metaphysics*, Collingwood emphasises the point that he does not aim at constructing a metaphysical theory:

> This is not so much a book of metaphysics as a book about metaphysics. What I have chiefly tried to do in it is neither to expound my own metaphysical ideas, nor to criticize the metaphysical ideas of other people; but to explain what metaphysics is ... and how it is to be pursued (EM, civ; Vanheeswijck, 1997: 171).

Metaphysics, therefore, is the study of reality, although this is inextricably linked with an account of the processes by which we create and apprehend reality. Collingwood's philosophy transcends the dualism between realism and idealism: thought both 'apprehends' and 'constructs' (cf. Mink, 1969: 112–3). As Vanheeswijck points out,

> Precisely because of its hermeneutic approach, Collingwood's project differs from that of the history of ideas on which it relies so heavily. Collingwood's conviction is that those who impose a new pattern of meaning onto the life and thought of their time do more than simply apply a different film of thought to an indifferent reality. They transform the nature of reality itself ... Spiritual changes transform reality as much as physical changes do (Vanheeswijck, 1994: 120).

For Collingwood, absolute presuppositions are

> ... catalytic agents which the mind must bring out of its own resources to the manipulation of what is called 'experience' and the conversion of it into science and civilization (EM, 197).

However, as Collingwood points out at the beginning of *An Essay on Philosophical Method*, if science and civilisation are to develop beyond a rudimentary level, it is necessary for us to reflect on them.

> There are some things which we can do without understanding what we are doing; not only things which we do with our bodies, like locomotion and digestion, but even things which we do with our minds, like making a poem or recognizing a face. But when that which we do is in the nature of thinking, it begins to be desirable, if we are to do it well, that we should understand what we are trying to do. Scientific and historical thought could never go very far unless scientists and historians reflected on their own work, tried to understand what they were aiming at, and asked themselves how best to attain it. Most of all, this is true of philosophy (EPM, 1).

The purpose of both logic and metaphysics, then, is to provide an historical awareness of the thinking, with its absolute presuppositions and complexes of questions and answers, by which we create science and civilisation.

Collingwood's logic and metaphysics, therefore, provide an account of the world of process and change. In this respect, his philosophy constitutes a solution to the problems facing a Western civilisation that has not yet significantly moved beyond the Platonic and Aristotelian philosophy of being. The logic and metaphysics of the Greeks are inadequate in that they attempt to locate all meaning and value in a transcendent world, while failing to adequately account for the actual world of process and becoming. Collingwood's philosophy aims to overcome the crisis of the West (i.e. the need for a more adequate philosophy, or communal self-understanding) by reconciling normative values with the historical world. Hence, as I have argued, he narrows the gap between logic, as the study of thought, and metaphysics, as the study of reality.

Although, as some commentators have indicated, Collingwood's philosophy becomes something like hermeneutics, unlike most hermeneutical thinkers and continental philosophers, he retains the old names of logic and metaphysics. Although Collingwood's 'revolution' in logic and metaphysics attempts to transcend the philosophy of the Greeks, there is continuity with the past. There is in Collingwood's philosophy, I suggest, a middle ground between traditional philosophy (or Platonism) and postmodernism. The middle ground is the reconciliation of normative thinking with the world of becoming.

For Collingwood, however, the crisis of civilisation had many aspects. One of these aspects was the threat to an historical metaphysics from reactionary traditional philosophy and from irrationalism. These threats to metaphysics and to civilisation will be discussed in the next chapter, and will serve to provide a more detailed understanding of Collingwood's reformed metaphysics. I will also explain in more detail how Collingwood's philosophy in general provides a solution to the crisis of the West through reconciling normative thinking and historical change.

Chapter Seven

Metaphysics, History and Progress

As I have argued in the last two chapters, Collingwood regarded Western civilisation as confronted by a crisis due to the instability and inadequacy of its philosophical foundations. The philosophies of Plato and Aristotle, which Western culture to a large extent still depends upon, meant that our self-understanding was circumscribed by an abstract philosophy of being and failed to give an adequate account of historical reality. Collingwood's solution to this was a reform of both logic and metaphysics, in order to provide an account of becoming, not being. As I have also argued earlier, Collingwood's solution to the crisis of the West ought to be seen in the context of Romanticism and historicism and sought to improve on previous attempts to reform philosophy, for example, by Kant, Hegel and Nietzsche.

Collingwood regarded his reformed metaphysics, and with it the ideal of an historically self-conscious civilisation, as threatened by reactionary philosophy and irrationalism. In Part II of *An Essay on Metaphysics* he refers to this threat as 'anti-metaphysics'. This chapter will discuss Collingwood's response to anti-metaphysics and how in both his reformed metaphysics and his philosophy as a whole Collingwood responded to the crisis of civilisation by reconciling normative thinking with historical change.

For Collingwood, 'anti-metaphysics' means a kind of thought that regards metaphysics as a delusion and an impediment to the progress of knowledge, and demands its abolition. He describes three kinds of anti-metaphysics: progressive anti-metaphysics, reactionary anti-metaphysics and irrationalist anti-metaphysics (EM, 82–3). Collingwood reminds us that '… metaphysical analysis, the discovery that certain presuppositions actually made are absolute presuppositions, is an integral part or an indispensable condition … of all scientific work' (EM, 84). In the interests of science it is necessary that the work of metaphysics should be done. 'Science' in this context means not natural science, but orderly and systematic thinking on every subject, and not 'theoretical' thinking alone, but 'practical' thinking as well (EM, 85). According to Collingwood, 'If a case arises when, for the sake of progress in any scientific enquiry, there is need for a certain piece of analysis to determine whether a certain presupposition newly brought to light is a relative one or an absolute one …' and if professional metaphysicians are not willing or able to do this piece of analysis, then persons who do not profess to be metaphysicians, but are concerned for the progress of scientific enquiry in this actual case, have to undertake it for themselves (EM, 85).

This results in amateur metaphysicians: that is, metaphysical work done by persons who do not regard themselves as qualified to do it, but find they have to do it because a metaphysical problem has arisen out of their own special work to which the professional metaphysicians do not seem to be attending, and unless this problem is solved their own special work cannot go forward. Examples of this can be found in the introductory chapters of large scale works in natural science, history, law, and economics, especially works which are regarded as original and important contributions to knowledge.

The amateur metaphysicians may come to resent the fact that they are doing the work of professional metaphysicians and regard their own work as anti-metaphysics, an attack on metaphysics. This Collingwood refers to as 'progressive anti-metaphysics', but in fact it is metaphysics, sometimes good and sometimes bad (EM, 88). For example, the development of Newton's physics and modern physics meant putting forward new metaphysical propositions and warning people against the metaphysics of the professional metaphysicians (EM, 90). Professional metaphysicians, in this case, were bad historians and failed to keep in touch with the advance of ordinary science, and mistakenly thought that metaphysics has to do with 'eternal' problems — which in practice means the problems of the last generation, not this generation (EM, 86).

Collingwood argues that the case of reactionary anti-metaphysics is similar to the case of progressive anti-metaphysics in terms of the loss of effective contact between metaphysics and science. However, in this instance, the professional metaphysicians have moved ahead of ordinary science. Ordinary science here would have to create its own metaphysics, which would be reactionary as compared to professional metaphysics. The reactionary anti-metaphysician embraces past works in metaphysics as his 'doctrine', considering them in abstraction from the historical context to which they were relevant. He condemns contemporary metaphysics as false, thereby also condemning the science it is derived from. The reactionary in metaphysics is also a reactionary in ordinary science (EM, 92).

Collingwood indicates that '... reactionary anti-metaphysics became a living force in the nineteenth century' (EM, 93). After the revolutionary movements of the eighteenth century, Collingwood asserts, the nineteenth century saw in science and politics a counter-revolution. In order to consolidate the work of the eighteenth century, it was thought that the revolutionary spirit that created them must be held in check. Although conceiving itself as an age of progress, the nineteenth century, until within twenty or thirty years of its close, was, with regard to fundamental principles, an age of reaction (EM, 93).

According to Collingwood, James Watt's principles of the reciprocating steam engine and John Locke's theory of the English parliamentary system were introduced in the eighteenth century and continued to be used for much of the nineteenth, but became obsolete in the late nineteenth century. Those with a vested interest in their maintenance opposed two new developments. There was a new physics which was to produce what we now know as the physics of relativity, and there was a new history, cutting itself loose from the age-old method of scissors and paste, which was to revolutionise the accepted view of the human world. Nineteenth-century reactionaries fought against these tendencies using the slogans 'back to Kant' and 'no more metaphysics' (EM, 95).

Kant, Collingwood explains, laid down the lines on which natural science was content to travel during the central part of the nineteenth century. The new physics and new geometry involved a breach with the Kantian system: a breach foreseen and some of its consequences worked out by Hegel (EM, 95). Reactionaries, therefore, attempted to maintain the pseudo-metaphysical *status quo* and represented the conviction that all questions about fundamental principles had been settled and should not be re-opened (EM, 96).

According to Collingwood, the immaturity of historical technique in the eighteenth century found its characteristic expression in the doctrine that historical events were the effects of causes in the world of nature: nature seemed to be an absolute presupposition of all historical thinking. This illusion was dispelled by the development of historical thought in the nineteenth century. If the eighteenth century historians' grasp of historical method had been firmer they would have said that man's historical activities were conditioned not by nature but by what he was able to make out of nature. The so-called conditioning of history by nature is in reality a conditioning of history by itself (EM, 98).

The Lockian system in politics presupposed nationality (as well as private property), where nationality was conceived as 'natural': an absolute presupposition of all political activity whatever (EM, 97). For the modern historian, however, nationality is a relative presupposition. Nationality can make history only because history has made nationality and is constantly destroying and remaking it. Those who wanted to retain the political principles of the eighteenth century, therefore, represented reactionary anti-metaphysics. The historian had worked out the metaphysics against which the political reactionaries tried to defend themselves (EM, 99).[1]

Collingwood, therefore, regarded his reformed historical metaphysics as threatened by reactionary pseudo-philosophy. However, it was also confronted by the threat of irrationalism. Reacting to the inadequacies of traditional philosophy derived from Ancient Greece, certain modern intellectual movements tended to reject normative thinking and metaphysics completely, giving rise to scepticism and nihilism. Collingwood refers to these tendencies as 'irrationalist anti-metaphysics'. He describes two kinds of

---

[1]   Collingwood's discussion of 'reactionary anti-metaphysics' casts an interesting light on Hughes' account of German historicism. Hughes remarks that the separation of Germany from the main stream of Western European social thought tormented the minds of Troeltsch and Meinecke: 'Why was it, they asked themselves, that from "shallow" philosophies of history and society the British and the French had been able to develop political practices that were both viable and humane, whereas the Germans, with their "deeper" understanding, not only failed to achieve a social equilibrium, but as the twentieth century advanced, were ever more obviously succumbing to the "demon" of naked physical power?' (Hughes, 1959: 184). The German school of historical idealism, Hughes contends, taught Europeans to be dissatisfied with merely intellectualist explanations and to seek out the living and growing stuff of history and society themselves. Yet in the sense of applied wisdom this teaching came to next to nothing. The great political innovations of the nineteenth century were based on presuppositions derived from the century preceding and, in a philosophical sense, already out of date. Again, from Germany, figures such as Nietzsche and Dilthey were to serve as the heralds of the intellectual renewal of the 1890s (Hughes, 1959: 185). According to Collingwood, however, reactionary anti-metaphysics was as much prevalent in Germany as elsewhere (cf. EM, 95).

irrationalist attack on metaphysics, one that emerges from psychology, and another from logical positivism.

In revealing the absolute presuppositions in any given piece of thinking, metaphysics is one branch of the science of thought (EM, 101). Psychology claims to be the science which describes how we think, and if this is so it would embrace metaphysics (EM, 103). But this claim, Collingwood contends, is questionable. He argues that unlike any kind of bodily or physiological functioning, thought is a self-criticising activity. Whereas judgement is passed on a body by its environment, the mind judges itself. Not content with the simple pursuit of ends, the mind also pursues the further end of discovering for itself whether it has pursued them successfully. Hence the sciences of body and mind respectively must take this difference into account. Unlike the science of body, the science of mind '… must describe the self-judging function which is part and parcel of all thinking and try to discover the criteria upon which its judgements are based' (EM, 108).

The Greeks, Collingwood points out, recognised this dual aspect of the mind and constructed a science of theoretical thought called logic and a science of practical thought called ethics (EM, 108). In view of the attention to the idea of a criterion or standard of judgement, in Latin *norma*, these sciences have been traditionally called normative sciences. But, Collingwood argues,

> … the word 'normative' may prove misleading, as it conveys by its form the suggestion that the standard or criterion to which it refers is a criterion belonging to the practitioner of the science thus described, and used by him to judge whether the thinking which he studies has been well or ill done; as if it were for the logician to decide whether a non-logician's thoughts are true or false and his arguments valid or invalid, and for the student of ethics to pass judgement on the actions of other people as having succeeded or failed in their purpose. This suggestion is incorrect. The characteristic of thought in virtue of which a science of thought is called normative consists not in the possibility that one man's thoughts may be judged successful or unsuccessful by another, real though that possibility is; but in the necessity that in every act of thought the thinker himself should judge the success of his own act. (EM, 109)

Therefore, he substitutes '… for the traditional epithet "normative" the more accurate term "criteriological"' (EM, 109). It seems then that, coinciding with his historicist reform of metaphysics, Collingwood replaces the term 'normative' with the term 'criteriological' because the criteria for judgements are not separate from or transcending judgements themselves: rather they are immanent to a particular context.

Collingwood asserts that the sixteenth-century proposal for a new science called psychology arose from the recognition that what we call feeling is not a kind of thinking, not a self-critical activity, and therefore not the possible subject matter of a criteriological science (EM, 109). Psychology, as the study of the 'psyche', or a science of feeling, was designed to fill the gap between logic and ethics on the one hand, and physiology on the other (EM, 110).

According to Collingwood, 'The intellectual task of the eighteenth century was the liquidation of Europe's debt to Greece' (EM, 112). Eighteenth century religious innovations were an attack upon Christian doctrines and institutions in so far as these expressed a mentality moulded by Greek influence. Scientific innovations attacked biology, as biology was the last refuge of teleological natural science. Thus, eighteenth century biology argued that organisms were nothing but complexes of material particles and operated solely according to mechanical principles. Similarly, in the theory of knowledge it was argued that operations of thought were nothing but aggregations and complexes of feelings, special cases of sensation and emotion. This 'materialistic epistemology' aimed to wipe out the old sciences of thought, logic and ethics, and replace them with psychology, the science of feeling (EM, 114).

Collingwood explains that a revolt against the old logic and ethics may have been desirable and beneficial '… for it might very well be true that people who professed those sciences had misunderstood their normative character, and had claimed a censorship over the thoughts and actions of other people …' (EM, 114). However, epistemological materialism proceeded on the assumption that thought did not possess the power of self-criticism, the criterion of truth and falsehood, by reference to which thought judges itself. Therefore, the new psychological science of thought proposed by epistemological materialism was a pseudo-science of thought (EM, 115). The difference between logic and psychology, Collingwood indicates, is that psychology has a clear and conscious determination to ignore the self-critical part of thought.

The advance of epistemological materialism in the nineteenth century meant that psychology was accepted as the science of thought and logic rejected as an out-of-date pseudo-science. But these claims, Collingwood argues, down to the present day, have always continued to be based on the principles of epistemological materialism. Psychology fails to understand thought as an attempt to think truly and avoid thinking falsely, and fails to distinguish thinking from feeling (EM, 117).

Despite the triumphs of psychology when it has attended to its proper business, the study of feeling, it does not survive critical inspection when it deals with such matters as art, religion, civilisation and the intellectual structure of institutions belonging to other civilisations. An example of this is Freud's *Totem and Taboo* (EM, 118). Because psychology ignores the distinction between truth and falsehood, Collingwood contends, it is implicitly teaching that there is no difference between science and sophistry, and is covertly describing itself as no science at all (EM, 120–1). For example, Collingwood accuses W. McDougall's discussion of animal behaviour of being an attempt to associate thinking with 'a random scratching and clawing about' (EM, 126).

Collingwood declares that European civilisation is based on the belief that truth is the most important thing in the world and that scientific thinking is the most valuable thing a person can do. In this kind of civilisation, 'Religion would be predominantly a worship of truth ... and the god's presence to the worshipper a gift of mental light' (EM, 133). Philosophy would be predominantly an exposition of scientific thought and orderly action, and especially the problem of establishing standards by which on reflection truth can be distinguished from falsehood. Politics would be predominantly the attempt to build up a common life by the methods of reason and subject to the sanctions of reason. Education, social structure and economic life would also place orderly and scientific thinking in the most honourable and commanding position (EM, 134).

According to Collingwood, the growth of irrationalism is leading to an '... epidemic withering of belief in the importance of truth and in the obligation to think and act in a systematic and methodical way' (EM, 135), and substituting the worship of truth for the worship of emotion and a cultivation of certain emotional states. The success of this attack on civilisation is conditional on the victims' suspicions not being aroused. Immunity from criticism for irrationalist agents is ensured by putting forward their propaganda under the pretence that it is a special science (EM, 136).

With the irrationalist attack on civilisation, there has been a tendency '... to ignore and vilify the traditional theology of religion and to regard religion as an affair of the emotions' (EM, 137). In philosophy there has been a tendency to belittle the notion of scientific thought, to magnify emotion at the expense of intellect and the developing of a kind of ethical intuitionalism. In politics, Collingwood asserts, there has been a tendency to become impatient with the work of politically educating an entire people, to choose leaders not for their intellectual powers but for their ability to excite mass-emotions, and to suppress discussion in favour of propaganda (EM, 139).

A civilisation perishes (Collingwood continues) if the people who share it are no longer convinced that the form of life which it tries to realise is worth realising:

> If European civilization is based on the belief that truth is the most precious thing in the world and that pursuing it is the whole duty of man, an irrationalist epidemic if it ran through Europe unchecked would in a relatively short time destroy everything that goes by the name of European civilization (EM, 140).

In this condition scientific workers would no longer be able to continue their work.[2] Science will not grow

> ... except where the scientist as the priest of truth is not only supported but revered as a priest-king by a people that shares his faith. When scientists are no longer kings, there will be (to adapt a famous saying of Plato's) no end to the evils undergone by the society that has dethroned them until it perishes physically for sheer lack of sustenance (EM, 141).

Collingwood's attack on psychology, as he remarked in *An Autobiography*, implied no hostility towards psychology proper, as a science of feeling, and when dealing with the problems of psychotherapy (A, 95). But psychology, in so far as it claims to be the science of thought and ignores the criteriological part of thought, is part of a nihilism that threatens civilisation.

From the psychological attack on metaphysics, Collingwood turns to the positivistic. Positivists believed that only knowledge attained by the methods of natural science was valid. Unlike the psychological attack on logic, positivists were concerned with the question of whether or not a process of thought had satisfied the scientific criterion of validity. However, in defining this criterion, they mistakenly argued that, in scientific enquiry, firstly, facts were ascertained by the senses, and then, secondly, they were classified by thought. Concepts, hypotheses and laws were defined in terms of the observation of facts (EM, 144).

Contrary to positivism, Collingwood argues that by means of our senses we do not observe any facts, we only undergo feelings. Positivism, in this respect, Collingwood contends, was reverting to a long-exploded error of the Middle Ages. Positivists failed to see that 'fact' is a term belonging to the vocabulary of historical thought:

---

[2]   The point that irrationalism in society fatally undermines scientific work is discussed by Peter Drucker in his account of Nazi Germany in *The End of Economic Man* (1939).

'Positivism thus implied, but did not furnish, a theory of historical knowledge as a foundation for its theory of natural science' (EM, 145).

Furthermore, the positivist argument that every notion is a class of observable facts implied that scientific thought has no presuppositions. If the function of thought is to classify observed facts, this implied that there must be facts available for classification before thought can begin to operate. Once facts are available there would be no need to presuppose anything: you just set to work and classify them. But, Collingwood explains, the work of observing facts is really done by the senses with assistance from the intellect. What the positivists called 'observing' facts is really historical thinking, which is a complex process involving numerous presuppositions (EM, 146).

Continuing the eighteenth-century programme of waging war against Greek elements in modern thought, the positivists attacked metaphysics because of its subject matter. They had never discovered that there were such things as absolute presuppositions. Presuppositions were misunderstood as general propositions about matters of fact, advanced on credit and awaiting verification (EM, 147). For the positivists, presuppositions were either facts arrived at from observation and verifiable through observation, or else nonsense (EM, 148).

In practice, Collingwood asserts, positivists practiced both metaphysics and pseudo-metaphysics. Through sound metaphysical analysis, they detected absolute presuppositions which were implied in the methods of natural science, then justified them on positivistic principles as generalisations from observed fact. This is because they thought themselves bound to justify any presuppositions which natural science thought fit to make (EM, 149). For example, John Stuart Mill discovered that natural scientists are convinced that all events happen according to laws. Mill mistakes this absolute presupposition for a proposition and tries to prove it true, but his argument is circular (EM, 151–2). Similarly, Bradley's claim that 'metaphysics is the finding of bad reasons for what we believe upon instinct', while equating absolute presuppositions with 'what we believe upon instinct', signifies that he also thinks that absolute presuppositions must be justified by appeal to observed facts, but, not realising that he is engaging in pseudo-metaphysics, has grown disillusioned with the process (EM, 153–4).

According to Collingwood, logical positivism developed further this erroneous approach to metaphysics, using the following syllogism, which had been put forward by A.J. Ayer, in *Language Truth and Logic* (1936): 'Any proposition which cannot be verified by appeal to observed facts is a pseudo-proposition. Metaphysical propositions cannot be verified by appeal to observed facts. Therefore metaphysical propositions are pseudo-propositions, and therefore nonsense' (EM, 162).

For Collingwood, however, Ayer's position is an attack not on metaphysics, but on pseudo-metaphysics. Characteristically, suppositions are mistaken for propositions (EM, 163). For Ayer, so-called 'metaphysical propositions' are not verifiable and are therefore 'pseudo-propositions'. As such, Collingwood argues, they are not propositions. This gives rise to the question of what they really are (a question that Ayer does not answer) and the answer is suppositions (EM, 165). Ayer, Collingwood explains, proved merely that metaphysics is not a set a propositions claiming to give knowledge of a reality which transcends the phenomenal world.

Accordingly, the logical positivist demand for the elimination of metaphysics, Collingwood suggests, is the outcome of a desire to '... belittle what one cannot share, and destroy what one cannot understand' (EM, 166). Ayer's ideas of ethics and theology are, Collingwood proposes, foolish ideas from our childhood which we have a resentment towards in later life. We reject with argument the traces of that real or supposed teaching still discernible in ourselves (EM, 167).

According to Collingwood, the logical positivist attack on metaphysics is an attack on the foundations of natural science. To deny the doctrine that thought has presuppositions is to attempt to reduce all thinking to its most confused and unscientific level (EM, 170-1).[3] The logical positivist attack on metaphysics, then, is part of the irrationalist threat to civilisation. For Collingwood,

> The fate of European science and European civilization is at stake. The gravity of the peril lies especially in the fact that so few recognize any peril to exist. When Rome was in danger, it was the cackling of the sacred geese that saved the Capitol. I am only a professorial goose, consecrated

---

[3]   Collingwood, furthermore, argues that Samuel Alexander was infected by positivism in regarding the idea that every event has a cause as a summary statement of observed facts, rather than as a presupposition (EM, 176-7). Alexander mistakenly constructed his metaphysics on the assumption that all human beings everywhere and always accepted Mill's law of universal causation and everything enunciated in Kant's 'System of Principles'. But these principles, absolute presuppositions of eighteenth-century science, had only a short historical life in a limited part of the world (EM, 179-80).

with a cap and gown and fed at a college table; but cackling is my job, and cackle I will (EM, 343).

As Collingwood argues, therefore, the well-being of civilisation is inextricably bound up with the well-being of science. Furthermore, the preservation of science is the same thing as the growth of science: 'Science is a plant of slow growth … and for a plant the end of growth is the end of life …' (EM, 141). The advancement of science and the existence of science, he asserts, '… are not two things but one …' (EM, 342).

However, for Collingwood, it seems that the advancement of science and the preservation of civilisation are not safeguarded by metaphysics alone. As I have already suggested, according to Collingwood's account of metaphysics and the logic of question and answer, the meaning of a set of absolute presuppositions is only fully realised in the context of the questions and answers that it actually gives rise to. The work of the metaphysician, in revealing absolute presuppositions and providing an historical account of how one set of absolute presuppositions has changed into another, is an indispensable condition for the advancement of science. But for a science, that is, 'systematic or orderly thinking about a determinate subject matter' (EM, 4), to progress it is also necessary to have knowledge of the relative presuppositions, questions and answers that have occurred in the history of that particular science.

This kind of historical knowledge must be possessed by the scientist in order to make an advance in any particular science or practice and by the philosopher in order to reflect on that science or practice and determine whether or not an advance has been made. It seems, however, that, for Collingwood, this kind of detailed historical knowledge of how a science or practice has developed over time is not primarily the concern of the metaphysician. Instead it is the business of philosophy, not metaphysics, to interpret the whole of a science or practice in order to say whether or not progress has occurred.

The interpretation that I am putting forward here is illuminated by the view of Oldfield. As Oldfield describes it,

> Collingwood's analysis of the theory of absolute presuppositions is to work backwards from statements to the questions to which they are answers, or from propositions to the presuppositions which underlie them, until we reach rock bottom with presuppositions which are not answers to questions, and which are therefore absolutely not relatively presupposed. If we reverse this procedure, and start with absolute presuppositions working forwards, then we have a much more fruitful way of linking the theory of absolute presuppositions with Collingwood's theory of historical knowledge. If we stand at the mouth of a river, we

have only to walk along its bank to find its source: if, on the other hand, we stand at its source, while some courses will definitely be ruled out, there is a variety of courses which might have been taken (Oldfield, 1995: 196).

It seems that Oldfield agrees with Mink's claim that the questions which absolute presuppositions give rise to are prospectively open, but retrospectively determinate (cf. Mink, 1969: 132). According to Oldfield, 'Questions arise from constellations of absolute presuppositions, but there is no logical entailment between them and the questions which do arise. One constellation can give rise to a number of relative presuppositions' (Oldfield, 1995: 196). Oldfield argues that

> ... for the theory of absolute presuppositions to illuminate Collingwood's theory of historical knowledge, what has to be incorporated is an analysis of what relative presuppositions have in fact been given rise to by particular constellations of absolute presuppositions (Oldfield, 1995, 196–7).

As an example of particular relative presuppositions that absolute presuppositions have given rise to, one needs to discuss the history of science and the history of history. Oldfield draws attention to three different intellectual traditions that Collingwood analyses in *The Idea of History*, each of which was in its time inimical to the development of historical knowledge: Greek mathematical thinking of the sixth century; medieval theology; and the concern with natural science from the sixteenth to the nineteenth centuries. At the same time, Collingwood offers an account of the development of a different tradition of thinking which not until the late nineteenth century and early twentieth century was able to offer a theory of knowledge which did proper justice to historical thought (Oldfield, 1995: 197). Each of the former three traditions had its period of dominance, when its concerns coloured the whole field of intellectual inquiry. The achievement of Herodotus in the field of historical knowledge lay 'smothered' for centuries, until revived by Vico, and developed thereafter mainly by Kant, Hegel, Marx, Simmel, Dilthey and Croce (Oldfield, 1995: 198).

Although my argument is not the same as Oldfield's, I think that Oldfield's distinction between 'working backwards' and 'working forwards' is especially useful. For Collingwood, I suggest, 'working backwards' in order to provide an account of the absolute presuppositions that underlie science is essentially the task of the metaphysician. But for philosophy to examine whether or not progress has occurred in a science or practice it must take into account, not just absolute presuppositions, but also the scientific thinking, or 'working forwards', to which absolute presuppositions have given rise.

Accordingly, on this interpretation, Collingwood's reformed metaphysics is a solution to the crisis of Western civilisation and rejects both reactionary philosophy and irrationalism. However, it needs to be supplemented by a broader philosophy of history and of the history of science. Metaphysics, then, does not provide an account of the advancement of science and civilisation. But it does facilitate this advance, or progress, by revealing absolute presuppositions. The historical change from one constellation of absolute presuppositions to another is not in itself progressive.

The argument that I am putting forward here, however, is quite different from the interpretation of Martin[4]. Martin argues that the transition from one set of absolute presuppositions to another can be seen as progressive. According to Martin, metaphysics involves a modified scale of forms, where the overlaps are partial and spread out over time, in contrast with the 'logical' model in *An Essay on Philosophical Method* where all theories confront one another together (Martin, 1998a: xlii). Martin, referring to Collingwood's short essay on progress at the end of *The Idea of History*, points out that Collingwood thought that we can talk of 'progress' when referring to two contemporaneous but competing theories within a science, or regarding two stages in the development in one and the same science (Martin, 1998a: xliii). For Martin, just as we can say that one scientific theory, or phase of scientific development, marked an improvement over a competing theory or earlier phase, so we can say that one ingredient set of absolute presuppositions marked an improvement over another (Martin, 1998a: xliv). Therefore, Martin asserts, a modified scale of forms *could* be offered for the whole sequence of absolute presuppositions of a given science within the overall process of its development. In this way, metaphysics can be seen as progressive (Martin, 1998a: xlv).

Referring to Collingwood's discussion of 'the existence of God' in Part IIIA of *An Essay on Metaphysics*, Martin argues that the metaphysician can say that in the practice of science, with the history it actually has had and in the process of development it has actually undergone, the monotheistic presupposition goes with improved science in that particular process of development and, hence, can be regarded as superior in a (modified) scale of forms to the presuppositions of polytheism. In Martin's view, the metaphysician compares

---

[4] My argument is also quite different from that of Michael Beaney, which I do not discuss here. See Beaney, 'Collingwood's Conception of Presuppositional Analysis' (2005).

different phases in the history of a science with each other, but not with whole ways of life (Martin, 1998a: xlvi).

Martin contends, then, that the main task of metaphysics is the comparative one of assessing progress, of showing that it has occurred as between theories occupying two different stages in a historical process of development and differentiation. The crucial judgement of explanatory improvement can be accomplished, between two scientific theories covering roughly the same ground, by subjecting the presuppositions of each theory to scale of forms analyses (Martin, 1998a: l). The work of metaphysics is not merely descriptive, but normative or critical (Martin, 1998a: lii). Martin argues that the metaphysician may also want to identify problems in present science and to suggest how these problems might be resolved (Martin, 1998a: xlvii). Accordingly, referring to Collingwood's discussion of causation in Part IIIC of *An Essay on Metaphysics*, Martin regards Collingwood as criticising Newtonian and post-Newtonian ideas of causation in theoretical natural science and replacing them with a more suitable set, which could be shown to solve certain problems in the earlier ideas while keeping a grip on the solid achievements there (Martin, 1998a: lxvii).

Like Martin, Hinz also argues that metaphysics is progressive. According to Hinz, the criteriological aspect of thought means that the process of development with which metaphysics is concerned must be shown to be progressive (Hinz, 1994b: 132). The metaphysician regards the successive systems in a process of development as contentious versions of a single practice (Hinz, 1994b, 135). For Hinz, 'dialectical argument informed by the criteria for progress supplied by the particular process of development in question' demonstrates how progress has been made in a practice (Hinz, 1994b, 135–6).

I suggest, on the contrary, that Martin and Hinz are mistaken in their view that the transition from one set of absolute presuppositions to another is progressive and that Martin's interpretation of Collingwood's discussions of causation and 'the existence of God' is mistaken. Martin and Hinz are correct in their contention that there can be progress in a science or practice. However, progress occurs in a science or practice as a whole, not in its absolute presuppositions, and it is not the task of the metaphysician to assess whether or not progress has occurred.

As we have seen, for Collingwood, absolute presuppositions are not true or false. Therefore, 'It is a mistake ... to fancy that by investigating the truth of their absolute presuppositions a metaphysician could show that one school of science was fundamentally right and another fundamentally wrong' (EM, 52–3). Metaphysics, Collingwood explains, does not show which schools of scientific thought are justified in the light of metaphysical criticism and which are not. The metaphysician does not criticise absolute presuppositions: he or she finds out what they are (EM, 54). This view of metaphysics as aiding the progress of science through revealing absolute presuppositions, but not as judging whether or not progress has taken place, is evident in Collingwood's discussion of 'the existence of God' in Part IIIA of *An Essay on Metaphysics*.

According to Collingwood, the existence of God is an absolute presupposition of all the thinking done by Christians (EM, 186). Because it is not a proposition it is neither true nor false. However, the metaphysical proposition that 'somebody believes that God exists', if true, can be proved, and if false, can be disproved (EM, 188). Thus, Anselm's ontological proof proves the proposition that 'we believe in God'. People who cannot see that metaphysics is an historical science, Collingwood argues, have allowed themselves to become indignant over the fact, as they think it, that this argument starts from 'our idea' of God and seems to proceed thence to 'God's existence' (and in this they are following Kant). But Anselm's proof is a metaphysical argument, and therefore an historical argument. It proves that '… because our idea of God is an idea of *id quo maius cogitari nequit* we stand committed to belief in God's existence' (EM, 190).[5]

Collingwood argues that the Greek philosopher, Thales, in maintaining that the world and everything in it was made of water, was attempting to introduce unity into a pre-existing mass of scientific work which was polymorphic in character (EM, 202–3). The collection and study of isolated blocks of material, each drawn from a single realm of nature, was finding itself handicapped by the obscurity of the relations between one such block and another. Thales, therefore, was fighting for the principle that in spite of all the differences between different natural realms and the different sciences that

[5] Collingwood's use of Anselm's ontological proof here is consistent with his unpublished 'Lectures on the Ontological Proof of the Existence of God' of 1919, where Collingwood had argued that metaphysics tells us what we are logically committed to believing in. It is also consistent with his use of the Ontological Proof in *An Essay on Philosophical Method*, where he argued that the object of metaphysical thought is non-hypothetical and real (EPM, 124). As I have argued, then, Collingwood's metaphysics transcends the distinction between belief and reality, and the belief (or absolute presupposition) in God is argued to be real.

study them there is one thing that is nature, and one science that is natural science (EM, 206). He was attempting to replace a polymorphic natural science with a monomorphic one, and this was bound up with the attempt to replace a polytheistic by a monotheistic religion (EM, 207).

According to Collingwood,

> The high-water of this reformation is recorded in Aristotle's *Metaphysics*, where the central problem is to expound the presuppositions of a science of nature ... in which the balance was evenly held between the oneness of things and their manyness (EM, 210–1).

However, Collingwood contends, Aristotle thought that the existence of nature is not a presupposition, but an observed fact, and this metaphysical error was corrected by Christianity (EM, 215). Similarly, Aristotle thought that motion was an observed fact, but it is a presupposition (EM, 216–7). Therefore, Aristotle failed in his metaphysical analysis, a metaphysical mistake that was a commonplace of Greek thought, and this implied a breakdown of Greek science (EM, 218). Hence, Collingwood argues, the Greco-Roman world was moribund from internal causes, specifically because it had accepted as an article of faith, as part of its 'pagan' creed, a metaphysical analysis of its own absolute presuppositions which was at certain points erroneous. This metaphysical error killed pagan science, and pagan civilisation with it (EM, 224).

Early Christian writers saw that the 'pagan' world was failing to keep alive its own fundamental convictions, because owing to faults in metaphysical analysis it had become confused as to what these convictions were. The remedy consisted in abandoning the faulty analysis and accepting a new and more accurate analysis, which they called the 'Catholic Faith' (EM, 225). These presuppositions needed to be made, they said, by anyone who wished to be 'saved': saved, that is, from the moral and intellectual bankruptcy, the collapse of science and civilisation, which was overtaking the 'pagan' world. Saving people, Collingwood explains, means inducing them to live in a different way, a way that is not impracticable (EM, 226). The new way of living would involve a new science and a new civilisation, and, Collingwood argues, the presuppositions that go to make up this 'Catholic Faith' have been the fundamental presuppositions of natural science ever since (EM, 227).

Thus, for Collingwood, through revealing absolute presuppositions, metaphysics facilitates the advancement of science and civilisation, and if the metaphysician's task is done badly, the consequences for civilisation are grave (as Collingwood argues was the case with the collapse of Greco-Roman civilisation). However, crucially, Collingwood does not argue that the metaphysician replaces one set of absolute presuppositions with a better set. Rather, early Christian metaphysical thinking provided a more accurate account of what the absolute presuppositions of European civilisation actually were.

This view of the task of metaphysics is also evident in Collingwood's discussion of causation in Part IIIC. Having outlined three senses of the word 'cause',[6] Collingwood argues that during what he calls the 'Kantian period', roughly speaking from Kant to Einstein, the fabric of natural science rested on an insecure foundation (EM, 333). In so far as it arose out of the idea of causation, this insecurity consisted in two metaphysical dilemmas: the anthropocentric dilemma and the anthropomorphic dilemma. The anthropocentric dilemma was between the idea of natural science as practical, of the Baconian or experimental type, and the idea of a theoretical natural science, which aimed at knowledge of what the natural world is in itself. According to Collingwood, the latter was the orthodox or accepted view of natural science during the Kantian period. But the issue as between the two alternatives was not clearly envisaged, and in the latter part of the century it began to be replaced by the former view (EM, 334).

The anthropomorphic dilemma concerned the question of whether the natural scientist presupposes that the world of nature is animated by something like a human mind or psyche, or whether he or she makes no such presupposition. The latter, Collingwood asserts, was the orthodox view of natural science during the Kantian period, but once more the issue was not clearly defined. The natural science of the period regarded itself as a non-anthropomorphic natural science, but it failed to realise that within its faith in causation there lay concealed, because of a lack of metaphysical analysis, an element of anthropomorphism.

According to Collingwood, the 'materialism' of nineteenth-century anti-metaphysical thinkers was 'anthropomorphic at the core'

---

[6]   Sense I is typical of history: 'here that which is "caused" is the free and deliberate act of a conscious and responsible agent and "causing" him to do it means affording him a motive for doing it'. Sense II is typical of what Collingwood called 'the practical sciences of nature': 'here that which is "caused" is an event in nature, and its "cause" is an event or state of things by producing or preventing which we can produce or prevent that whose cause it is said to be'. The leading idea here is that of a means-end relationship. Sense III is typical of the theoretical natural sciences, such as physics and chemistry, where things happen independently of the human will (EM, 285–6; cf. Martin, 1998a: lix–lx).

(EM, 336). He argues that while physicists were escaping from the Kantian confusion by the

> ... heroic measure of reconstructing their own science in such a way that the idea of causation no longer figures in it at all, philosophers, especially those of the reactionary and obscurantist schools which put forward the programmes of 'realism' and 'logical positivism', show their desire to perpetuate whatever confusions there were in nineteenth-century science by reiterating the contradiction that vitiated the nineteenth-century idea of causation (EM, 336-7).

Superficially, this might seem simply to be an account of one set of absolute presuppositions being replaced by a 'better', or more coherent, set. But, with regard to causation, the primary task of the metaphysician, for Collingwood, was accurately to reveal the absolute presuppositions that would ground modern science, in contrast with the reactionary anti-metaphysics of the 'realists' and the logical positivists, who embraced contradictory absolute presuppositions as their 'doctrine'.

Collingwood's view that absolute presuppositions are not progressive and that the task of the metaphysician is simply to reveal what the absolute presuppositions of a given practice are is also discussed in 'The Function of Metaphysics in Civilization' (published in the revised edition of *An Essay on Metaphysics*). According to Collingwood, 'The presence of a given item in a metaphysical system is a question of fact, not a question of logic' (EM, 384). The metaphysician has to settle the question of what relations there are between the items of a metaphysical system '... not on any abstract logical or dialectical methods of his own devising, but by studying the actual way in which the people whose thought he is analysing treat their presuppositions' (EM, 384). For Collingwood,

> ... the only kind of system that the metaphysician expounds is the kind of system which he finds to exist in the minds of the people whose thought he is studying; and hence, if he studies a pluralistic science like that of the ancient Greeks he will necessarily produce a pluralistic metaphysics, whereas if he studies a monistic science like that of the Renaissance and modern times he will necessarily produce a monistic one. (EM, 389)

In response to the question as to whether a monistic metaphysical system may not be better than a pluralistic one or *vice versa*, Collingwood asks:

> If modern metaphysics is so much better than ancient, the improvement in natural science which is cited in evidence of this ought to be reinforced by a parallel improvement in all other branches of theoretical and practical thinking: e.g. in morals, in law, in politics, in economics, in reli-

gion, in art, etc. Can this be maintained, or can it not rather be argued that in modern times we have specialized in certain directions and have progressed there at the price of retrogression elsewhere? This is often said, and I do not know how to refute it. (EM, 391)

Hence, we may have to qualify the statement that modern science is vastly better than the ancient, by pointing out that there is no real standard of comparison between them. Perhaps the ancients did the spadework in science, preparing a soil out of which we moderns are winning our harvests, and '... if so, is not the richness of these harvests a proof, not of our superiority to the ancients, but of the excellence of their pioneer work?' (EM, 392) There is, then, no way of answering the question definitely, Collingwood claims, except by surrendering to what he calls the 'trousers criterion': 'We wear trousers, therefore trousers are the best things to wear, and everybody who doesn't wear trousers is in that respect inferior to ourselves' (EM, 392).

Regarding the question of progress, therefore, it seems that the role of metaphysics in Collingwood's philosophy is comparable to the role of art. Whereas the objective of metaphysics is to uncover and clarify what the absolute presuppositions of a given piece of thinking are, the artist uncovers and expresses emotions.[7] Like the absolute presuppositions that the metaphysician reveals, the emotions that the artist expresses (as we have seen in Part One) are not in themselves 'better' or 'worse' than any other expressed emotions, but the act itself of accurately expressing emotions is indispensable for the advancement of civilisation.

As I have argued, therefore, Collingwood provides a solution to the predicament of Western civilisation (a predicament brought about by the inadequacy of traditional philosophy and the need to avoid irrationalism) by reconciling normative and historical thinking. For Collingwood, metaphysics is a normative, or criteriological, science in that, unlike psychology as the pseudo-science of thought and positivism, metaphysics has as its object 'high grade thinking' and absolute presuppositions: making use of the former in order to identify the latter. The philosophy of history (and of the history of science) in the wider sense is also normative in that, by examining both absolute presuppositions and the relative presuppositions that they have given rise to, it assesses whether or not progress has occurred in a science or practice.

---

[7]   The metaphysician does, however, employ an explicit methodology in order to discover absolute presuppositions, whereas for the artist there is not necessarily a distinction between means and ends in expressing emotions.

Collingwood's apparent 'relativism', in regarding transitions from one set of absolute presuppositions to another as not progressive, does not contradict the fact that judgements about progress can be made regarding science. Collingwood's theory of absolute presuppositions is not relativist, I have argued, precisely because, contrary to Martin, it is connected with his dialectical logic of question and answer. Martin, as we have seen, denies that absolute presuppositions are connected with the logic of question and answer, and in order to avoid having to charge Collingwood with relativism, he argues that Collingwood's transition from one set of absolute presuppositions to another is progressive.

Further support for the distinction I am drawing between metaphysics and philosophy in the wider sense can be found in Chapter XV of *An Essay on Metaphysics*. In this chapter (entitled 'A Positivistic Misinterpretation of Plato'), Collingwood, referring to Plato's *Republic*, first distinguishes between mathematical, or scientific, thought and dialectical thought. Mathematical thought depends on and argues from hypotheses or presuppositions. Dialectical thinking involves removing the hypotheses or un-supposing presuppositions. An example of mathematical thinking is: 'let ABC be a triangle, and let the angle ABC be a right angle; then prove that the square on AC is equal to the sum of the squares on AB and BC'. This piece of mathematical thinking is based on the assumption 'let ABC be a triangle and let the angle ABC be a right angle'. Throughout this particular work one must stand by that assumption (EM, 157).

An example of dialectical thinking, Collingwood asserts, is the kind of thinking that is going on in the *Republic* itself. The general question is: what is justice? The presupposition that justice is a craft or a skill is removed. Polemarchus unwittingly believes this but it is shown to be nonsensical. Thrasymachus then argues that injustice is a special kind of skill, and justice is a lack of skill. Here too the consequences are found to be nonsensical. Therefore, justice cannot be subsumed under the notion of craft at all, and the presupposition is removed. However, Collingwood then goes on to distinguish between dialectic and metaphysics:

> The dialectician may have to bring 'hypotheses' to light before he can remove them. In bringing 'hypotheses' to light the dialectician resembles the metaphysician. But in 'removing' them he is doing something which it is certainly not the metaphysician's business to do (EM, 158).

The 'hypotheses' that Collingwood refers to here must be relative presuppositions, not absolute presuppositions, as absolute presuppositions cannot be removed. Revisiting my use of Oldfield's argument, the metaphysician in this context can be seen as 'working backwards' in order to reveal absolute presuppositions and the dialectician as 'working forwards' in order to make normative judgements about progress in science.[8] Metaphysics, then, is primarily an historical science, or a branch of history, in contrast with philosophy in its wider sense, which reflects on history.[9]

The interpretation that I have advanced, however, might seem to need qualification, to a slight extent. As I have already indicated, referring to the logic of question and answer in *An Autobiography*, Collingwood claimed that what is ordinarily meant when a proposition is called 'true' is this: '... the proposition belongs to a question-and-answer complex which as a whole is "true" in the proper sense of the word ...' (A, 38). Martin argues that this means that absolute presuppositions can be true in an indirect manner.[10]

A question-and-answer complex that is 'true', that is, one which occupies a higher position in a scale of forms as compared with a lower complex on the same scale, will have different absolute presuppositions than the lower. However, it is not clear that there would be any necessary connection between a 'higher' complex and the particular content of a set of absolute presuppositions. It could perhaps be said that a higher science or question-and-answer complex will encompass historical self-consciousness and that therefore the absolute presuppositions of such a science or complex will necessarily include those of historical thinking. The science of history has its own presuppositions (EM, 84–5).

---

[8]   Connelly thinks that Collingwood made a mistake on this point. According to Connelly, we ought to regard 'hypotheses' as hypotheses about the content of our absolute presuppositions, hence closely linking metaphysics with the role of philosophy as described in *An Essay on Philosophical Method* (Connelly, 2003: 140n). Contrary to Connelly, I suggest that they are hypotheses primarily made by the scientist, not the metaphysician, although, as the work of the scientist may overlap with that of the metaphysician, some hypotheses may also be about absolute presuppositions.

[9]   As Beaney remarks, in *An Essay on Metaphysics* there is no suggestion that *philosophy* is an historical science, only that *metaphysics* is (Beaney, 2001: 118).

[10] As Martin indicates, this idea that a complex of statements can be true *as a whole*, though not in each of its parts, is not one that we find repeated in Collingwood's *Essay on Metaphysics* (Martin, 1998a: lxxix). However, despite its omission from *An Essay on Metaphysics*, we can nevertheless take this idea to be an important part of Collingwood's logic of question and answer. In *An Autobiography*, Collingwood claims to be providing an account of his logic of question and answer, but in *An Essay on Metaphysics* he purports to provide a 'theory of presuppositions', and only 'so much of this theory as seems necessary for my present purpose' (EM, 23). Perhaps Collingwood did not state this detail of his logic of question and answer in *An Essay on Metaphysics* as he had already done so in *An Autobiography*.

On the other hand, as Shipley speculates, Collingwood's argument that only a question-and-answer complex as a whole can be true lends support to the view (which I have defended) that absolute presuppositions can be neither true nor false and yet be meaningful (Shipley, 2001: 173). Hence Shipley casts doubt on the need for Martin's reconstruction of Collingwood's philosophy. I contend, therefore, that a set of absolute presuppositions cannot be better or worse than another set, although our knowledge of them certainly can improve or deteriorate. This point regarding the relation between fundamental principles and wider cultural practices is further illuminated by the argument of Ortega y Gasset. But this is something I will discuss a little further on.

For Collingwood, the normative judgement that philosophy makes as to whether or not progress has occurred in a science or practice depends on historical knowledge. The argument that natural science cannot progress without historical knowledge is developed in *The Idea of Nature*. In this book, Collingwood argues that natural science is not a self-contained and self-sufficient form of thought, but depends for its existence upon another form of thought, history, which is different from it and cannot be reduced to it (IN, 175–6). For Collingwood, 'a scientific fact' is a class of historical facts:

> A scientific theory not only rests on certain historical facts and is verified or disproved by certain other historical facts; it is itself an historical fact, namely, the fact that someone has propounded or accepted, verified or disproved that theory. If we want to know, for example, what the classical theory of gravitation is, we must look into the records of Newton's thinking and interpret them: and this is historical research (IN, 177).

Hence, Collingwood claims at the end of *The Idea of Nature* that 'we go from the idea of nature to the idea of history' (IN, 177).[11]

In his 1936 essay 'Progress as Created by Historical Thinking' (in the revised edition of *The Idea of History*), Collingwood argues that

> ... if a community of fish-eaters had changed their method of catching fish from a less to a more efficient one, by which an average fisherman could catch ten fish on an average day instead of five, this would be called an example of progress (IH, 325).

The older generation, however, might think that the old method is better than the new '... because the way of life which it knows and values is built around the old method, which is therefore certain to

---

[11]   As Boucher indicates, in investigating the idea of nature, Collingwood resolves nature itself into history. The modern idea of nature asserts the principles of minimum space and time, and these principles have their counterparts in history (Boucher, 1995a: 21–2).

have social and religious associations that express the intimacy of its connexion with this way of life as a whole' (IH, 325). To a person of the older generation, therefore, the change is no progress, but decadence.

According to Collingwood, to choose between these two ways of life is impossible unless one has actual experience of each way of life, or '… the sympathetic insight which may take its place for such a purpose' (IH, 326). Historical changes in a society's way of life are very rarely conceived as progressive even by the generation that makes them: 'It makes them in obedience to a blind impulse to destroy what it does not comprehend, as bad, and substitute something else as good' (IH, 326). But in order to conceive a change as a progress, the person who has made it must have historical knowledge of what he has abolished: '… the revolutionary can only regard his revolution as progress in so far as he is also an historian, genuinely re-enacting in his own historical thought the life he nevertheless rejects' (IH, 326). To legitimately use the word 'progress', the person who uses it must compare two ways of life

> … both of which he can understand historically, that is, with enough sympathy and insight to reconstruct their experience for himself … Then, having fulfilled that condition, he is entitled to ask whether the change from the first to the second was a progress (IH, 329).

Collingwood's conception of progress is evidently a development from his view of dialectical logic that he first put forward in his early manuscripts, *Truth and Contradiction* and *Libellus de Generatione*. For Collingwood,

> If thought in its first phase, after solving the initial problems of that phase, is then, through solving these, brought up against others which defeat it; and if the second solves these further problems without losing its hold on the solution of the first, so that there is gain without any corresponding loss, then there is progress. And there can be progress on no other terms. If there is any loss, the problem of setting loss against gain is insoluble (IH, 329).

Collingwood contends, however, that we cannot know whether one period of history taken as a whole showed progress over its predecessor. The historian cannot take a period as a whole because 'there must be large tracts of its life for which he has either no data, or no data that he is in a position to interpret' (IH, 329). We cannot speak of progress in happiness, comfort or satisfaction:

> Different ways of life are differentiated by nothing more clearly than by differences between the things that people habitually enjoy, the condi-

tions which they find comfortable, and the achievements they regard as satisfactory (IH, 330).

Similarly, there is no progress in art or morality.

Nevertheless, Collingwood explains, although in one sense there is no progress in morality, in another sense there is moral progress:

> Part of our moral life consists of coping with problems arising not out of our animal nature but out of our social institutions, and these are historical things, which create moral problems only in so far as they are already the expression of moral ideals. A man who asks himself whether he ought to take voluntary part in his country's war is not struggling with personal fear; he is involved in a conflict between the moral forces embodied in the institution of the State, and those embodied not merely in the ideal, but in the equal actual reality, of international peace and intercourse. Similarly the problem of divorce arises not out of the whims of sexual desire, but out of an unresolved conflict between the moral ideal of monogamy and the moral evils which that ideal, rigidly applied, brings in its train. (IH, 330–1)

Hence, for Collingwood, there can be progress in a civilisation, not in terms of individual appetites and desires, but in terms of shared practices. Similarly, there can be progress in economics, politics, law, science, philosophy and religion. The example of the fishing community, however, suggests that, in assessing whether or not progress has occurred in a science or practice, we must consider that science or practice in the context of its widest aspects and implications and in the context of its contribution to a 'way of life' as a whole, in so far as we have knowledge of it.

In an article called 'A Philosophy of Progress', (published in *Essays in the Philosophy of History*) Collingwood similarly argued:

> Goodness, like beauty and happiness, is not a product of civilisation. A man's moral worth depends not on his circumstances, but on the way in which he confronts them. It was a good act to abolish slavery, but the men who are born into a slaveless world are not automatically made good men by that fact. All it can do for them is to confront them with moral problems of a new kind (EPH, 115).

Nineteenth-century believers in progress mistakenly

> … thought that external circumstances, by being better, made men better. You might as well say that we are better soldiers than Napoleon because our guns have a longer range, or better musicians than Bach because our orchestras are larger (EPH, 115).

However, Collingwood contends that the idea of progress is a legitimate one. Why, he asks, (referring to the example of architecture) should we say that our new architecture is better than any of its predecessors? 'The answer is simple. If we do not think it better, why do we build it?' (EPH, 117) Similarly, Collingwood argues that

> ... the development of political life down to the present day has undeniably been a progress in the sense that it has led to the creation of political systems more supple, more adaptable, more responsive to individual initiative from within, and to alterations of conditions without, than systems of the past (EPH, 118).

Collingwood asserts that an increase in the power of the individual does not mean a diminution in the power of society:

> ... any increase in freedom, intelligence, and self-reliance in individuals is automatically reflected in society, which is not a mythical superhuman being but just individuals themselves in their mutual relations. As the individual gains in power, his social and political life gains in power too; for the rigidity of a primitive political system is not strength but weakness. The increase in the power of political institutions, which sometimes makes people fear for individual liberty, is thus one of the most certain proofs of human progress, and is both the effect and the cause of an increase in individual liberty itself (EPH, 119).

Our political institutions may be unsuited to people of previous ages, but elements from these previous institutions have all

> ... gone to make modern political life what it is; and in so far as modern political life is based on the values which we consider the most important, this evolution must, to us, appear as a progress (EPH, 120).

Therefore, in Collingwood's view, the question of whether progress occurs in history depends on the question:

> Have you the courage of your convictions? If you have, if you regard the things which you are doing as things worth doing, then the course of history which has led to the doing of them is justified by its results, and its movement is a movement forward (EPH, 120).

Historical thinking, Collingwood argues, not only discovers progress, but it creates this progress itself. This is because progress only happens '... by the retention in the mind, at one phase, what was achieved at a preceding phase' (IH, 333). Therefore:

> If Einstein makes an advance on Newton, he does it by knowing Newton's thought and retaining it within his own, in the sense that he knows what Newton's problems were, and how he solved them, and, disentangling the truth in these solutions from whatever errors prevented Newton from going further, embodying these solutions as thus disentangled in his own theory ... Newton thus lives in Einstein in the way in which any past experience lives in the mind of the historian ... but re-enacted here and now together with a development of itself that is partly constructive or positive and partly critical or negative (IH, 333–4).

Van der Dussen draws attention to Collingwood's assertion in his 'Lectures on the Philosophy of History' of 1926 that

> history is nothing but the attempt to understand the present by analysing it into its logical components of necessity, or the past, and possibility, or the future; and this is an attempt that is made by everybody and at all times (IH, 422; van der Dussen, 1995: 266).

As van der Dussen indicates, the idea of progress can be understood as having the function of serving as a guiding principle in solving present problems and in deciding which possibilities and opportunities should be realised (van der Dussen, 1995: 260 and 266).

For Collingwood, therefore, through historical thinking the advancement of science and civilisation, that is, the philosophical judgement that science and civilisation have advanced, is made possible. Historical knowledge, I have argued, includes knowledge of absolute presuppositions and the questions, answers and relative presuppositions that they have given rise to.

As Oldfield indicates, however, Collingwood recognised that the territory of the historian was wider than reflective thought about the actions of other people:

> It included, for instance, the customs, habits and institutions of the past, and the changes which occur in them over time, not all of which could be traced to the intentions and purposes of the people who may have been ultimately responsible for them (Oldfield, 1995: 184).

Boucher, in his Introduction to the revised edition of *The New Leviathan*, demonstrates that although Collingwood regarded history as the re-enactment of past thought, knowledge of absolute presuppositions can be included in this. According to Boucher,

> Given the inseparability of absolute presuppositions from the thought, or actions, which absolutely presuppose them, the re-enactment of the thoughts, or actions, necessarily entails implicating that from which they are inseparable (Boucher, 1992: xxx).

Boucher also argues that re-enactment can be extended to the domain of rational emotions (Boucher, 1992: xxxvi). I suggest, therefore, that Collingwood's conception of history as the re-enactment of past thought can be seen as consistent with his view of the task of the metaphysician. Part of the task of the historian is to re-construct or bring in to the light of consciousness what was 'unconscious' thought, and to make the implicit explicit (cf. Vanheeswijck, 1994: 114).

Oldfield points out that the achievement of historical knowledge is by inferential argument from that which is present: namely, the evidence which the past has left behind, and evidence is anything that can be so used (Oldfield, 1995: 187). Thought is always re-enacted in a new context, and this new context must be receptive to that thought. For example, in his unpublished folktale manuscript Collingwood wrote:

> If magic were a form of belief or custom peculiar to primitive peoples and absolutely foreign to the mind of civilized man, the civilized historian could never understand it (Collingwood, 2004: 129; cf. Oldfield, 1995: 189).

Oldfield draws attention to Martin's suggestion that there appears to be an inconsistency between the demands of the re-enactment theory and the implications of the doctrine of absolute presuppositions, and Martin's view that there may be some cultures where the kind of agency demanded by the re-enactment theory may simply be absent (Oldfield, 1995: 193).[12] Oldfield explains that from the fact that Collingwood said that change between absolute presuppositions could be radical, both Martin and Stephen Toulmin inferred, incorrectly, an incommensurability between different absolute presuppositions, such that trans-historical understanding is problematic. Contrary to Martin and Toulmin, Oldfield rightly argues that '… the problem does not arise if absolute presuppositions are interpreted dialectically' (Oldfield, 1995: 194). Change in absolute presuppositions is not discontinuous: instead a new set of absolute presuppositions will be a 'modification of the old' (EM, 48; Oldfield, 1995: 194–5). We can have historical knowledge of absolute presuppositions, therefore, because traces of the past survive in the present, allowing the past to be re-enacted, and hence the absolute presuppositions of past epochs can be revealed.

The example of conceptual change that Oldfield (cf. 1995: 195) takes, from Collingwood's *Autobiography*, is useful in showing how we can have knowledge of the past because the historical process is continuous and it leaves traces of itself in the present. In *An Autobiography*, Collingwood argues that Plato's *Republic* and Hobbes's *Leviathan*, so far as they are concerned with politics, are concerned with different problems, for Plato's 'State' is the Greek *polis*, and Hobbes's

---

[12] As we have seen, Martin argues against the connection between absolute presuppositions and the logic of question and answer. Similarly, Martin disagrees with the attempt by some interpreters to link the recovery of absolute presuppositions with the re-enactment of past thought. Martin argues that the re-enactment doctrine was meant only to explain actions — to explain an action by reference to the thoughts, beliefs and motivations of an agent (Martin, 1998a: xxxi). The idea that absolute presuppositions are to be explained by re-enactment is, according to Martin, a 'deep mistake' (Martin, 1998a: xxxiii).

is the absolutist State of the seventeenth century. Nevertheless, there is a connection between Plato and Hobbes, but the connection is not

> ... the sameness of a 'universal', and the difference the difference between two instances of that universal. But this is not so. The sameness is the sameness of an historical process, and the difference is the difference between one thing which in the course of that process has turned into something else, and the other thing into which it has turned. Plato's *polis* and Hobbes's absolutist State are related by a traceable historical process, whereby one has turned into the other ... (A, 62).

As Collingwood argues, therefore, the historian can only study a past event because it leaves traces of itself which survive in the present world.[13] History is not concerned with 'events', but with 'processes', and 'processes' are things which do not begin and end but turn into one another:

> ... if a process P1 turns into a process P2, there is no dividing line at which P1 stops and P2 begins; P1 never stops, it goes on in the changed form P2, and P2 never begins, it has previously been going on in the earlier form P1. There are in history no beginnings and no endings. History books begin and end, but the events they describe do not. If P1 has left traces of itself in P2 so that an historian living in P2 can discover by the interpretation of evidence that what is now P2 was once P1, it follows that 'traces' of P1 in the present are not, so to speak, the corpse of a dead P1, but rather the real P1 itself, living and active though encapsulated within the other form of itself P2 (A, 98).

For Collingwood, '... the essence of history lies not in its consisting of individual facts ... but in the process of development leading from one to another' (IH, 169; cf. Martin, 1998a: xxxv).

As we have seen, therefore, in Collingwood's view, the progress and advancement of civilisation and the solution to the crises that it faces depend on a philosophy of historical and dialectical thinking. For Collingwood, Platonism and the West, in so far as it is still dependent on Platonism, are in crisis and the solution is the working out of a philosophy where the criteria for value and truth are immanent to the historical process, and not located in an ideal transcendent world.

As Collingwood noted in 'A Footnote to Future History', the transition from Platonism to a comprehensive historicist philosophy has not yet been fully realised. For Collingwood, then,

> This seems to be the end of an era. A world catastrophe is generally supposed to divide two purely different phases of history. But this is a mis-

---

[13] Croce also distinguished between history and chronicle. History, unlike chronicle, lives on in the present: it 'vibrates in the soul of the historian' (cf. Boucher, 1985: 7–8).

take. A catastrophe is not the end, nor yet the beginning; like the storms of adolescence, it is the rebirth of an organism already established in vigorous growth and capable of inflicting the uttermost torments upon itself in order to pass through them into the balanced life of maturity (FFH, 9–10).

'Such a catastrophe', Collingwood thinks, 'undoubtedly awaits our civilisation', although '… it may not come for another nine centuries: our present conflicts, like the agonies of the expiring Roman Republic, are but a ripple on the surface of history' (FFH, 10). Therefore, the role of the philosopher is to guide a new historical philosophy through the 'storms' of development and change before it is more fully realised in the form of a concrete civilisation. As we have seen, however, unlike Hegel, Collingwood does not regard philosophy as culminating in any final position, and nor is the development in any way pre-determined. As Collingwood remarks in 'The Three Laws of Politics' (published in *Essays in Political Philosophy*), the future '… has to be made by us, by the strength of our hands and the stoutness of our hearts' (EPP, 223).

As I have argued in Part One, in Collingwood's view, it is through aesthetic experience that we first begin to apprehend the world. This is also true to some extent of religion. Art and religion are regarded as stages, which the mind must pass through, prior to the emergence of higher levels of consciousness. Hence the dialectical solution to the crisis of civilisation is foreshadowed in the activities of art[14] and religion.

---

[14] In *Speculum Mentis*, in an early inchoate version of what he later stated as his logic of question and answer (cf. Hinz, 1994a: 64), Collingwood regarded art as being an integral part of this logic. Aesthetic experience and imagination are associated with the attitude of supposal. But, Collingwood argues, imagination, or supposal, does not exist in a vacuum. Supposal and assertion are not independent of one another but correlative. Knowledge, Collingwood contends, is '… the interplay of question and answer in the soul's dialogue with itself …' (SM, 77), and supposal and questioning are seen as '… at bottom the same thing …' (SM, 78). As questioning is essentially a suspension of the activity of asserting, Collingwood speculates that 'art, as pure imagination, imagination without assertion, may be paradoxically defined as a question which expects no answer: that is, a supposal' (SM, 79). But, to ask any question we must already possess information: 'so even if art is pure imagination, it must spring from a soil of concrete fact … This basis of fact in turn requires a basis of imagination, for no fact can be known until it has been sought by the imaginative act of questioning, and this question itself requires a further basis of fact, and so on *ad infinitum*' (SM, 79–80). For Collingwood, then, 'The process of knowledge is therefore, strictly speaking, not so much an alternation of question and answer as a perpetual restatement of the question, which is identical with a perpetual revision of the answer. If it is objected that this reduces all the diversity of knowledge to a bare identity in which there is only one judgement judging one truth, our answer — to

Using the arguments of *Speculum Mentis* (SM, 138–46) and *The Idea of History*, Hinz provides an astute and compelling explanation of the correlation between religion and history in Collingwood's solution to the crisis of civilisation. Hinz explains that the ground for the revitalisation of Western civilisation must reside in its own principles, and this pointed towards a 'new interpretation of Christianity' (Hinz, 1994a: 195). For Collingwood, like the world of nature, the world of historical fact does not exist 'in itself', but as known by acts of thought which 'make' it. As Hinz indicates,

> The world of historical fact, however, is not nature but historical process — the activity of thought itself, which includes the activity by which the world of nature is 'made'. Since, on the Christian view, God makes nature, it follows that the world of historical process is identical to God. Christianity, in holding that God is the creator of all things, propounds the notion of creation *ex nihilo*, a conception which is elucidated and made fully intelligible in the theory of *historical process as a self-creative activity*. (Hinz's italics; 1994a: 197)

The conception of the fall from grace, the separation of God and man, signifies man's self-imposed estrangement from the source of spiritual wholeness, which corresponds to man's ignorance of himself as a historical being. Therefore, Hinz argues:

> With respect to Collingwood's philosophy the significance of the Incarnation is that *the work of historical process itself inaugurates the union of God and man* ... The doctrine of Incarnation corresponds to the realization that the source of all value is historical process itself, through which all value is generated. Thus the activity of historical process brings about *the realization that the justifying grounds for all systems of thought and value are historically conditioned.* Just as the Incarnation is an act of God which is at the same time the death of God, the activity of historical process brings an end to the belief in any transcendent source of value (Hinz's italics; 1994a: 198).

The Christian conception of a fusion of God and man in a new unity, Hinz continues, is accomplished only if man cooperates in the effort and partakes in the divine nature. Hence, '... man is united with God and so comes to a knowledge of himself as free historical activity only when he engages in historical thinking' (Hinz, 1994a: 199). The rise of historical consciousness means that historical thinking is now a commonplace of humanity. Properly re-construed, Christian principles can overcome nihilism (Hinz, 1994a: 199). As

be given in full later on — will be that this identity contains all diversity within itself' (SM, 80). Collingwood, of course, later distinguished questioning from presupposing, and distinguished art, as imagination and consciousness, from thinking, as questioning, answering and presupposing.

Hinz rightly argues, therefore, Christianity, for Collingwood, expresses in an allegorical form the solution to the crisis of Western civilisation that Collingwood articulated in his metaphysics and philosophy of history.

Collingwood's historicist philosophy also articulates a solution for the causes and symptoms of cultural crisis pertaining to his philosophy of art and the suppression of emotion that I examined in Part One. For example, the Enlightenment rejection of the emotional and superstitious side of Christianity that Collingwood criticised in 'Fascism and Nazism' for depriving Western civilisation of its 'vital warmth' and emotional vigour (EPP, 187) is also criticised in *The Idea of History* as a failure to see the superstition of past ages as a necessary stage in human development (IH, 76–81). Collingwood's philosophy of history constitutes a response to the suppression of emotion and the fragmentation of human experience that he criticised in *Speculum Mentis* and in his philosophy of art.

Collingwood's dialectical account of truth, however, as an open-ended process of development, which began with his modification of the coherence theory of truth in his early manuscripts, also constitutes a refinement of the 'unity of the forms of experience' argument in *Speculum Mentis* and *Ruskin's Philosophy*. As we have seen, in Collingwood's later philosophy progress in a science or practice can only be considered to have occurred when it is considered in the context of its contribution to a 'way of life' as a whole. But a way of life, or culture, is not static and complete: it has value only in so far as it assimilates and explains what is outside and different. This idea was first expressed in *Truth and Contradiction*, when Collingwood defined truth as that '... which expresses most, which includes most successfully within itself a number of diverse and by themselves conflicting points of view' (TC, 8).

Collingwood's solution to the crisis of civilisation, then, is an improvement and refinement of the Romantic idea of culture. This improvement was implicit in Collingwood's criticism of Ruskin's confusion about how greatness in art sometimes coincided with the downfall of civilisation (cf. EPA, 37–8). It seems that Ruskin subscribed to a more static view of culture. Hence, like Collingwood's modification of the coherence theory of truth, the development of his dialectical philosophy meant an improvement and fine-tuning of the Ruskin-inspired idea of the unity of the forms of experience as a solution to the crisis of modernity.

To sum up, therefore, in Collingwood's view, historical consciousness provides the ground for normative judgements about progress to be made. Only through historical thinking can civilisation overcome decadence and advance and prosper. Collingwood argues:

> This understanding of the system we set out to supersede is a thing which we must retain throughout the work of superseding it, as a knowledge of the past conditioning our creation of the future. It may be impossible to do this; our hatred of the thing we are destroying may prevent us from understanding it, and we may love it so much that we cannot destroy it unless blinded by hatred. But if that is so, there will once more, as so often in the past, be change but no progress; we shall have lost our hold on one group of problems in our anxiety to solve the next. And we ought by now to realize that no kindly law of nature will save us from the fruits of our ignorance (IH, 334).

The idea that Western civilisation is faced with a crisis precipitated by the inadequacy of the Platonic ontology of being, to be resolved by a philosophy of becoming, is also strongly present in the works of Ortega y Gasset and Nietzsche. Furthermore, like Collingwood, for both Ortega and Nietzsche, it is not the truth or falsity of fundamental principles or individual judgements, but their ability to generate vitality and enhance life as a whole, which is important.

Ortega's philosophy betrays a remarkable resemblance to Collingwood's, especially in the importance placed on fundamental beliefs and in the need for a historicist philosophy as a solution to a cultural crisis that is brought about by the inadequacy of an abstract philosophy of being derived from the Greeks. The work of Ortega confirms the point that Collingwood's philosophical concerns with the crisis of Western modernity ought not to be seen as singular and isolated. Instead they are a part of a broader historicist 'tendency' in early twentieth-century philosophy.

Ortega played a key role in the development of 'crisis' thought in the early twentieth century, and his importance as a 'crisis' theorist is emphasised by Graham:

> The fact is that most of his works either develop or apply concepts related to crisis, for Ortega took the understanding of this crisis — as the first step toward resolution — to be the chief 'mission' of his life and thought, quintessentially the mission of the intellectual (Graham, 1997: 226).

Like Collingwood, part of the business of philosophy, for Ortega, is to define new faiths (cf. Dobson, 1989: 169), and philosophy's present task is to describe the new type of reason which, replacing naturalistic reason, will provide a more adequate understanding of human life. As Graham indicates, both Collingwood and Ortega, as historicists, were influenced by Dilthey, Rickert, Simmel, Mommsen and Meyer. Both borrowed Dilthey's distinction between 'inward' and 'outward' knowledge and both regarded Dilthey as failing sufficiently to overcome 'naturalism' and to distinguish clearly enough between history and the natural sciences (Graham, 1997: 133).

Ortega and Collingwood also both developed philosophies of history that regarded epistemology and ontology as properly inseparable. Despite Collingwood being seen as an Idealist and Ortega as a 'realist', opposition between them was more apparent than actual, and such labelling can be seen as superficial (cf. Graham, 1997: 148). Both develop theories of truth that (to some extent) go beyond realism and Idealism. As I will explain, Ortega, like Collingwood, regards truth as that which allows the widest perspective on life.

Ortega's conception of the crisis of Western civilisation and the historicist solution to it is particularly evident in *History as a System*, and because it is probably his most important work, a brief outline of it may prove illuminating. As Victor Ouimette points out, Ortega, in *History as a System*, began to develop the distinction between ideas that a person has, and beliefs that he or she is, with beliefs having an influence far more profound than mere ideas (Ouimette, 1982: 124). According to Ortega, the structure of human life depends primordially on the beliefs on which it is grounded. Beliefs always constitute a system in so far as they are effective beliefs: they function as beliefs resting on one another, combining with one another to form a whole (HS, 167). The diagnosing of any human existence must begin by an ordered inventory of its system of convictions, and it must establish which belief is fundamental, '... breathing life into all the others' (HS, 168).[15]

For Ortega, the European's fundamental convictions changed profoundly in the early twentieth century. The generation of 1900 was the last of a cycle which was characterised by a faith in reason, which is expressed by Descartes (HS, 169). This rationalism, Ortega contends, ushered in the modern age, whose death agony we are now witnessing. For Descartes, the world is to become transparent to the human mind, and everything is to be reduced to clarity (HS, 170). Europe came by this faith, having lost, in the fifteenth century, its faith in God and revelation. Hence, the fifteenth and sixteenth

---

[15] Ouimette explains that unlike ideas, one lives from one's beliefs and is inseparable from them. Beliefs are taken for granted and assumed in all of our activities. They are implicit and largely unconscious suppositions from which we set out. The existence of ideas depends on will, but beliefs are inescapable because they are involuntary (Ouimette, 1982: 126).

centuries were two centuries of crisis, and from this crisis Western man was saved by a new belief: faith in reason. In Ortega's view, 'The Renaissance is the parturient disquiet of a new confidence based on physico-mathematical science, the new mediator between man and the world' (HS, 174).

But by the twentieth century this faith in science had decayed. Ortega argues that within its genuine territory, nature, science has transcended our hopes, but it has nothing to say about human life (HS, 178–9). 'Life is haste and has urgent need to know what it is up against, and it is out of this urgency that truth must derive its method' (HS, 182). Scientific utopianism and 'the idea of progress, placing truth in a vague tomorrow, has proved a dulling opiate to humanity' (HS, 182). Therefore, Ortega argues, we must shake ourselves radically free from the physical, natural approach to the human element: the collapse of physical reason leaves the way clear for vital, historical reason (HS, 183).

When naturalistic reason studies man, Ortega explains, it seeks to reveal his nature, and it entrusts the study of man's psychic mechanism to psychology, a natural science. 'The prodigious achievement of natural science in the direction of the knowledge of things contrasts brutally with the collapse of this same natural science when faced with the strictly human element' (HS, 186). This is because man is not a thing and man has no nature, '… and in consequence we must make up our own minds to think of it in terms of categories and concepts that will be radically different from such as shed light on the phenomena of matter' (HS, 186). According to Ortega, the moral or cultural sciences, the *Geisteswissenschaften*, which arose in opposition to the natural sciences in fact attempted to do the same as the natural sciences, by opposing the concept of spirit to nature (HS, 187–8). Idealists were guilty of the same mistake Descartes made when he defined the self by opposing *res cogitans* to *res extensa* (HS, 189).

Therefore, for Ortega, in the concept of nature the European man is heir to Parmenides and Eleaticism: 'This Greek destiny continues to weigh on us, and in spite of some notable rebellions we are still prisoners within the magic circle described by Eleatic ontology' (HS, 192). Ever since Parmenides, the orthodox thinker searches for a fixed static consistency, and following Aristotle, the 'nature' of things. Until Kant no one had '… begun to see clearly that thought is not a copy or mirror of reality but a transitive operation performed on it, a surgical intervention' (HS, 194). Kant has taught us that thought has its own forms and projects these on to the real. Thus '…

we must learn to disintellectualize the real if we are to be faithful to it. Eleaticism was the radical intellectualization of being' (HS, 195). In naturalism what veils human phenomena to our minds is the idea of *res* founded on identical being, and fixed, static, predetermined. But 'Naturalism is, at bottom, intellectualism, i.e., the projection on to the real of the mode of being peculiar to concepts' (HS, 196).

The concept of spirit, Ortega explains, is a disguised naturalism. Spirit '... is already, to begin with, what it is going to be', and 'Hegel's movement of the spirit is a pure fiction, since it is a movement within the spirit, whose consistency lies in its fixed, static, pre-established truth' (HS, 197). The entity whose being consists in identical being possesses already all it needs in order to be. Identical being is substance, or thing. For Ortega, then, we need to transcend the idea of nature, as

> ... this idea can have no authentic reality: it is something relative to the human intellect, which in its turn has no detached, independent reality ... but is only real when functioning in a human life, by whose constitutive urgencies it is moved (HS, 198).

Ortega asserts that man is 'no thing, but a drama' (HS, 200). Each one has to make human life for himself or herself and has to determine what he or she is going to be. One makes choices in accordance with the general programme one has mapped out for one's life. I am free by compulsion, whether I wish to be or not. Accordingly, we must '... elaborate a non-Eleatic concept of being ... The time has come for the seed sown by Heraclitus to bring forth its mighty harvest' (HS, 203). In human life the 'substance' is precisely change, which means it cannot be thought of 'Eleatically' as substance. The being of whatever is alive '... must be thought of in concepts that annul their own inevitable identity' (HS, 205). All concepts that seek to think of authentic reality must be 'occasional' concepts (HS, 206).

According to Ortega, what we have been acts negatively on what we can be: one is still a Christian in the form of having been a Christian (HS, 208). The same might be said about being 'a democrat', being 'a liberal', being 'feudal'. Man's being, then, '... is irreversible; he is compelled ontologically always to advance on himself ...' (HS, 209). Society is primarily the past, and the determination of what at each moment society is going to be, depends on what it has been, just as in individual life. In the public opinion of the present, an enormous amount of the past continues active (HS, 210).

The past forms part of our present, in that it is active in us now. Man's authentic being consists in 'being what one has not already been', and, Ortega proposes, as we cannot hope to rid the term 'being' of its traditional static signification, we should be well advised to dispense with it (HS, 213). For Ortega, unlike physico-mathematical reason, 'to comprehend anything human, be it personal or collective, one must tell its history ... Life only takes on a measure of transparency in the light of *historical reason*' (HS, 214).

According to Ortega, man invents for himself a program of life that gives a satisfactory answer to the difficulties posed for him by circumstances. But experience makes apparent the shortcomings and limitations of the said program of life. He thinks out another program of life, drawn up in the light of the first. In the second, the first is still active: it is preserved in order to be avoided. On the second project of being, there follows a third, and so on (HS, 215). Therefore: 'He goes on accumulating being—the past; he goes on making for himself a being through his dialectical series of experiments. This is a dialectic not of logical but precisely of historical reason ...' (HS, 216).

Ortega asserts that 'Man, in a word, has no nature; what he has is history' (HS, 217). That man's being progresses can only be affirmed *a posteriori* by concrete historical reason. In our present 'crisis', Ortega argues, in our present doubt concerning reason, we find included the whole of our earlier life: 'We are other than the man of 1700, and we are more' (HS, 219). To progress is not simply to change one's form of life. Progress demands that the new form

> ... should rise above the old and to this end should preserve it and turn it to account, that it should take off from the old, climbing on its shoulders as a high temperature mounts on lower ones. To progress is to accumulate being, to store up reality (HS, 219).

In Ortega's view, therefore,

> History is a system, the system of human experiences linked in a single, inexorable chain. Hence nothing can be truly clear in history until everything is clear ... Every historic term whatsoever, to have exactness, must be determined as a function of all history, neither more nor less than each concept in Hegel's *Logic* has value only in respect of the niche left for it by the others (HS, 221–2).

History is a science of the present, and the past is the active force that sustains our today.

According to Ortega, 'Man stands in need of a new revelation. And whenever he feels in contact with an absolute reality distinct from himself, there is always revelation' (HS, 223). Man

> ... loses himself in the infinite arbitrariness of his inner cabalism when he cannot essay this and discipline it in the impact with something that

smacks of authentic, relentless reality. Reality is man's only true peda-
gogue and ruler (HS, 227–8).

The physical world, or nature, turns out to be an apparatus of man's
own manufacture that he interposes between authentic reality and
himself:

> Every disillusionment consequent on depriving of faith in some reality
> on which he had set store brings into the foreground and permits the dis-
> covery of the reality of what remains to him … (HS, 229).

Having lost his faith in physico-mathematical reason, man is compelled to take his stand on his disillusioned life. Having arrived at
this point through the dialectical series of his experiences, which is
the transcendent reality, 'Man … is brought up against himself as
reality, as history' (HS, 230). 'Historical reason' reveals a reality
which is the self underlying his theories. Historical reason is '… still
more rational than physical reason, more rigorous, more exigent'
(HS, 232). Unlike physical reason, historical reason accepts nothing
as mere fact. Instead it shows how these facts have come about: they
are nothing more than interpretations that man has manufactured at
a given juncture of his life (HS, 232–3).

Like Collingwood, then, for Ortega, the progress and advancement of civilisation can only take place through historical thinking.
Also, like Collingwood, there might appear to be some degree of
ambivalence in Ortega's philosophy as to whether or not fundamental convictions themselves are progressive. Ortega's position on this
point, however, is clearer in *Man and Crisis*, and is consistent with the
interpretation of Collingwood that I have defended: that is, fundamental principles are not in themselves progressive, although the
sciences or practices that make up a civilisation can be.

Overlapping with the argument of *History as a System*, in *Man and
Crisis* Ortega argues that history

> … advances dialectically, although that basic dialectic of life is not, as
> Hegel believed, a conceptual dialectic composed of pure reason, but the
> dialectic of a reason much broader, and richer than pure reason—the
> dialectic of life, of living reason (MC, 176).

Ortega asserts that

> The medieval universe was made up of absolutes … Today nothing is
> what it is, but stands always in a state of transition toward being in
> another wise. Each thing can be something else, everything has in it a lit-
> tle of everything. We are in the era of the cats that are neither black nor
> white, but grey (MC, 211).

Ortega suggests that today we are confronted by a cultural crisis, and crisis differs from normal change. Normal change is where 'yesterday's system of convictions gives way to today's, smoothly, without a break ...' (MC, 85). An historical crisis occurs when '... the system of convictions belonging to the previous generation gives way to a vital state in which man remains without these convictions, and therefore without a world' (MC, 86). There are no new positive beliefs to replace the traditional ones. Consequently, life as crisis is a condition in which man holds only negative convictions, and as he '... is not truly decided about anything, man, and indeed the masses of men, move from black to white with the greatest of ease' (MC, 87). But

> ... in order that man may stop believing in some things, there must be germinating in him a confused faith in others ... These new enthusiasms soon begin to stabilise themselves in some dimension of life, while the rest of life continues in the shadow of bitterness and resignation. It is curious to note that almost always the dimension of life in which the new faith begins to establish itself is art (MC, 88).

Ortega argues that in order to make decisions about my existence I must have a repertoire of convictions, or opinions, about the world. But those opinions must be truly mine, and

> ... I adopt them only because I am fully convinced of them. This is possible only if I have thought them out from their very roots and they have come forth nourished and advanced by undeniable evidence. Now, nobody can give me this evidence ready made; it takes shape for me only when I analyze for myself the matter in question, when I take it to myself and form my own convictions about it. For me to have an opinion about something is merely a matter of knowing on what facts to rely to determine my own position in regard to a thing. Several possible ideas on a question may occur to me; but I must come to agreement with myself in order to see which one of them it is that convinces me, which one is my *real* opinion. An opinion which I have formed for myself in this manner and which I base on my own evidence is truly mine; it contains what I truly think about the matter, and therefore when I think thus I am in agreement with myself. I am myself. And the series of actions, of conduct, which that genuine opinion engenders and which it motivates will be genuinely my life, my real and authentic being (MC, 90).

In this way, according to Ortega, man is 'centred in himself' and he does not '... permit himself to be alienated or converted into what he is not' (MC, 91).

Many things, Ortega asserts, we do not understand very well because we have not tried to rethink them on our own account. We hide behind the selves of other people and flee from our genuine life which is synonymous with solitude (MC, 92). Man, unlike animals, is able to retire from the world, to withdraw inside himself (MC, 95). According to Ortega, 'Culture is only the interpretation which man gives to his life, the series of more or less satisfactory solutions which he invents in order to handle his problems and the needs of his life' (MC, 97). But,

> For the very reason that an effective solution has been created ... subsequent generations do *not* have to create it, but to inherit and develop it ... the inheritance which frees one from the effort of creation has the disadvantage of being an invitation to inertia. He who receives an idea from his forebears tends to save himself the effort of rethinking it and recreating it within *himself*. This recreation consists in nothing more than the task of him who created the idea, that is, in adopting it only in view of the undeniable evidence with which it was imposed on him ... On the other hand the man who does not create an idea but inherits it finds between things and his own person a preconceived idea which facilitates his relationship with things as would a ready-made recipe. He then will be inclined not to ask himself questions about things, not to feel genuine needs, since he has in hand a repertory of solutions before he feels the needs which call for these solutions. So that the man who is already heir to a cultural system accustoms himself ... to using mental processes ... for which he has no evidence, because they were not born out of the depth of his own genuine self (MC, 97–8).

Hence one lives 'on top' of a culture or system of opinions that come from a collective irresponsible 'I', which does not know why it thinks what it thinks. Meanwhile, the culture, which in its origin was simple, becomes complicated. The individual, effective and primitive 'I', Ortega contends, is replaced by the conventional, complicated, cultivated 'I'. Every culture ends in man's socialisation, or collectivisation: '... the maximum degree of man's alienation or otherness' (MC, 99). For example, the complexity of culture was one of the principal causes of the crisis suffered at the end of the Middle Ages. The clearest and most continuous desire from the fifteenth century to Descartes was the desire for simplification (MC, 100). Ortega argues that the man who is too cultivated and socialised must free himself from his received culture in order to return to himself. Accordingly there are periods of 'return to nature', for example, the Renaissance, Rousseau and romanticism (MC, 101).

From this perspective, Ortega explains, the words 'problem' and 'solution' thus take on a new meaning. Something is a problem when I do not know what my genuine attitude towards it is: 'The essential basic problem ... is ... to be in agreement with myself, to find myself' (MC, 109). The solution is to be very clear what one's sincere attitude is toward each and every thing. The humblest peasant is so clear about his actual convictions that he has hardly any problems. But

> There are few of these countrymen left now; culture has reached them, and so has the topical, and that which we call socialization; and they are beginning to live on ideas received from the outside and to believe things they do not believe (MC, 110).

The cultivated man, then, '... runs the risk of losing himself in the jungle of his own knowledge; and he ends up by not knowing what his own genuine knowledge is' (MC, 110). This is the position of the average modern man, who does not know which thoughts he believes. He feigns beliefs in order to ease the pretence in which he lives, drugging himself with those attitudes which are easiest, most topical, most according to formula (MC, 111).

In a 'classic age' or 'golden age', according to Ortega, man lives with a repertory of sincere beliefs about his surroundings (MC, 114). He has, however, solved his own problems, not those of other eras. He feels in accord with himself; there is a perfect equilibrium between man and his surroundings.

> But it is obvious how carefully one must tread when giving to the classic the value of a norm. Strictly speaking, only the classic is classic, that is, perfect, for itself. To wish that another era would live in the classic manner is to invite it to internal falsification. What seems profitable and exemplary about the classic age is not the particular content of its ideas, but the balance between them and its life, the congruence with which it habitually behaves (MC, 115).

Ortega's philosophy, therefore, transcends both rationalism and relativism. As Ortega argues in *What is Philosophy?*, things do not exist either inside or outside of consciousness, but rather together with my thoughts about them. Neither independent thought nor independent world exist in themselves: they are mere constructions or inventions. Reality is the coexistence of myself with things. Dobson explains that '... the truth of a statement or belief is, in Ortega's mature opinion, to be judged from the point of view of its efficacy in the economy of the individual life' (Dobson, 1989: 156–7), and in this Ortega resembles Collingwood. For Ortega, '*Authentic truth*, then, will be a function of *authentic life*, and only inferior or partial truths will be available to those who live their lives inauthentically' (Dobson's italics; Dobson, 1989: 160).

For both Collingwood and Ortega, therefore, the solution to the crisis of Western modernity is a historicist philosophy. Through a philosophy of historical thinking Western man can achieve authentic self-understanding, the Greek ontology of being is transcended and civilisation can advance.

Harold C. Raley indicates that 'Ortega elevated history to a prominence as a valid philosophical component that it almost certainly had never before enjoyed in Spain, or, with a few exceptions (Dilthey, Hegel, etc.), in European thought generally' (Raley, 1971: 4). As we have seen, for Ortega, like Collingwood, history is not equated with the mere past: anything worthy of the name 'history' does not pass away completely but continues to exist in the present, though in an altered form (cf. Raley, 1971: 5). It is idle to look for human reality in abstract Reason, but it is equally absurd to renounce all reason. It is impossible to reduce man to an unchanging essence or to an unchanging 'nature', but this does not mean that man must remain incomprehensible (Raley, 1971: 9).

Raley points out that according to Ortega, until now, philosophy has always been utopian. Each system tried to speak for all times and all men, and lacked 'the vital, historical, perspectivist dimension' (cited from Raley, 1971: 16). On the other hand, 'the doctrine of the point of view demands that within the system there be merged the vital perspective from which it sprang ...' (*The Modern Theme*, cited from Raley, 1971: 16). Life, for Ortega, is historical and perspectivistic (Raley, 1971: 17). Far from being relativistic, as critics allege, under the new criteria of perspective, circumstance, and historicism,

> ... philosophy acquires a more urgent and pragmatic aim. Relieved of the onerous task of deciphering eternal truth, it assumes the responsibility of defining or redefining man's course through the ages (Raley, 1971: 21).

In this respect, Raley argues that Ortega's philosophy is close to existentialism, and on the many points where their thought coincides, he is the predecessor of both Sartre and Heidegger (Raley, 1971: 23). However, Ortega saw existentialism as a one-sided view of human life. Human life does not exclusively consist in anguish, or dread, or care, or being unto death. It is not reducible to any of the usual 'existential characteristics': 'If human life has a characteristic, it is its openness to many possibilities' (Ferrater Mora, 1963: 77; cited in Raley, 1971: 26).

Similarly, as Mink has noted, Collingwood's philosophy has affinities with pragmatism and existentialism. Mink argues that some of the principles of Collingwood's logic of question and answer—for example that all propositions are answers to questions, and that they are not true or false but 'right' or 'wrong' in the sense that they help or fail to help us get ahead in the process of inquiry—are intelligible only as characteristic of a pragmatic, rather than a correspondence, coherence or semantic conception of truth (Mink, 1969: 9). According to Mink,

> We do not have a name to describe or an articulated theory to explain the movement of thought which transformed, after the First World War, what we call, in its earlier forms, 'Romanticism'. But I think it is likely that the future historians of our time will see Collingwood along with pragmatists and existentialists as tributaries of a common stream (Mink, 1969: 12).

According to the historicist philosophies put forward by Collingwood and Ortega, then, individual principles, judgements and categories are not in themselves 'true'. Instead truth and value are to be found in a way of life, or culture, as a whole. Cultures or ways of life, however, are not self-contained. A culture can become decadent or fossilised if its development is taken as complete and its principles are taken as eternal truths. As we have seen, Collingwood's philosophy transcends the coherence theory of truth, in that true philosophy strives to assimilate what has yet to be explained. Similarly, Ortega's historicism is a progressive attempt to strip away abstractions until one is left with the reality of history and open-ended process.

Like Collingwood and Ortega, for Nietzsche[16] also, the development of historical thinking coincided with a need to respond to the crisis of modernity by replacing a philosophy of being with a philosophy of becoming[17]. As with Collingwood and Ortega, Nietzsche distinguishes the worth of individual principles and judgements

---

[16] In my overview of Nietzsche's philosophy here I draw upon Hinz's *Self-Creation and History: Collingwood and Nietzsche on Conceptual Change* (1994a).

[17] According to Hinz, Collingwood and Nietzsche address the problem of resolving the 'postmodern' crises facing present-day Western culture – its nihilism, barbarism, and relativism – and provide a philosophical basis for its solution, 'nihilism' and 'barbarism' '... being understood as names for a "moral" or "spiritual" disease which threatens the integrity and vitality of Western civilization as a system of thought and value' (Hinz, 1994a: 3). Reflection on Collingwood and Nietzsche furnishes a valuable way of understanding one of the fundamental antagonisms in contemporary philosophical thought and 'postmodern' society: the move towards deconstruction and other radical modes of interpretation on the one hand, and the insistence on adhering to criteria of rationality and tradition on the other (Hinz, 1994a: 3). Collingwood and Nietzsche, Hinz contends, demonstrate that only a proper explanation of the 'death of God' can furnish a liberating movement beyond the merely religious, theological, scientific and metaphysical points of view: 'Thus, Collingwood and Nietzsche both acknowledge the end of metaphysics in the traditional sense' (Hinz, 1994a: 8). As we have already seen, however, Collingwood claims to be revealing the true nature of metaphysics by arguing that it has always been an historical science, and by insisting on the name 'metaphysics' he, unlike Nietzsche, retains a continuity with the past.

from the value of a culture or a life as a whole. Nietzsche's distinction, however, between 'truth' and 'life' is more emphatic and radical than with Collingwood and Ortega. As I have already mentioned in Part One, for Nietzsche, consciousness is a development of instinctive activity and reason is a reflection of irrational drives. The goal of reason, therefore, is not knowledge or truth. As a result, Nietzsche's solution to the nihilism of the West is quite different from Collingwood's and Ortega's.

For Nietzsche, we impose order and direction on the world through the activity of valuation[18]. The standard according to which the self gives value is conduciveness to life, or the further creativity of the self in question (Hinz, 1994a: 54). But, as Hinz explains, according to Nietzsche, the valuations adopted by the sick and the weak are products of decadence, bad conscience and *ressentiment*, and can become an indirect means for the weak to dominate over the strong, by exalting its own mode of valuation as the nature of valuing as such and by according 'honour' to a world of eternal truth and being (Hinz, 1994a: 56–8). Hence, morality has become a form of valuation which attacks the essential valuational activity of life itself, and so kills the very thing it feeds on (Hinz, 1994a: 61).

Valuations reflect the need '… to impose upon chaos as much regularity and form as our practical needs require' (Nietzsche, 1968: 515) and, by schematising the world, they impart to it the character of 'being' (Hinz, 1994a: 76). As Hinz indicates, Nietzsche is critical of the fact that greater honour is given to abstractions than to the valuational process by which these things are created (Hinz, 1994a: 80). Through decadent modes of valuation, reason has been exalted and assumes a tyranny over the self (Hinz, 1994a: 81).

For Nietzsche, in Hinz's account, rather than being a science of 'what is', philosophy must be a study of the activity of transfigurative creation whereby systems of valuation come to be (Hinz, 1994a: 121). Genealogy construes values as a function of will-to-power, that is, attempts by a form of life to create the conditions for its continued existence and self-overcoming. Because philosophy must study not some unchanging mental substance or fixed human nature, but the flux of becoming, there is a need for 'historical philosophising'. In order to be 'cured' of Platonism, the philosopher must study systems of thought in a psychological and historical fashion (Hinz, 1994a: 124).

---

[18] According to Hinz, Nietzsche's 'valuation' correlates with Collingwood's presupposing, both of which provide '… the context of *a priori* criteria in terms of which self-creation proceeds beyond the activity of art' (Hinz, 1994a: 52).

According to Nietzsche, therefore, there is no 'truth' or 'falsehood' as such. The opposition of true and false is part of a perspective which makes the world (cf. Hinz, 1994a: 79). In *The Will to Power*, Nietzsche argues that logical thinking is made possible only by taking for granted the assumption that there are identical cases (Nietzsche, 1968: 512). The categories of reason '... represent nothing more than the expediency of a certain race and species — their utility alone is their "truth"' (Nietzsche, 1968: 514). The formation of logic, Nietzsche asserts, depended on '... the utilitarian fact that only when we see things coarsely and made equal do they become calculable and usable to us' (Nietzsche, 1968: 515).

Hence, for Nietzsche, Aristotle's law of contradiction, that we are unable to affirm and to deny one and the same thing, is not a reflection of reality, but part of the axioms of logic which are '... a means and measure for us to create reality ...' (Nietzsche, 1968: 516).

> Supposing there were no self-identical 'A', such as is presupposed by every proposition of logic (and of mathematics), and the 'A' were already mere appearance, then logic would have a merely apparent world as its condition. In fact, we believe in this proposition under the influence of ceaseless experience which seems continually to confirm it. The 'thing' — that is the real substratum of 'A'; our belief in things is the precondition of our belief in logic. The 'A' of logic is, like the atom, a reconstruction of the thing — if we do not grasp this, but make of logic a criterion of true being, we are on the way to positing as realities all those hypotheses: substance, attribute, object, subject, action, etc.; that is to conceive a metaphysical world, that is, a 'real world' (this, however, is the apparent world once more) (Nietzsche, 1968: 516).

Accordingly, the implicit claim of logic to assert something about the true-in-itself is 'quite coarse and false' (Nietzsche, 1968: 516). Nietzsche continues:

> Our subjective compulsion to believe in logic only reveals that, long before logic itself entered into our consciousness, we did nothing but introduce its postulates into events: now we discover them in events — we can no longer do otherwise — and imagine that this compulsion guarantees something connected with 'truth'. It is we who created the 'thing', the 'identical thing', subject, attribute, activity, object, substance, form, after we had long pursued the process of making identical, coarse and simple. The world seems logical to us because we have made it logical (Nietzsche, 1968: 521).

Similarly, in *Beyond Good and Evil*, Nietzsche contends that it is a prejudice of metaphysicians that things of the highest value cannot be derivable from the transitory world, and must, rather, have their origin in the intransitory 'thing in itself': 'The fundamental faith of the metaphysicians is the *faith in antithetical values'* (Nietzsche, 1990: 2). Consequently, for Nietzsche, the standard of value according to which genealogical inquiry explains and assesses systems of thought is not truth, utility or justice, but 'life' (Hinz, 1994a: 127). Nietzsche argues:

> The falseness of a judgement is to us not necessarily an objection to a judgement: it is here that our new language perhaps sounds strangest. The question is to what extent it is life-advancing, life-preserving, species-preserving, perhaps even species-breeding; and our fundamental tendency is to assert that the falsest judgements (to which synthetic judgements *a priori* belong) are the most indispensable to us, that without granting as true the fictions of logic, without measuring reality against the purely invented world of the unconditional and self-identical, without a continual falsification of the world by means of numbers, mankind could not live — that to renounce false judgements would be to renounce life, would be to deny life. To recognize untruth as a condition of life: that, to be sure, means to resist customary value-sentiments in a dangerous fashion; and a philosophy which ventures to do so places itself, by that act alone, beyond good and evil (Nietzsche, 1990: 4).

In Nietzsche's view, genealogy provides an account of the way in which valuations are interpreted by consciousness, and how interpretations arise and supersede one another,[19] and genealogy is part of the necessary destructive preliminary to a revivification of the Western world (Hinz, 1994a: 130–2).

Nietzsche argues (as Hinz explains) that nihilism is the culminating condition of Western culture and it is confronted by 'nihilism' because of the dominance of decadent modes of valuation based on *ressentiment* (Hinz, 1994a: 161). The decadent mode of valuation establishes a perspective where its own mode of valuation is absolute and unconditional, and the source of all value is regarded as situated in 'the beyond', outside the realm of becoming. However, Nietzsche asserts, this mode of valuation 'devalues' itself. Truthfulness as a moral value becomes the very means by which the falsification, or idealisation, of the world is at last revealed. The rational demand to eradicate dogma ultimately results in the discovery of

---

[19] In a society, culture, or system of thought at any given time there are dominant and recessive elements, where the competing valuations make it unstable and ever liable to change. Unlike Collingwood, who regards conceptual change as produced by continual development, for Nietzsche, conceptual change is characterised by discontinuity and is brought about by novel irruption (Hinz, 1994a: 129). Contrary to Nietzsche, however, it could be argued that conceptual change can only be understood because we impose some kind of conceptual apparatus on it. Thus, Collingwood rightly argues that the past can only be understood because it leaves traces of itself in the present. There is a limit, then, to how much chaos and 'novel irruption' that a knowable historical process can contain.

reason's own dogmatic foundations (Hinz, 1994a: 164–66). Hence the value of truth is recognised as a problem, and the will to truth gains self-consciousness. In order to create new values, what is initially needed is to carry nihilism to its 'logical conclusion' (Hinz, 1994a: 170).

Nietzsche provides an acute diagnosis of the crisis of modernity and his critique of Platonism and abstract rationalism has much in common with the views of Collingwood and Ortega.[20] But, while Collingwood and Ortega develop an alternative logic to the one that they criticise, Nietzsche, as I will explain, does not put forward a solution in *rational* terms.

Nietzsche contends that Western civilisation must attempt self-overcoming through a transvaluation of all values. The transvaluation involves the irruption of a new will-to-power into history and the establishment of a new perspective. For Nietzsche, according to Hinz's account, the beginnings of a remedy are in the idea of eternal recurrence. In the hands of those who can endure it, it becomes a principle of reinterpretation. This idea creates an 'order of rank', which allows for the development of a new 'aristocracy' through whom the self-overcoming of humanity can be achieved (Hinz, 1994a: 175).

The development of a higher, self-creative type of being, the *Ubermensch*, is itself an ideal. Humanity must become conscious of itself as the creative source of values and cultivate a scepticism towards convictions and prejudices. The will to truth must be used to promote self-creative activity rather than hindering it. Nietzsche, then, is not opposed to conviction as such, only to complete submission to them (Hinz, 1994a: 176–78). As Hinz argues, 'Knowledge here serves first and foremost the value of creative fecundity rather than truth' (Hinz, 1994a: 179). In the establishment of a new order with a new interpretation and new principles, the will-to-power is fundamental (Hinz, 1994a: 180).

It seems, therefore, that whereas Collingwood's solution to the crisis of the West is something that can be known, Nietzsche's is intu-

---

[20] Nietzsche's objection to logic because it does not allow for contradiction correlates with similar arguments by Collingwood and Ortega. However, Collingwood and Ortega, along with the Italian Idealists followed on from this to develop a post-Hegelian 'logic of contradiction'. Croce asks 'And who has ever destroyed or eradicated the truth of Hegel, that the principle "A is A, and not-A is not-A" must be profoundly modified, since reality is not static but living, not fixed but changing, and therefore demands the new principle that "A is both A and not-A", so that rationalist logic gives place to the dialectic?' (Croce, 1949: 12)

ited. As Hinz puts it, Nietzsche's appeal is not primarily to one's reason. Whereas Collingwood's philosophy is intended to be judged by primarily rational standards, it would seem that Nietzsche's philosophy is intended to persuade by virtue of the force of its rhetoric (Hinz, 1994a: 214).

Because, for Nietzsche, the basic principles of Western Civilisation are grounded in artistic failure and *ressentiment*, his proposed remedy is more severe: the revaluation of all values. Collingwood, on the other hand, rejects the idea that the cause of the crisis of civilisation rests ultimately in the basic principles of Western culture itself. Hinz contends: 'Because of Collingwood's philosophy we can concede much of the substance of Nietzsche's concerns about the state of Western culture, and yet still have some reason for thinking that the demise of Western civilization is not an *inevitable* outcome of the direction it has traditionally taken' (Hinz, 1994a: 221). While Collingwood's philosophy consistently provides a rational ground for acting, Nietzsche's philosophy is not one that a person could simply agree with: a genuine agreement could only be a call to one's own creative act (cf. Hinz, 1994a: 222).

In conclusion, therefore, Collingwood's philosophy is intended as a response to a crisis in Western civilisation and the solution to the crisis is an improvement in our self-understanding through a historicist and dialectical philosophy. What is now needed is a discussion of how Collingwood's solution to cultural crisis in terms of logic, metaphysics and philosophy of history manifests itself in the practices of civilisation and politics. In some sense, then, in Part Three, we move from theory to practice, although, as I will explain, in Collingwood's view, theory and practice are intimately related. As we will see, Collingwood's dialectical theory of truth as the ability to assimilate and explain what is different from and outside of one's individual principles and judgements becomes evident in his morality of duty, a reform of social contract theory, and a dialectical response to the problems of economics and bureaucratic administration.

Part Three

Dialectic, Civilisation and Politics

Chapter Eight

The Phenomenology of Mind

In Part One and Part Two I have examined Collingwood's diagnosis and response to the crisis of Western civilisation, which he presents in his philosophy of art and his logic and metaphysics, or alternatively his philosophy of emotion and his philosophy of thought. For Collingwood, as we have seen, our first apprehension of the world comes through aesthetic activity, and it is through art that we first become aware of cultural crisis. However, what we become conscious of in art is made detailed and explicit in thought proper. Thus in Collingwood's theory of logic and metaphysics and his philosophy of history the crisis of the West manifests itself as a failure to move beyond a reliance on rationalistic thinking and the solution is the development of a dialectical philosophy. The dialectical philosophy meant a reform of logic and metaphysics, and advancing the idea of thinking and truth as an open-ended process of development.

Part Three explores how Collingwood's dialectical philosophy, which includes the philosophy of emotion, leads to a reform in our conceptions of morality, society and politics. Thus this section will provide a more detailed and enhanced view of his diagnosis and response to the ills of modernity and draw together some of the conclusions from the first two parts.

In Collingwood's view, there is an extremely close relation between theory and practice. In *An Autobiography* he criticised the 'realist' dogma that theory has no effect on practice. Collingwood asserted that it is a truth that ought to be familiar to every human being

> ... that in his capacity as a moral, political, or economic agent he lives not in a world of 'hard facts' to which 'thoughts' make no difference, but in a world of 'thoughts'; that if you change the moral, political, and economic 'theories' generally accepted by the society in which he lives, you change the character of his world; and that if you change his own 'theories' you change his relation to that world; so that in either case you change the ways in which he acts (A, 147).

The relation between theory and practice, therefore, was one of mutual dependence. Thought depends on what we have learned from our experience of acting, and action depends on how we think of ourselves and the world (A, 150). Similarly, at the beginning of *Speculum Mentis*, Collingwood declared that

> All thought exists for the sake of action. We try to understand ourselves and our world only in order that we may learn how to live. The end of our self-knowledge is not the contemplation by enlightened intellects of their own mysterious nature, but the freer and more effectual self-revelation of that nature in a vigorous practical life (SM, 15).

Furthermore, Collingwood held that the influence of the 'realist' view that theory is irrelevant to practice taught people to think of philosophy as a 'futile parlour game' and prepared the ground for the threats to civilisation by irrationalism and Fascism (A, 50 and 166–7).

Regarding the precise nature of the relation between theory and practice, Collingwood argued in 'Political Action'[1] that theory is not directly concerned with finding a solution to practical problems, but aims '... to clear them of misunderstandings which make their solution impossible' (EPP, 94). However, it is evident that for Collingwood practical reason, to some extent, is itself philosophical. As I will discuss in more detail further on, the highest forms of practical reason and moral thinking correspond with the highest form of theoretical reason. Collingwood in the *Autobiography* asserted that the theoretical activities of

> ... scientific, historical, or philosophical thinking depended quite as much on 'moral' qualities as on 'intellectual' ones, and that 'moral' difficulties were to be overcome not by 'moral' force alone but by clear thinking (A, 150).

For Collingwood, '... the plane on which, ultimately, all problems arise is the plane of "real" life: that to which they are referred for their solution is history' (A, 114).

---

[1]   This essay appears in *Essays in Political Philosophy*, pp. 92–109.

The rejection of any sharp distinction between theory and practice[2] was also evident, as we have seen, in *An Essay on Philosophical Method*. There Collingwood argued that experience and theory are names for any two successive stages in a scale of forms of philosophical knowledge, where the higher stage explains the lower (EPM, 172). For Collingwood, then, all of us are philosophers, to some extent, in our everyday lives, and we engage with theory in our ordinary moral thinking. Collingwood's *rapprochement* between theory and practice meant overcoming the distinction between the contemplative life and the practical life as a division between two classes of specialists (A, 150). Collingwood's response to the crisis of Western civilisation, therefore, culminates in *The New Leviathan*, which outlines a theory of mind, morality, society and politics, and makes explicit his dialectical philosophy.

As we have seen in Part Two, for Collingwood, the philosophical foundations of Western culture presupposed a static conception of being, which is ultimately nihilistic. According to his moral and political philosophy (which I now discuss here in Part Three), this crisis of civilisation is evident in the dominance of abstractly rationalistic forms of thought and action, associated with natural science. The solution to this problem is the development of an account of mind both where each of the levels of consciousness makes an important contribution to human life and where mind is seen as a process of development that is dialectical and leading to greater degrees and kinds of self-consciousness. Thus, the characterisation of thinking and truth as an open-ended process of development, assimilating and explaining diverse points of view, in Collingwood's reform of logic and metaphysics, is demonstrated and made use of in his social and political thought.

In Part Three, particularly in this chapter and the next, I will make extensive reference to David Boucher's *The Social and Political Thought of R.G. Collingwood* (1989). Boucher's important and ground-breaking book first brought to prominence Collingwood's political philosophy and *The New Leviathan*. Hence in my exposition

---

[2]   With this reading of the relation of theory and practice in Collingwood's thought, I am inclined to qualify Connelly's view that the function of theory is 'essentially negative' in that it helps our practice by clarifying what our fundamental principles about morality are (Connelly, 2003: 175). Following on from the argument of Part Two of this study, I suggest that the function of philosophy is not merely to clarify what our opinions are but also to consider how they manifest themselves in particular kinds of practice. I would question what seems to be Connelly's effective identification of the purpose of philosophy with metaphysics, and moral philosophy with a 'metaphysics of morals'.

of the way in which Collingwood's dialectical philosophy reveals itself in his account of mind, morality and politics, it will be necessary to engage with this text frequently.

Collingwood's dialectical method, which is expressed in *An Essay on Philosophical Method* as the theory of the scale of forms, was developed in his early work, including the moral philosophy lectures, and the moral philosophy lectures formed the basis of what was to become *The New Leviathan*. As Boucher indicates, then, a version of the scale of forms emerges in *The New Leviathan*, and *An Essay on Philosophical Method* and *The New Leviathan* are related as theory and its application (Boucher, 1989: 28). Boucher explains that

> ... the principles of method which inform *The New Leviathan* are in substance, with minor changes in detail, those exemplified in varying degrees in *Speculum Mentis*, *Outlines of a Philosophy of Art*, and later *The Principles of Art*, as well as in the lectures on moral philosophy, and articulated as theory in *An Essay on Philosophical Method* (Boucher, 1989: 37).

The New Leviathan was also a culmination of Collingwood's attempts to bring about rapprochements both between philosophy and history and between theory and practice. Boucher argues that *The New Leviathan* is the concrete exemplar of the union of philosophy and history, citing a letter to Malcolm Knox in 1936 where Collingwood claims: 'What I do wish to resolve without residue into history is the *Philosophy of Spirit*, or Theory of Mind, or Science of Human Nature' (Boucher, 1989: 38). In 'Notes on Historiography' (which was written during the same voyage on which he wrote *An Essay on Metaphysics*) Collingwood made his now famous assertion that 'Philosophy as a separate discipline is liquidated by being converted into history', and also claimed that 'history is the only kind of knowledge'(Boucher, 1989: 38 and 49).[3] *The New Leviathan*, as Boucher explains, was a concrete demonstration of the rapprochement between philosophy and history, because Collingwood developed the argument there that history means self-knowledge of the mind and knowledge of what mind has done in the past (Boucher, 1989: 50–1).

Following on from *The Idea of History*, Collingwood declares that the argument of *The New Leviathan* is constructed on what Locke called the 'historical plain method', and concentrates on 'facts',

---

[3]   Boucher points out that in this Collingwood was following the example of his Italian sources of inspiration: Croce and Gentile (Boucher, 1989: 38). Similarly, in a letter to E.R. Hughes in December 1939, Collingwood said that he would continue to devote his life to 'the idea of a union of philosophy and history', an idea that 'could save Europe' (Boucher, 1989: 50).

things done, or deeds (NL, 9.1–11). The historical study of mind involves studying the activities of mind. It does not ask what mind is, only what it does, and not what mind always and everywhere does, only what it does on certain occasions (NL, 9.16–8). Contrary to Locke, however, for Collingwood, the study of human mind using the historical plain method would not result in knowledge of a universal human nature. Collingwood rejects the idea of mind as substance, and, as we have already seen, argues that mind is activity and is creative of itself and its environment.[4]

Collingwood argues that the sciences of mind, unlike the natural sciences, only give us knowledge about things of which we were already conscious (NL, 1.71). The answer to any question in a science of mind is provided by reflection: 'The sciences of mind, unless they preach error or confuse the issue by dishonesty or involuntary obscurity, can tell us nothing but what each can verify for himself by reflecting on his own mind' (NL, 1.85). This is consistent with the dialectical principle that Collingwood advanced in *An Essay on Philosophical Method*: that in a philosophical inquiry what we are trying to do is not to discover something of which until now we have been ignorant, but to know better something which in some sense we always knew — to know it better in the sense of coming to know it in a different and better way (EPM, 11).

For Collingwood, in *The New Leviathan*, a mind develops when it has the mental energy to do so:

> There are no laws of development or progress. Occasions arise when certain kinds of progress, certain steps in development, are possible for a mind. They are never necessary. Whether the mind takes the step that is possible for it depends entirely on the mind's practical energy (NL, 7.28–29).

Collingwood states that he is concerned only with the modern European mind, as that is enough for deciding how to deal with the attack on modern European civilisation, as represented by Fascism and

---

[4] Boucher draws attention to an affinity between Collingwood and Gentile on this point. Gentile, in viewing mind as pure act, reached a philosophical position termed 'absolute immanence', whereby the mind attains self-consciousness by bringing about a unity in historical reality. Boucher cites de Ruggiero's summing up of Gentile's doctrine: 'Philosophy, in creating its own history, creates itself. Hence an absolute immanence of philosophical truth in the historical process, which is at the same time the phenomenological process of spirit' (Boucher, 1989: 112). Although Collingwood did not follow Gentile's views without modification, Gentile's views show us that Collingwood's use of the word 'facts' does not mean 'facts' in abstraction from the acts that created them: 'The word *fact*, then, is Collingwood's term for that which is the unity of the immanent and transcendent aspects of experience' (Boucher, 1989: 113).

Nazism (NL, 9.2–21). He aims to give a catalogue of the mind's functions, to be arranged serially, albeit in an irregular series (NL, 9.32–9.4).

Collingwood's methodology is obviously Hegelian.[5] However, as I have argued in Part Two, Collingwood also reforms Hegel's dialectic by getting rid of the Absolute and developing the idea of an open-ended process of development. Hence, Collingwood argues that the development of the mind is not predictable (NL, 9.43), and it only develops if it has the energy to do so. He refers to this as the 'law of contingency': 'the earlier terms in a series of mental functions do not determine the later' (NL, 9.48).

Another principle which Collingwood introduces into the study of mind is the 'law of primitive survivals': '*When A is modified into B there survives in any example of B, side by side with the function of B which is the modified form of A, an element of A in its primitive or unmodified state*' (NL, 9.51). Apes have evolved into men; but there are still apes (NL, 9.52). The lower levels of mind survive in the higher as objects of reflection. Thus, this resembles the idea of a scale of forms in *An Essay on Philosophical Method*.

According to Boucher, the 'law of primitive survivals' qualifies the doctrine of *An Essay on Philosophical Method*. It means that there is no longer a complete overlap of forms on the scale. Something of the lower form remains 'pure' in the higher form: that is, modification is only partial and never complete. Following from this, the law of primitive survivals is at variance with his principle of the 'fallacy of precarious margins', which, as we have seen,

> … consists in assuming that the overlap which has already affected a certain area of the class in question can be trusted not to spread, and that beyond its limits there lies a marginal region in which the instances exhibit only one of the specific forms, uncontaminated by the presence of the other (EPM, 48; Boucher, 1989: 96).

However, Collingwood did argue further on in *An Essay on Philosophical Method* that the higher of any two adjacent forms fails to include the lower in its entirety because there is also a negative aspect of the lower, which is rejected by the higher (EPM, 90). This

---

[5]   The Hegelian aspect to Collingwood's phenomenology of mind is noted by Gary Browning. Browning points out that the notion of the mind ascending forms and functions to achieve a self-recognition of itself as free, social and self-moving which is presented in *The New Leviathan* rehearses a similar journey to that followed by mind in Hegel's *Phenomenology of Spirit* (Browning, 1995: 104). Browning's interpretation of Collingwood is more fully presented in *Rethinking R.G. Collingwood: Philosophy, Politics and the Unity of Theory and Practice* (2004).

seems to suggest that the principle of the 'fallacy of precarious margins' was modified in the text of *An Essay on Philosophical Method* itself.

Collingwood's account of the development of mind in *The New Leviathan* supplements and modifies his account of mind in *The Principles of Art*. In doing so, *The New Leviathan* provides a more detailed exposition of the levels of consciousness and the dialectical development from one to the other than we saw in his philosophy of art. Collingwood's theory of mind culminates in an account of morality as duty, and the way in which this dialectical account of mind and duty provides a solution to the problem of the crisis of civilisation, or the nihilistic consequences of an over-reliance on rationalistic thinking, will become evident in the course of the overview I now provide.

Collingwood begins his dialectic of mind in *The New Leviathan* by discussing the relation between mind and body. 'The problem of the relation between body and mind', he asserts, is a bogus problem, based on the false assumption that man is partly body and partly mind (NL, 2.41–2). In fact, body and mind are the same thing, known in two different ways. From the point of view of natural science, the whole of man is body. From the point of view of the sciences of mind, the whole of man is mind. The problem of the relation between body and mind, then, resolves itself into the problem of the relation between the sciences of body and the sciences of mind, each of which are a valid search for the truth, with their own methods and problems (NL, 2.43–63). Adopting the methods of one to solve the problems of the other is the 'fallacy of swapping horses' (NL, 2.71).

However, Collingwood contends that there is a psychological sense of the word 'body', for example, 'bodily appetite', 'bodily pleasure' and 'bodily exertion' (NL, 3.2). Lying in a hot bath is referred to as a 'bodily pleasure', whereas reading Newton's *Principia* is not. The word 'bodily' here refers to a certain group of feelings (the pleasure of warmth on the skin and so forth), as opposed to the pleasure of thinking in a certain way (NL, 3.4–43). Hence, a 'bodily' pleasure means a pleasure arising out of 'feelings', that is, sensations and the emotions directly connected with them (NL, 3.44).[6]

[6] Boucher interestingly contends that this is a modification of the principle in *The Idea of History* that historical knowledge consists solely in the re-enactment of past purposive thought. In *The Idea of History* Collingwood maintained a sharp distinction between rational thought and feelings, or psyche: a distinction that continues in both *The Principles of Art* and *An Essay on Metaphysics*. The inclusion of the psychical level of experience in the science of mind in *The New Leviathan*

According to Collingwood, consciousness is an activity which is a constituent of the mind. In contrast, feeling is an *apanage* of the mind. It is what simple consciousness is conscious of. Mind, then, *is* consciousness and *has* feeling (NL, 4.14–2). Consciousness in its specialised form finds feeling in a correspondingly specialised form as 'ready made' and 'immediately given' (NL, 4.22).

Knowledge is a highly specialised form of consciousness. In order to know anything one must achieve second-order consciousness, or reflection on simple consciousness (NL, 4.3–31). This means that we attend to an object, focussing our consciousness on it, make suppositions about it, subject it to questioning, and attempt to answer the question (NL, 4.33–36). Second-order consciousness is the level at which conceptual thinking takes place. The object of second-order consciousness, therefore, is not found ready-made or 'given', but is produced by the act of selective attention. Out of the confusion in which feeling is given to simple consciousness, selective attention makes a pattern and reduces the confusion to order (NL, 4.52–6).

In Collingwood's view, 'Knowledge rests on a foundation of feeling' (NL, 5.1). All thought has a certain degree of difficulty, causing emotional strains in the mind, which in extreme cases can lead to insanity. The solidity or robustness of a person's sensuous emotional nature affords a sane basis for his or her thinking and consists of two kinds of strength: vividness and tenacity (NL, 5.11–14). On methodological grounds Collingwood argues that there are no objects of feeling, thus agreeing with Descartes and disagreeing with Locke. Both the Cartesian view and the Lockean view fit the facts, but the Cartesian theory is preferable as it means that a theory of feeling does not need objects as well as modes (5.2–39).[7]

In second-level consciousness the activity of attending to, or selecting, feelings takes place within a context of evocative thinking. This is the process by which we encounter appetite in the forms of hunger and love, and we become conscious of passion in the forms of fear and anger. Hunger, Collingwood explains, is not a feeling, but an appetite: a complex thing '… consisting of feelings and ghosts of feelings combined into a certain pattern by the practical work of consciousness' (NL, 7.1). Hunger or appetite involves an act of prac-

---

means that reason now studies the sensations, feelings and appetites which 'feed and support' it. History must now concern itself with thought at all the preceding levels of consciousness, and thought in *The New Leviathan* begins at the level of simple consciousness, that is, at the level he had previously termed the psyche (Boucher, 1989: 117–9).

[7]   For Descartes, for example, colour is a mode, not an object, of action (NL, 5.34–35).

tical consciousness, namely conceptual thinking, or selective attention (NL, 7.19–23). In second-order consciousness, the act of
selective attention is accompanied by '… the act of *evocative thinking*:
the act of arousing in yourself, by the work of thought, feelings you
do not find as "given" in yourself' (NL, 7.32). The evocation of feelings provides a context where feelings that are present are contrasted with feelings that are absent. One tries to attain the absent
feeling because of its 'pleasure potential' (NL, 7.43). Appetite, then,
makes partially determinate what was completely indeterminate
(cf. Boucher, 1989: 124). When in a condition of appetite, one is not
conscious of either the feeling-state one has or the feeling-state one
wants as having any determinate characteristics, except that each
contrasts with the other (NL, 7.52–3).

Thus, for Collingwood, 'Appetite is what thought makes out of
feeling when thought develops by its own activity from mere consciousness to conceptual thinking. It is both a specialized form of
consciousness (namely conceptual thinking) and a specialized form
of feeling produced out of simple feeling by that form of consciousness' (NL, 7.6). 'Appetite is a name for the inherent restlessness of the
mind' (NL, 7.69). The mind is driven unconsciously from an indeterminate here-and-now towards some indeterminate there-and-then
in a quest '… due to no choice, guided by no reason, directed on no
goal. Choice and reason and goal are not among the sources or conditions of appetite, they are among its products' (NL, 7.69).

Collingwood divides appetite into the hunger-type and the
love-type. Appetite involves a movement from an actual self
towards an ideal self. Hunger is a wanting to be strong. The ideal self
in this case is a self that is indefinitely strengthened. Love, on the
other hand, is a wanting to be attached. The ideal self is a self that has
achieved a relation with something other than itself, a 'not-self', of
such a kind that one's present dissatisfaction is removed (NL,
8.12–16).

Love, therefore, is an appetite for a relation with a not-self. In the
struggle towards this relation, the not-self is created, and the self
establishes itself as a focus of activity with an identity of its own,
unique and different from every not-self. Prior to this there is no self
or not-self, only a chaos of consciousness and feeling in which appetite works (NL, 8.44–47). Love is a modification of hunger, or the
impossible quest for omnipotence. Love comes about when blind
appetite suffers repeated disappointments in its quest for omnipotence, despairs of that quest, and seeks instead strength from something not itself (NL, 8.52–5). According to Collingwood,

> The birth of love is the act of limiting your demands: substituting for the
> quest of absolute satisfaction ... the quest of many partial and incom-
> plete satisfactions, each derived from a specialized relation to this, that,
> or the other not-self (NL, 8.58).

However, in frustrating the satisfaction of a limited set of
demands, the not-self has the power to throw one into a passion, and
passion has two forms: fear and anger (NL, 10.2). Collingwood
rejects the rationalistic accounts of fear, given by Hobbes and
Spinoza, which explain fear by reference to our supposed reasons
for being afraid. Fear does contain an intellectual element, not of
propositional thinking (for example, 'this may hurt me'), but of conceptual thinking: the idea of a not-self, and a contrast between it and
oneself. Fear is simply a practical reaction to this contrast (NL,
10.26–27). Love turns into fear when one starts thinking of the
not-self no longer being in the passive role of accepting adoration,
but being alive and having an independent character of its own (NL,
10.3–32).

Collingwood similarly rejects the rationalistic accounts of anger
given by Hobbes and Spinoza. There is the same intellectual element
in anger as in fear, namely the contrast between yourself and something other than yourself. The difference is practical. The first thing
one feels inclined to do on encountering opposition is to give way to
it. But fear is self-contradictory. Like hunger it is insatiable, and
yielding to it completely would be self-annihilation. The flight from
self-contradiction arises from despair, and combined with resilience
or adaptability, passion changes from fear to anger. Anger means
fighting against the not-self and is accompanied by shame, the
renunciation of the cowardly self for being afraid (NL, 10.45–49).
Shame and anger, Collingwood explains, are a critical point in the
whole development of mind. Anger is a bridge between the lower
levels of consciousness and the higher forms where propositional
thinking develops (NL, 10.5–51).

At the third level of consciousness we encounter desire and happiness. With desire, truth and error, and self-knowledge, originate.
Unlike appetite, desire involves knowing what you want. It involves
asking and answering a question and contemplating alternatives:
'which do I want, *a* or *b*?' The idea of alternatives is abstracted from
the experience of fear and anger as two alternative reactions to the
not-self (NL, 11.1–14). According to Collingwood, you find out what
you want by going through a process of fear and anger (NL, 11.17).

Appetite has no negative form: there is only its presence and its
absence. But desire has a negative form: aversion or loathing. Desire

involves propositional thinking. Appetite and absence of appetite, as objects of knowledge, become desire and aversion (NL, 11.21–24). Also, one can have true and false desires. In answering the question 'which of these alternatives do I want?' the answer given is either true or false (NL, 11.32). The first step in knowing yourself is knowing what you want (NL, 11.39). 'Good' is the name for the object of our desires. The mind bestows goodness on whatever it desires. Thus, for Collingwood, '... desire first makes us able to know (knowledge being the theoretical function of which desire is the practical counterpart); and good is the first thing we come to know' (NL, 11.69).

Collingwood follows Aristotle by arguing that the general name for the things we desire and think good is called 'happiness'. Happiness is a combination of internal well-being, or virtue, and external well-being, or power (NL, 12.2–22). Happiness and unhappiness are freedom from and subjection to passion or the force of circumstances (NL, 12.34). Interestingly, Collingwood criticises Nietzsche for confusedly asserting that what one wants is not happiness but power. Our word 'happy', Collingwood explains, is derived from Aristotle and a title used by Roman emperors, and '… what was good enough for Greek philosophers and Roman emperors is good enough for us' (NL, 12.44).

Unhappiness is a familiar element in contemporary civilisation. Despite having a different conception of the nature and content of mind from that of Hobbes, Collingwood praises Hobbes for emphasising that the social, economic and political structures which exert such power over us are our own creations. There is a sense of despair when we realise that those very agents whose protection we expected to enjoy are perpetrators of the very evils they were meant to end. But despair is parasitic upon hope, and the solution is to strengthen the hope until it overcomes the nightmare, by constructing a science of politics for the modern world (NL, 12.9–97; cf. Boucher, 1989: 128 and 130). *The New Leviathan*, therefore, is intended as a remedy for the ills of modernity.

According to Collingwood, the next level of consciousness is choice. Choice is distinguished from preference. Preference means that one desires *a* and suffers aversion to *b*. Choice, on the other hand, presupposes freedom. The question of whether or not we have free will, Collingwood argues, is a pseudo-problem, involving 'the fallacy of misplaced argument'. Instead, '… freedom is a first-order object of consciousness to every man whose mental development has reached the ability to choose' (NL, 13.18).

Freedom of the will is, positively, freedom to choose and, nega-tively, freedom from being at the mercy of desires, and its achieve-ment is involuntary (NL, 13.25–26). One achieves freedom through accepting unhappiness: that is, by accepting badness and weakness, and renouncing virtue and power. Through an act of self-denial, therefore, instead of happiness, a person gains self-respect, or the consciousness of being free (NL, 13.3–31). We escape from any par-ticular desire by naming it: a doctrine common to Spinoza, fairy-tales, and psychoanalysis (NL, 13.41–47).

Collingwood indicates that the doctrine that a person acquires free-will by conquering his or her passions is fundamental to Confu-cianism, Buddhism, Christianity and Islam, and that the denial of this doctrine in modern Europe is popularly referred to as 'pagan-ism' (NL, 13.48–51). But, he explains, this so-called 'paganism' is an escapist fantasy. The proposal to abandon freedom, in the shape of an organised and scientific Christian world, in exchange for a better pagan world is inconsistent. We cannot choose to get rid of choice: abandoning freedom cannot be a free act, but can only happen due to psychological causes (NL, 13.52–5).

The achievement of free-will marks the reaching of mental matu-rity. However, in some people self-liberation may be achieved but remain pre-conscious. A person is made conscious of being free by arousing his or her self-respect, something extremely important in government and education (NL, 13.6–64). Also when self-respect is achieved, it may still be precarious and it may be felt that desire is still not completely conquered. This leads to asceticism where peo-ple bolster up their self-respect by deliberately doing things they would rather not, something which dies away at mental maturity (NL, 13.67–68).

This fourth level of consciousness involves a distinction between 'the will' and 'the deed'. However, as Collingwood argues:

> A voluntary act is not *preceded by* a decision to do it; it *begins with* a deci-sion to do it. But the process from the will to the deed is at every stage under the control of the will; the will is not content to initiate the process, leaving the details to be completed by the other hand; it fills in the details itself as it goes on (NL, 13.8–81).

A will is an example of practical thinking, and as practical it expresses itself by the initial stage of action. The rest of the action, the part that is as yet unperformed, is 'intended':

> The development of the process from the will to the deed involves the progressive conversion of intention or decision into performance. There are perhaps occasions on which thought turns wholly and without resi-

due into deed; more often the process is incomplete, and some of what begins as intention ends as — what shall we say? — frustrated intention (NL, 13.85).

In the phenomenology of mind that Collingwood presents in *The New Leviathan*, language occupies a crucial place.[8] Each conversion from one level of consciousness to another is brought about by a linguistic act. Collingwood's theory of language in *The New Leviathan* is a modification of that propounded in *The Principles of Art*. What was, in *The Principles of Art*, psychical experience now becomes simple consciousness, or first-level consciousness. Language, which had only appeared at the second level of experience, namely consciousness or imagination, now emerged at the level of simple consciousness. Collingwood, then, abandoned the distinction between language, which is expressive, and intellectualised language, which has meaning. All language now has meaning.[9]

Language is defined as '… any system of bodily movements, not necessarily vocal, whereby the men who make them *mean* or *signify* anything' (Collingwood's italics; NL, 6.1). Language is an abstraction from discourse. Whereas discourse is the activity by which a person means anything, '… a language is the system adopted, the means employed, the rules followed, in this activity' (NL, 6.11). Discourse is continuous, the 'rests' and 'pauses' being an integral part of it. It begins as continuous activity and is then broken up into words — vocal words or gesture words — by selective attention (NL, 6.12–14). The vehicle of discourse is a succession of sensations with their emotional charges. Discourse is

> … the activity of *meaning something (a) by something else (b)*, where meaning *a* is an act of theoretical consciousness, and *b* is a practical activity, the production in oneself or others of a flow of sounds or the like which serve you as the vehicle of that meaning (NL, 6.19).

We become conscious of our feelings by means of language. Naming a feeling awakens consciousness of it. It remains pre-conscious until it is named (NL, 6.26–28). The act of naming a feeling itself also remains preconscious until one reflects upon it. According to Collingwood,

> This is the difference between linguistic activity in general and that reflective, critical form of it which is called 'literature' or 'poetry' or in general 'art'. The artist or poet, like other men, achieves consciousness of his feelings only so far as he finds words for them; but he is conscious not

---

[8]   Boucher declares that 'The importance of language in Collingwood's philosophy of mind cannot be overestimated' (Boucher, 1989: 134).

[9]   Here I am making use of Boucher's account (1989: 138).

only of the feelings but of the linguistic activity, and works at perform-
ing this activity as well as he can (NL, 6.29).[10]

Collingwood remarks that it is a commonplace today that not only
is language the means by which knowledge is communicated from
one person to another, making possible social life, but it is '... an
activity prior to knowledge itself, without which knowledge could
never come into existence' (NL, 6.41). Unlike in *The Principles of Art*,
in *The New Leviathan*, Collingwood credits Hobbes with the discovery of this truth, and cites from p.14 of Hobbes' *Leviathan*:

> ... without words, there is no possibility of reckoning of Numbers; much
> lesse of Magnitudes, of Swiftnesse, of Force, and other things, the reck-
> onings whereof are necessary to the being, or well-being of man-kind
> (NL, 6.46; cf. Boucher, 1989: 139).

In Collingwood's view, therefore, language and consciousness
develop in unison:

> Language in its simplest form is the language of consciousness in its sim-
> plest form; the mere 'register' of feelings, as wild and mad as those feel-
> ings themselves; irrational, unorganized, unplanned, unconscious. As
> consciousness develops, language develops with it. When conscious-
> ness becomes conceptual thought, language develops abstract terms.
> When consciousness becomes propositional thought language develops
> the indicative sentence as the standard verbal form in which to state the
> proposition. When consciousness becomes reason language becomes
> demonstrative discourse wherein sentences are so linked together as to
> state verbally 'the Consequence of one Affirmation to another' (NL,
> 6.58–59).

In *The New Leviathan*, then, (to sum up what I have outlined so far)
Collingwood modifies and extends the theory of mind that he presented in *The Principles of Art*. As we have already seen in Part One,
for Collingwood, the lower levels of consciousness constitute a
foundation for the emergence and development of mind at higher
levels. Because of this, aesthetic experience plays a crucial role in our
self-understanding and in our understanding of civilisation and the
problems which beset it. Art is seen as the beginning of the process
by which we create the self and the world, and in this emphasis on
the importance of art Collingwood is demonstrably working in the
Romantic tradition.

In *The New Leviathan*, this position is developed such that what
was previously termed the psyche is more completely integrated

---

[10] Collingwood does not discuss the corruption of consciousness in relation to ar-
      tistic activity in *The New Leviathan*, presumably because he had already dis-
      cussed it in *The Principles of Art*. Here his main concern is to explain how one
      progresses from simple consciousness to thought.

into the life of mind and Collingwood's theory of language is modified accordingly. Furthermore, in contrast with *The Principles of Art*,
The New Leviathan provides a more detailed account of the levels of
consciousness (simple consciousness, appetite, passion, desire,
choice and reason) and the dialectical development from one to
another.

Regarding the point that the emergence of reason and society
depends fundamentally on the lower levels of consciousness,
Collingwood can profitably be compared with Ortega y Gasset. In
'The Sportive Origin of the State',[11] Ortega argues that we can divide
animal and human activity into two classes: one original, creative,
vital, spontaneous and disinterested, and the other of utilitarian
character, in which the first is put to use and mechanised: 'Utility
does not create and invent; it simply employs and stabilizes what
has been created without it' (HS, 17). Life, Ortega argues, presents
itself as an effort of two different kinds, one made for the sheer
delight of it, which becomes most manifest in sport, and the other '…
an exertion in which we are urged on and worn out by a necessity
imposed on us and not of our invention or desire', the classic
instance of which is what we call work (HS, 18). On this view,

> Sportive activity seems to us the foremost and creative, the most exalted,
> serious, and important part of life, while labour ranks second as its
> derivative and precipitate. Nay more, life, properly speaking, resides in
> the first alone; the rest is relatively mechanic and a mere functioning
> (HS, 18).[12]

Ortega contends that in every vital process the first impulse is
derived from '… an energy of supremely free and exuberant character' (HS, 19). Life then selects among the possibilities created, some
of which consolidate in the form of useful habits. According to
Ortega,

> Abundance of possibilities is a symptom of thriving life, as utilitarian-
> ism, the attitude of conforming oneself to the strictly necessary, like the

---

[11] This essay is published in *History as a System and other essays toward a philosophy of history*, (1961) pp. 13–40.

[12] This is an idea that Nietzsche alludes to in *Beyond Good and Evil*: 'Mature man-
hood: that means to have rediscovered the seriousness one had as a child at
play' (BGE, 94). As we have seen, Nietzsche also emphasises the crucial role of
the pre-rational levels of mind in human life. However, for Nietzsche, unlike
Collingwood and Ortega, appetite and desire are not merely pre-rational, but irrational, and cannot lead to knowledge or truth. Comparisons and contrasts between Nietzsche and Collingwood on the subject of the phenomenology of
mind and the idea of duty will be discussed further on in this chapter.

sick man who begrudges every expenditure of energy, discloses weakness and waning of life (HS, 19).

Life, then, needs overflow:

> He who rests content with barely meeting necessity as it arises will be washed away. Life has triumphed on this planet because it has, instead of clinging to necessities, deluged it with overwhelming possibilities, so that the failure of one may serve as a bridge for the victory of another (HS, 21).

Similarly, in 'Man the Technician',[13] Ortega asserts that '... man begins where technology begins' (HS, 117). But,

> ... the meaning and final cause of technology lie outside itself, namely in the use man makes of the unoccupied energies it sets free. The mission of technology consists in releasing man for the task of being himself (HS, 118).

Technology can mobilise its ingenuity and perform the task life is and, within limits, realise the human project, but it does not draw up that project. The vital program is pre-technical, and depends on 'original desire' (HS, 119).

However, desiring is not easy. Every wish for this or that particular thing, Ortega explains, is ultimately connected with the person you want to be, and one can distinguish between the pseudo-wish and the genuine wish. Not knowing how to wish may mean that '... one of the basic diseases of our time is a crisis of wishing ...' (HS, 120–1).[14] The material wealth and superabundance of contemporary civilisation surpasses that of all other ages, 'Yet we suffer from an appalling restlessness because we do not know what to do with it, because we lack imagination for inventing our lives' (HS, 121).[15] Consequently, Ortega suggests that those in special charge of the human project are poets, philosophers, politicians, founders of religions, and discoverers of new values. The engineer is dependent on them, and has a secondary role (HS, 121).

The crucial role played by the lower levels of consciousness in human life, therefore, is vividly emphasised by Ortega. Ortega's

---

[13]   This essay is published in *History as a System and other essays toward a philosophy of history*, pp. 87–161.

[14]   This is something discussed by Gadamer in *Reason in the Age of Science* (1981: 81).

[15]   Ortega distinguishes three stages in the evolution of technology: technology of chance, technology of the craftsman, and technology of the technician (HS, 142). At the third stage, technology is the source of practically unlimited human activity, and finding ourselves in principle capable of being almost anything, we find it even more difficult to know what we actually are (HS, 150–1). Our time, '... being the most intensely technical, is also the emptiest in all human history' (HS, 151).

emphasis in this respect can, I suggest, enrich our understanding of Collingwood's dialectic of mind. For both Collingwood and Ortega, responding to the ills of contemporary civilisation means recognising the importance of the lower levels of consciousness in order to avoid the self-deception of abstractly rationalistic forms of thinking (and this supplements what I have argued in Part One). But the solution to the crisis of civilisation also occurs at the higher levels of mind, in terms of the development of dialectical and historical thinking (as I have argued in Part Two). In the life of mind, however, dialectical thinking manifests itself in a historical morality, and the way in which Collingwood's historical account of morality constitutes a response to cultural crisis is something that I will now explore.

Collingwood's response to the crisis of civilisation with the development of a dialectical and historical philosophy is not only evident, as we have seen, in the use of a dialectical methodology in his theory of mind. It is also evident in the way that Collingwood's phenomenology of mind assimilates and transcends various inadequate theories. Collingwood displayed a growing admiration for Hobbes in his later career, and, as Boucher indicates, Hobbes's tendency to equate morality with the 'springs of human nature' provided an alternative to the excessive intellectualism of Plato.[16] However, Collingwood found Hobbes's subjectivism to be deficient (cf. Boucher, 1989: 66).

For Collingwood, as Boucher demonstrates, Hobbes's hedonism was a considerable advance on the ethics of the Greeks, because, unlike the latter, it emphasised the fact that action is self-willed, creative, and spontaneous, and not something imposed upon the individual from outside the self. But Hobbes, like Descartes, failed to move beyond the one-sidedness of subjectivism. According to Collingwood, all forms of subjectivism rest on a misconceived distinction between subject and object (Boucher, 1989: 77). Hobbes conceives the self as something fixed and complete, standing in opposition to a world which is hostile. But in Collingwood's view, in the 'Lectures on Moral Philosophy': 'The self is really in constant flux, a process of creating itself and its world' (cited from Boucher, 1989: 78). Hence, in his 1921 'Lectures on Moral Philosophy', Collingwood argued: 'The task is to think on from Plato to Hobbes

---

[16] Furthermore, Boucher suggests that a second reason why Collingwood admired Hobbes is that the former, like his distinguished predecessor, endeavoured to ground his theories of ethics and politics in a philosophy of human nature, or philosophy of mind. A third factor to bear in mind is that Collingwood saw certain similarities between the revolt against civilisation which was occurring in his own day with the rise of Fascism, and the events of Hobbes's day (Boucher, 1989: 67).

and then from Hobbes to something new which shall overcome the defects of Hobbes' (cited from Boucher, 1989: 67).

Collingwood's theory of mind also absorbs and transcends utilitarianism. For Collingwood, utilitarianism constitutes a modification of hedonism, in that it appeals to a criterion, or standard, of what feelings ought to be, and uses as its criterion the feeling of society as the greatest happiness of the greatest number. However, the radical subjectivism and autonomy of the will, the strong points of hedonism, are sacrificed by subjecting the individual to an external authority which is beyond question. The greatest happiness is an object which stands outside the individual (cf. Boucher, 1989: 78). Nonetheless, utilitarianism does have genuine philosophical value, although one-sided, in that it demonstrates that utility 'is one of the permanent and necessary categories of ethical thought' (Collingwood, 1923: 25; cited from Boucher, 1989: 79).

According to Boucher, therefore,

> In relation to the general philosophical aims of the two *Leviathans*, Collingwood was attempting to formulate a different criterion of conduct from that of Hobbes, one which he hoped would overcome the deficiencies of the subjectivist and objectivist traditions. We can, then, take the title of *The New Leviathan* to mean *new* in the sense that it would attempt to establish the criterion of moral conduct on a different foundation; namely on the idea of duty rather than upon the principle of utility (Boucher, 1989: 80).

In keeping with his dialectical conception of philosophy, Collingwood did not think that his project entailed refuting what Hobbes had argued. Collingwood argued in the 'Lectures on Moral Philosophy' that we do not refute philosophies, but continue them (cf. Boucher, 1989: 80).[17]

For Collingwood, the forms of practical reason, which, as we will see, are utility, right and duty, are related not as species of a genus, but as an overlapping series of forms in which the lower includes within itself the potential of the higher. Neither utility, nor right, nor duty is exclusive or autonomous, and each is a characteristic of all action. Moral goodness, or duty, contains in itself, as indispensable elements, the subordinate goods of utility and rightness (cf. Boucher, 1989: 30–1). According to Collingwood,

---

[17]   This is also consistent both with his distinction between dialectical and eristical discussion in *The New Leviathan*, which I will discuss in the next chapter, and with his argument on p.11 of *An Essay on Philosophical Method* that in philosophy we aim to know better something which in some sense we always knew.

Duty is thus the truth of action; it is what action really is, it is so far as we act morally that we really act at all. Yet in acting morally we do not rid ourselves of such distinctions as that of means and end, law and the application of law, any more than we shake ourselves free of the physical world or leave our animal nature behind us. Moral action includes all these things within itself, makes of them the material out of which it builds its own world (Collingwood, 1929: 142).

Collingwood's attempts to specify the character of action can be distinguished into two categories. First, as Boucher points out, corresponding to the earlier part of Collingwood's career, there are those accounts of action which wholly, or substantially, conform to the sequence, at the level of the rational will, of utility, duty, and absolute ethics. The second sequence with which Collingwood characterises the concept of action is that of utility, right and duty, and was not published in a fully articulated form until *The New Leviathan* (Boucher, 1989: 82). In the second sequence, utility is associated with economic action, right is associated with politics, and duty is associated with morality, the highest form of action.[18]

Both sequences demonstrate how at each successive level capriciousness is gradually eliminated.[19] Caprice, Collingwood explains, is '… mere choice or mere decision, uncomplicated by any reason why it should be made in this way and not that …' (NL, 13.12). Of the two categories of answers that Collingwood gave to the problems of moral philosophy, I will concentrate on the second, as it is here that Collingwood provides his mature account of duty. In the second sequence, unlike in the first, right and duty are distinguished, and duty now includes within itself what was characterised as absolute ethics in the first sequence.

[18] This is discussed in *An Autobiography*, pp. 148–9, and by Connelly (2003: 189–90).

[19] Boucher also provides an instructive analysis of how in both sequences the Hegelian dialectic becomes modified into a scale of forms analysis, a difference expressed by Croce. For Croce, Hegel's important contribution to philosophy was the formation of the concept as concrete universal, the development of the doctrine of degrees of reality as opposed to coordinate species of a genus, and the recognition that opposites are not opposed to unity. According to Boucher, 'Hegel's error lay in conflating the ideas of distincts and opposites, which led him to misconceive the relation between a concept and its contrary as the dialectic of opposite concepts, whereas, Croce argues, the distinct concept has within itself its own opposite. Therefore the relation between concepts is not that of contradiction, but of implication. Collingwood's idea of the concept as a fusion of differences in kind with differences in degree, and a fusion of opposites and distincts, owes more to Croce, it seems, than it does to Hegel. Collingwood denied the dialectic of opposites and conceived the philosophical concept as a series of distinct degrees, each of which implicates the others and includes its opposite within itself' (Boucher, 1989: 84).

As we have already seen, for Collingwood, there is an intimate relation between theory and practice. In *The New Leviathan*, he distinguishes between practical and theoretical reason: whereas practical thinking is to ask and answer questions about oneself, for example, 'why am I doing this?', theoretical thinking asks and answers questions about what is not oneself (NL, 18.1). However, concern with how things are in themselves, is interrelated with the problems of relations between the self and other things. All real thinking, then, '... starts from practice and returns to practice; for it is based on "interest" in the thing thought about; that is, on practical concern with it' (NL, 18.13). Theoretical reason, Collingwood argues, always includes within itself an element of practical reason, and our practical attitude towards something has a strong bearing upon our theoretical attitude towards it (NL, 18.2).

In the first sequence of answers which Collingwood gave to the problems of ethics, the practical form of reason, utility, had its theoretical counterpart in science; duty had its counterpart in history; and absolute ethics had its counterpoint in philosophy. The second category of answers postulates a different set of relations. Utility gave rise to the teleological view of nature, which was held by the Greeks. The medieval view of right as obedience to law gave rise to the theoretical view of nature in terms of law and conformity to law. Duty gave rise to history as its theoretical counterpart (cf. Boucher, 1989: 94). Crucially, then, each of the forms of practical reason and the corresponding forms of theoretical reason is associated, albeit roughly, with different stages in Western civilisation or culture. In so far as there has been a development from utility and right to duty and from an emphasis on natural science to an emphasis on history, this represents a gradual advancement in European civilisation.

According to Collingwood, the Greeks thought of their practical life in utilitarian terms, and therefore thought of the world about them in utilitarian terms. According to Greek science Nature had her ends and devised means to those ends. This teleological view of Nature has a rational basis, but depends also on irrationality and caprice. It was retained throughout the Middle Ages and Renaissance, and displaced in the sixteenth century (NL, 18.3–34).

Thinking in terms of right, or regularian thinking, Collingwood asserts, came to Europe through Roman law and Jewish religion. As a result, in the Middle Ages right took precedence over utility such that '... the business of man was not to achieve ends but to obey laws' (NL, 18.42). When people began to think of the world around them in the same way, modern science arose, and with it the idea of a 'law of nature' (NL, 18.44). Again, however, this concept of nature is not fully rational as it depends on a certain level of irrationality or caprice, which it calls 'brute fact' (NL, 18.45).

According to Collingwood, the idea of obligation or duty has existed since ancient times, but has slowly become disentangled from ideas of right and utility. When applied to the world at large, the idea of duty leads to history:

> The consciousness of duty means thinking of myself as an individual or unique agent, in an individual or unique situation, doing the individual or unique action that I have to do because it is the only one I can. To think historically is to think of a world consisting of things other than myself, each of them an individual or unique agent, in an individual or unique situation, doing an individual or unique action which he has to do because, charactered and circumstanced as he is, he can do no other. (NL, 18.52)

For Collingwood, in contemporary times the world of nature is no longer the primary object of study. The world of human affairs and history is central, and the problems of nature are only peripheral (NL, 18.8–92).[20]

The transition from utility and right to duty will now be explored in more detail. According to Collingwood, there are two kinds of choice: capricious choice and rational choice. In capricious choice the agent is conscious of choosing, but not of the reason for making the choice (NL, 13.12). In rational choice, on the other hand, the person who chooses is conscious of having reasons why this, rather than that, was chosen. Collingwood argues that European history reveals three types of rational choice, or practical reason.[21] That is, to the question 'why did you do that?' there are three possible answers: firstly, 'because it is useful', secondly, 'because it is right', and thirdly, 'because it is my duty' (NL, 14.63–68).

---

[20] According to Boucher, the culmination of theoretical reason in history in *The New Leviathan* suggests that Collingwood's rapprochement between philosophy and history is complete. I would suggest, however, that the rapprochement can never be regarded as 'complete', because, as I have already argued, in Collingwood's view philosophical thinking is an open-ended process of development without any particular end point. Hence, whereas Croce saw an identity between philosophy and history, Collingwood posited a rapprochement (cf. Peters, 1999: 10). Boucher, however, rightly criticises Rubinoff, who argued that Collingwood envisaged a philosophical ethic which would supersede the ethic of duty. As Boucher explains, Rubinoff is deceived by the fact that duty in *The New Leviathan* transcends the inadequacies of duty in *Speculum Mentis* (Boucher, 1989: 94–5).

[21] As we have already seen, practical reason, for Collingwood, is the original form of reason and theoretical reason is a modification of it (NL, 14.3).

The first kind of practical reason, utility, involves a distinction between means and end. The relation between means and end is one of logical priority, that is, of ground to consequent. In planning, the choice of end logically necessitates the choice of means. Conversely, in execution, the means logically necessitates the end (NL, 15.4–44). However, Collingwood explains, this implication of means by end in planning, and the converse implication of end by means in execution, is characteristic of every form of practical reason: 'In respect of its positive element utility is identical with rightness and duty' (NL, 15.51).

What distinguishes utility from rightness and duty is its negative aspect: the limits of its rationality, or what it fails to explain. For example, as Collingwood argues, if I go to the tobacco shop to buy tobacco, there are different ways of paying for the tobacco. The means of payment are left indeterminate. The choice of payment is made by what, from a utilitarian point of view, is caprice: in other words, something that the utilitarian point of view leaves unexplained. Similarly, the end is indeterminate: the plan to purchase tobacco cannot tell me which brand to buy (NL, 15.63–6). Furthermore, utility gives us no reason for choosing one end rather than another. Many things may be useful for quite different ends.[22]

Each utilitarian action, then, is '… an indefinite individual, required to satisfy certain specifications but free to vary so long as those specifications are satisfied' (NL, 15.72). Utility, in Collingwood's view, '… explains nothing except the abstract conformity of the means-plan with the abstract specifications of the end-plan' (NL, 15.8). Everything else is irrational, where irrational means what my principles of explanation do not explain.

Collingwood rejects the utilitarian contention that 'right' is only utility under another name, and that utility is the only form of practical reason. Right, he explains, is whatever is conformable to a rule (NL, 16.15). The 'right' key for a given lock is any key which obeys the rules governing the relations between lock-form and key-form (NL, 16.2–22). Something may be useful without being right. The wrong key, or a bent wire, may sometimes open a lock, but that does not make it the right key (NL, 16.24). A rule is a generalised purpose to do things of a certain kind on all occasions of a certain kind (NL, 16.31). As well as making a rule, regularian action includes the decision to obey the rule or to disobey it. Although it is often a social

---

[22] This point is explored in 'Monks and Morals' (EPP, 147–8) and discussed by Connelly (2003: 194).

thing, the simplest case of regularian action is making rules for oneself.

However, regularian explanations, like utilitarian explanations, are only partial. They cannot explain why a person does *this* particular act, only why he or she does an act of this kind, one of the alternative actions which satisfy the specifications of the rule (NL, 16.63). Furthermore, the same act may be both right and wrong, if it is judged by different rules. Collingwood cites Kant's example: if there is a rule to tell the truth, and another to save human life, what do you do when an intending murderer asks you where his intended victim is hiding? Different rules define different ways of living. One has to choose, from among many different rules that appear to be applicable, which to follow in one's own unique circumstances. Collingwood argues that

> Even the best-thought-out rules leave much to caprice and accident …. the rules you are trying to obey are hard enough to obey as it is; do not make them harder by attaching to them a degree of importance which no rule can ever have (NL, 16.77).

As Collingwood argues in *An Autobiography*, in acting according to rules we are moving among certain standard types of situations. But the existence of a rule means that a certain body of experience has been accumulated before the rule could be known to anyone (A, 103). There are two kinds of occasion on which it is necessary to act without rules. Firstly, '… you find yourself in a situation that you do not recognize as belonging to any of your known types. No rule can tell you how to act. But you cannot refrain from acting' (A, 103–4). You must improvise a way of handling it. The second kind of occasion on which you must act without rules is when you know a rule for dealing with the kind of situation that you are in, but '… you are not content with applying it, because you know that action according to rules always involves a certain misfit between yourself and your situation'. The rule '… comes between you and the situation it enables you to grasp' (A, 104; cf. Connelly, 2003: 199–200).

The inadequacies of utility and right are transcended in duty. 'Duty' refers to a logically prior act of incurring a debt (NL, 17.11–2). Collingwood explains that, etymologically, 'duty' and 'ought' mean the same thing: the idea of a debt incurred by one act and discharged by another act (NL, 17.16). One of the special characteristics of duty is that it admits of no alternatives. There is only one of it, and nothing else will do instead. It is my duty and nobody else's, in so far as it remains my duty, and it is a duty to do 'this' particular act, not 'an act of this kind'. There is a one-one relation between duty and its consequent. With utility and right, there is a many-one relation: there are many different alternatives. Hence, Collingwood argues, dutiful action is the only one of the three kinds of rational action that is completely rational in principle: the only one that fully explains (NL, 17.5–55).

The idea of duty, however, is an abstraction, and thus incompletely determinate. Consciousness of duty, or conscience, tells me that I am under an obligation but not what the obligation is. This is something that I discover by thinking through what the situation requires (NL, 17.59, cf. Connelly, 2003: 203). To the question 'what is my present duty?' one can only answer: 'I have considered x, y, and z as claimants for the title of my present duty: x is a better answer than either y or z; but there may be a better answer than any, which I have overlooked' (NL, 17.81). The question of what my duty is does not admit of a conclusive and unequivocal answer, only one which is '*morally* certain' (NL, 17.81).

Duty in general, then, is abstract, but

> 'my present duty' ... is a phrase which at any given time applies to only one thing or person ... and many different acts have been at different times my present duty (NL, 17.83).

Collingwood sums up his account of duty by asserting that

> A man's duty on a given occasion is the act which for him is both possible and necessary: the act which at that moment character and circumstance combine to make it inevitable, if he has a free will, that he should freely will to do (NL, 17.8).

For Collingwood, therefore, the ability to think of our actions in terms of duty constitutes a solution to the malaise of contemporary culture epitomised by utilitarianism and rule-based morality. In Collingwood's view, rule-based morality and its associated form of theoretical reason, natural science, are inadequate for human self-understanding: an inadequacy that is overcome by duty and historical thinking.

As Collingwood argued in his *Autobiography*, the growth of natural science and human control over nature contrasted starkly with a lack of power to control human situations (A, 91). Greater knowledge of human affairs would be provided by history, that is, a reformed scientific history and not 'scissors-and-paste' history, where the historian asks questions and interrogates the evidence and where the past which the historian studies in some sense still lives in the present (A, 96–7). Thus, Collingwood declares that

The reason why the civilization of 1600–1900, based upon natural science, found bankruptcy staring itself in the face was because, in its passion for ready-made rules, it had neglected to develop that kind of insight which alone could tell it what rules to apply, not in a situation of a specific type, but in the situation in which it actually found itself. It was precisely because history offered us something altogether different from rules, namely insight, that it could afford us the help we needed in diagnosing our moral and political problems (A, 101).

The ills of modernity are resolved by duty, or history as embodied in practical reason.

In Part Two, I explained that Collingwood responded to the crisis of civilisation by developing a dialectical logic, metaphysics and philosophy of history. Duty, then, is the practical aspect of this dialectical philosophy. This is a point that is made clear by Helgeby. Helgeby argues that Collingwood's logic of question and answer is ontological in that it must be seen in the context of his theory of action and agency (Helgeby, 1994: 97–8).[23] To answer a question adequately is to act from what Collingwood called 'duty'. According to Helgeby,

> Collingwood thought that duty is reason obligating action; our actions are conclusions to our arguments. The question we ask ourselves at any given time is which amongst our competing desires will we pursue. We eliminate our various options because they suit our interests less, or go against principles we follow. Beyond such considerations, we are conscious that there is one act which is necessitated by our conception of ourselves and our situation. This is what we choose. (Helgeby, 1994: 105)

In acting according to duty, Helgeby asserts, there are two sources of compulsion in our choice. Firstly, we choose to do the only thing we can do at the risk of no longer acting rationally. Secondly, we have to choose the only thing we can do at the risk of no longer being the person we have become. To do otherwise would be '… the most vicious form of insincerity' (Helgeby, 1994: 105). Hence, Collingwood's dialectical solution to the ill effects of the abstractions of modernity is given a more complete form in his theory of mind and practical reason. Thinking and acting according to duty means practising dialectical and historical thinking.

There are two aspects to duty in this context that particularly deserve attention. Firstly, there is a seeming paradox in duty,

[23] As Helgeby remarks, the remedy for the crisis of civilisation was '… the restoration of our capacity to express our emotions and desires, and the extension of our capacity to know ourselves. Collingwood's concern with religion and art were central to his first task; his concern with history, metaphysics and reasoned action were central to the second' (Helgeby, 1994: 100). See also Helgeby's *Action as History: The Historical Thought of R.G. Collingwood* (2004).

whereby it excludes freedom associated with caprice. Duty, as we have seen, allows no options and is completely determined by one's consciousness of obligation. But, as Boucher comments,

> Someone who is aware of what he, or she, has to do, with no alternative left open, is completely obliged only in so far as the person is consciously resolved to do his, or her, duty. The resolution is an act of free will, 'and hence the apparent absence of freedom is not a genuine absence of freedom' (Boucher, 1989: 105; NL, 472).

Boucher cites de Ruggiero's position in *The History of European Liberalism*:

> The really free man is not the man who can choose any line of conduct indifferently — this being rather a frivolous and weak-willed man — but the man who has the energy to choose that which is most conformable to his moral destiny ... the man who acts according to duty (de Ruggiero, 1959: 351–2; Boucher, 1989: 105n).[24]

As Boucher indicates, then, the highest forms of freedom and rationality, duty and history, include within themselves their own criterion (Boucher, 1989: 108). In this respect, Collingwood's conception of duty, like his dialectical reform of logic and metaphysics, is '... representative of the immanent, or rational will, tradition' (Boucher, 1989: 109).[25]

The second point that deserves emphasis is that Collingwood's conception of duty transcends conventional notions of morality based upon rules and draws upon the Romantic idea of authenticity. Authentic action, as I argued in Part One, occurs when one makes decisions for oneself and is not determined by external influences. Each of us has an original way of being human and being true to ourselves, something which only each individual can articulate and discover.[26]

---

[24]   This also overlaps with the conception of freedom held by Ortega y Gasset, which will be discussed further on. The view of freedom here is developed in detail by de Ruggiero, particularly in pp. 351–57 of *The History of European Liberalism* (1959).

[25]   This is also apparent in the 1929 Lectures on Moral Philosophy, where Collingwood argues that 'Duty lies beyond the distinction of right and wrong, because that distinction assumes the existence of rules, and duty goes behind this assumption and takes upon itself the task of making and unmaking all rules except the one formal rule that rules must exist' (Collingwood, 1929: 132). Hence: 'It is the really moral man who cannot help being moral. His complete subjection to the law of duty is the measure of his complete command of the situation and of himself ... This is because at the level of duty all otherness between the mind and itself has disappeared, or rather has been transfused with identity' (Collingwood, 1929: 140–1).

[26]   Here I draw upon Taylor (1991: 27–9).

In the 1929 Lectures on Moral Philosophy, Collingwood explains that morality, or duty, means facing the responsibility of life lived by your own decisions: 'This responsibility means that you are responsible for your life, not to anyone else, but to yourself, in your capacity as judge of your own actions, the only judge from whose decision there can be no appeal' (Collingwood, 1929: 146). One respects others in the same way as one respects oneself, and self-respect, Collingwood asserts,

> … is at least a clearer approximation to the true nature of morality than anything depending upon right and wrong, praise and blame, and the other categories of moral life. The fact is that when we come face to face with the deepest problems of action these everyday moral terms lose their force and seem irrelevant to the realities of the problem. To classify actions into right and wrong, to praise people or to blame them for what they do, when one is face to face with things that really matter, is to amuse oneself with toys. No doubt the occasions on which one breaks through the tissue of ordinary moral life, with its conventions and assumptions and concealments, are comparatively rare: but we know very well when we do so, that these are the only occasions on which we are conscious of ourselves as really acting. (Collingwood, 1929: 147)

Therefore, 'The way in which we try to determine our course of action is by a resolute clearing of our vision, in order to see ourselves as we actually are' (Collingwood, 1929: 147). When we see ourselves truly, we have overcome the enemy against which we were fighting:

> The enemy is nothing else than the tissue of illusions which forms the practical life of our everyday world: pleasure, satisfaction, expediency, right, benevolence and all the other things that pass for moral principles because we are too listless to probe through them to the reality which in less vivid moments they conceal from us. For it is a great mistake to think that only our bodily appetites and openly selfish passions stand between us and genuine moral action. We are far more likely to be seduced by the idea of doing good to people, or of regulating our lives according to the best rules, than by any sensuous temptations. (Collingwood, 1929: 148)

At this point, Collingwood's theory of duty as the practical aspect of his dialectical solution to the crisis of civilisation, with its concurrence of freedom and determination and its affinity with the Romantic idea of authenticity, can be further illuminated by a comparison with Ortega y Gasset.[27] Collingwood's theory of duty, I suggest, closely corresponds to Ortega's conception of 'destiny'.

---

[27] More generally, Mink compares Collingwood's conception of duty to existentialism. Mink points out that what morality proper, or duty, affirms is that intentional action is always one act, not merely because of what one is, but also in or-

As I indicated in Part Two, the comparison of Collingwood with Ortega helps to situate Collingwood's philosophical concern with the crisis of Western civilisation in the context of the development of 'historicism' in the twentieth century. According to Ortega, as we have seen, like Collingwood, European civilisation is confronted by a crisis due to the predominance of naturalism and a static conception of being, which we have inherited from the Greeks. The solution to this predicament is the development of dialectical and historical reason. For Ortega, 'destiny' is a practical aspect of historical reason.

For Ortega, like Collingwood therefore, there is a dialectical relation between theory and practice, and between historical thought and practical reason. All thought begins with and returns to practice. In *Man and People* Ortega argues that man gradually transforms his environment, imposes himself on nature, and humanises it. There are three different moments, which are repeated throughout human history, in forms each time more complex and rich:

> 1. Man feels himself lost, shipwrecked among things; this is *alteracion*.
> 2. Man, by an energetic effort, withdraws into himself to form ideas about things and possible ways of dominating them; this is being within one's self, *ensimismamiento*, the *vita contemplativa* of the Romans, the *theoretikos bios* of the Greeks, *theory*. 3. Man again submerges himself in the world, to act in it according to a preconceived plan; that is action, *vita activa*, *praxis*.
>
> Accordingly *it is impossible to speak of action except in so far as it will be governed by a previous contemplation; and vice versa, contemplation, or being within one's self, is nothing but a projecting of future action.* (Ortega's italics; MP, 23)

---

der to become what one is not. Such a self-creative choice is a situation which comes into being and is constituted only as it is consciously affirmed, and 'It is at this point that Collingwood comes closest to the view of human nature which has been given currency in modern existentialism, but with a difference' (Mink, 1969: 91). Collingwood is more 'radically dialectical' than any existentialist: 'For an existentialist like Sartre, consciousness or *l'être-pour-soi* is completely cut off from the causal nexus of nature, although it evades the anxiety of total responsibility for its own self-creation by inventing pathological forms of in-authenticity in which it regards itself as a "thing", a determinate outcome of causal forces in its own past and in its contemporary world' (Mink, 1969: 91). Sartre posits a dichotomy of physical nature and human consciousness. For Collingwood, on the other hand, fourth-level consciousness is not an intrusion into the causal nexus of the natural world: 'It emerges from that world, to which it remains forever attached through its bodily processes and activities, and the level of all the lower levels of consciousness survive at higher levels. But as consciousness at lower levels reflects the world, at higher levels it transforms and expands it .... The freedom of consciousness is not "absolute" freedom; it is the freedom of men who are creatures of feeling, appetite, and desire as well as the creators of mind' (Mink, 1969: 91–2).

Thus for Ortega, action is '... not a random fisticuffs with the things around us' (MP, 29). Instead:

> *Action* is to act upon the environment of material things or of other men in accordance with a plan preconceived in a previous period of meditation or thought. There is no genuine action if there is no thought, and there is no authentic thought if it is not duly referred to action and made virile by its relation to action (MP, 29).[28]

To return to Ortega's account of 'destiny', then, in *The Revolt of the Masses*, Ortega asserts that 'All life is the struggle, the effort to be itself' (RM, 99). In a world where there is a superabundance of resources the average person may lose contact with the reality of life and think that he or she can do what he or she likes. But, Ortega contends,

> It is not that one *ought* not to do just what one pleases; it is simply that one cannot do other than what each of us *has* to do, *has* to be ... We can quite well turn away from our true destiny, but only to fall a prisoner in the deeper dungeons of our destiny (RM, 103).

For example, regarding those parts of destiny that are shared in common, Ortega explains that

> ... the European of today *must* be a liberal .... the most reactionary of Europeans knows, in the depths of his conscience, that the effort made by Europe in the nineteenth century, under the name of liberalism, is, in the last resort, something inevitable, inexorable; something that Western man today *is*, whether he likes it or no (RM, 103).

Whereas theoretical truths owe their meaning to being discussed and disputed,

> ... destiny — what from a vital point of view one has to be or has not to be — is either accepted or rejected. If we accept it, we are genuine; if not, we are the negation, the falsification of ourselves. Destiny does not consist in what we feel we should like to do; rather is it recognised in its clear features in the consciousness that we *must* do what we do not feel like doing (RM, 104).

Ortega adds that

> Abasement, degradation is simply the manner of life of the man who has refused to be what it is his duty to be. This, his genuine being, none the less does not die; rather is changed into an accusing shadow, a phantom which constantly makes him feel the inferiority of the life he lives com-

---

[28] Ortega contends that this true relation between contemplation and action has been persistently ignored, from the Greeks onwards. The Greeks believed that man's destiny was solely to exercise his intellect, and this doctrine of 'intellectualism' is something that we have inherited and continued with the Enlightenment and Idealism (MP, 30 and 47).

pared with the one he ought to live. The debased man survives his self-inflicted death (RM, 104n).

As is the case with Collingwood's conception of duty, for Ortega, the highest form of freedom excludes the freedom associated with caprice. The human being, Ortega asserts in *Man and People*, is '... free before and in the face of his destiny. He can accept it or resist it, or, what is the same thing, he can be it or not be it' (MP, 133). Our destiny is not only the past, but '... projects itself, in openness, toward the future' (MP, 133). We are not predetermined by our past, but freedom presupposes plans of action, and in creating them the past is 'the guiding thread of our inspirations'. Hence, 'destiny directs, it does not drag' (MP, 133). We cannot escape maintaining continuity with the past, even if we make a plan to negate it and do the opposite of what has been done (MP, 134). As Ouimette points out, then, for Ortega, human life is an endless series of actions intended to give man freedom to be himself in total authenticity (Ouimette, 1982: 116).

In terms of the attempt to respond to the rationalism of modernity by transcending a conventional rule-based morality with an account of action as historical and concrete, Collingwood and Ortega have an affinity with Nietzsche. According to Nietzsche, one must 'become what one is' (cf. Hinz, 1994a: 51–2) and this, I suggest, coincides with Collingwood's idea of duty whereby one acts according to the unique details of one's situation.

In *Beyond Good and Evil* Nietzsche asserts that it is a sign of nobility '... never to think of degrading our duties into duties for everybody; not to want to relinquish or share our own responsibilities; to count our privileges and the exercising of them among our *duties*' (Nietzsche's italics; Nietzsche, 1990: 272). Tanner, in his Introduction to *Beyond Good and Evil*, indicates that Nietzsche's distinction between those who are used to obeying and those who are used to commanding can be equated with the distinction between those who regard values as imposed, external and universal in their application and those who regard values as coming from within, created by those who are powerful enough for the task, and who delight in their sense of being different from others (Tanner, 1990: 23).[29] According to Nietzsche, 'The noble type of man feels *himself* to be the determiner

[29]   Nietzsche, Tanner points out, saw the Germans as highly advanced examples of slave morality, partly because of their delight in obeying the laws of the Reich and partly because of Kantian morality and the 'categorical imperative', a law founded in reason alone and equally applicable to all rational beings (Tanner, 1990: 24). Adherence to both of them results in the total legalisation of life. In

of values, he does not need to be approved of, he judges "what harms me is harmful in itself", he knows himself to be that which in general first accords honour to things, he *creates values*' (Nietzsche, 1990: 260).

In a book review for *Oxford Magazine* in 1918, Collingwood refers to Nietzsche's 'two-fold relation to Christianity' and

> ... his striking reaffirmation of Christian ethics,[30] in their conception of the tragic nature of life and the uselessness of code morality, as against the utilitarianism, the bourgeois respectability, the 'sofa-millennium', of his age ... (Collingwood, 2001: 146).

Collingwood's own later critique of the 'uselessness of code morality' and his development of the theory of duty originated in a romantic and historicist response to the crisis of Western civilisation, where Nietzsche played an important role.

As I have already argued, however, Collingwood, unlike Nietzsche, provides a reason-based solution to the crisis of Western civilisation and one which emerges from within the Western tradition. This difference between Collingwood and Nietzsche is particularly evident in Collingwood's insistence on the use of the word 'morality' to describe authentic action:

> I admit that morality is a bad name for absolute action, because morality very often seems to mean doing what other people think respectable because one is afraid of offending them; but if that is what morality means, we have already dealt with it under the head of economic action, for it is merely a case of expediency. I admit that duty is a bad name for it, because duty seems to mean blind obedience to rules traditionally received and obeyed in a spirit of gloomy loyalty; but if that is what duty means it is only a somewhat low and slavish form of political action. But it would be treason to the ideas of morality and duty to acquiesce in these degradations of them. When we consider the analysis of duty given by Kant, for instance, or the account of morality expressed by Spinoza, we see that no conception short of absolute action is adequate to contain the wealth of meaning and the depth of moral experience which these accounts contain. (Collingwood, 1929: 149)

Although Collingwood was critical of Kant in *The New Leviathan*, Kantian rule-based morality, along with the rest of the history of

---

such a context art is seen as a relief from serious things in life, and the great artist is reduced to the level of a great sportsman (Tanner, 1990: 25).

[30] Collingwood's claim that, in spite of Nietzsche's real anti-Christianity, 'In much that he says, Nietzsche is profoundly Christian ...' (Collingwood, 2001: 146) is consistent with the views of Nietzsche commentators: for example, R.J. Hollingdale's Introduction to the 1969 edition of *Thus Spoke Zarathustra*.

Western moral philosophy, is assimilated and transcended in Collingwood's philosophy, rather than wholly rejected.

In conclusion, then, Collingwood's view is that European civilisation progresses if we think dialectically and historically. Collingwood's solution to the crisis of abstract rationalism in practical reason was the development of an account of duty as concrete and historical, and this was the practical aspect of his solution to the crisis of civilisation in terms of a dialectical and historical philosophy.

Collingwood's dialectical philosophy, however, not only manifests itself in a historical morality, but also in a dialectical account of society and the state. His critique of the abstractions of modernity entails a reform of social contract theory, which will be examined in the next chapter. The way in which this dialectical theory of morality and society resolves particular manifestations of cultural crisis, relating to the role of capitalism and bureaucratic administration, will be explained in the final chapter.

Chapter Nine

The Politics of Dialectic

Collingwood's view, evident in his theory of logic and metaphysics and his account of morality as duty, that the advancement of civilisation depends on dialectical thinking and historical self-consciousness becomes further elucidated in his social and political theory. By the mid-1930s Collingwood's concern for the future of civilisation became accentuated by the rise of fascism and the undermining of liberalism. In order to combat this threat he sought to expound the fundamental principles[1] of a liberal society and civilisation, and this culminated in *The New Leviathan*.

Liberalism, according to Collingwood, meant

> ... the dialectical solution of all political problems: that is, their solution through the statement of opposing views and their free discussion until, beneath this opposition, their supporters have discovered some common ground on which to act (EPP, 177).

Accordingly, liberalism actively sought to foster the free expression of political opinions, and government would draw strength from the enlightened and co-operative criticism of its people (EPP, 177–8). In his *Autobiography*, Collingwood asserted that fascism meant '... the end of clear thinking and the triumph of irrationalism' (A, 167), and his account of society and politics in *The New Leviathan* was explicitly intended as a response to this irrationalism.

It seems that, in writing *The New Leviathan*, Collingwood was inspired by C.E.M. Joad's exhortation to return to the classical tradi-

---

[1] In this respect, it may be said that Collingwood's theory of politics and civilisation in *The New Leviathan* includes a metaphysics, or a history of our absolute presuppositions, concerning politics and civilisation and how they have been modified since the times of Hobbes and Locke. This is indicated by Connelly (2003: 76).

tion in philosophy to combat the crisis of civilisation (EPP, 196). But whereas Joad thought that Plato and Aristotle exemplified the classical tradition, Collingwood refers to Hobbes, Locke and Rousseau as classical (cf. Boucher, 1989: 142). The 'classical politics', the theory of politics put forward by Hobbes, and restated with minor differences by Locke and Rousseau, is not a definitive and final statement on the topic of political life, but it is classical in that every beginner in the subject must start with it (NL, 31.23).

Collingwood turned to the classical tradition in political theory, or social contract theory, because it emphasised the fact that society is created though the free-will of agents. Social contract theory recognises that the body politic is based not upon force, but authority (NL, xli). As Collingwood indicates, Hobbes' *Leviathan* demonstrates that society is but an 'artificial man' (NL, lix). However, for Collingwood, as I will explain in the course of this chapter, social contract theory is not fully adequate to respond to the irrationalism that threatens contemporary civilisation, and therefore it must be modified and extended in important ways.

The 'classical politics', Collingwood argues, is a product of the same seventeenth-century notion of scientific method as the 'classical physics' of Galileo and Newton (NL, 31.24). Like all modern sciences, it is based on *the principle of the limited objective*, according to which instead of trying to interpret every fact, one selects the facts that call for immediate attention and the rest are left to wait (NL, 31.61–68). Following *the principle of the limited objective*, the theorists of the classical politics limited their explanatory efforts to facts that could be explained by the idea of society (NL, 31.81). They drew their idea of society from the Roman idea of *societas*, which comes into existence through a 'social contract', or an agreement between persons of free will. Classical politics could use the Roman law of society only because partnership was a thing with which its authors were familiar, from the 'bourgeois' life of medieval and post-medieval Europe (NL, 31.9–93).

According to Collingwood, classical politics sees political life as a dialectic with two ends: 'society' and 'nature' (NL, 32.21–2). Society is the part of political life which consists in agreement between mentally adult persons for the purposes of joint action. What 'nature' is, classical politics does not describe in positive terms: it is the element in political life which is not society (NL, 32.23). On this view, political life is dynamic or dialectical, where what was not society is converted into society. Human beings who hitherto did not possess free will must be educated up to mental maturity by those who possess free will. They are educated out of the 'state of nature' and into the 'state of civil society' (NL, 32.27–32). Rousseau is seen as expressing this idea more clearly than any of the other classical political theorists, and as recognising that '... the work done in the council chamber is to recruit itself, with all that this implies. The life of politics is the life of political education' (NL, 32.34).

The classical political theorists did not expect the state of nature to vanish and be wholly superseded by a social condition. Hobbes pointed out that even in a civil society people remain in certain respects in the state of nature. Also Hobbes observed that progress is not inevitable and that the process of political life is reversible. The social element in a community may regress into the non-social (NL, 32.44). In Collingwood's view, however, the deficiency of classical social contract theory was that it did not achieve a theory of the non-social community and give a positive meaning to the phrase 'state of nature' (NL, 33.18). As Boucher indicates,

> The theorists of the classical politics, in acknowledging the perpetual danger of regression, merely postponed rather than eliminated the necessity for a theory of the non-social community (Boucher, 1989: 145).

Rousseau confusedly asserted that man is born free and everywhere found in chains (NL, 33.18). Collingwood responds that, in contrast to the abstractions of 'human nature', the facts of human infancy are a safer foundation for a science of human community:

> A man is born a red and wrinkled lump of flesh having no will of its own at all, absolutely at the mercy of the parents by whose conspiracy he has been brought into existence. That is what no science of human community, social or non-social, must ever forget (NL, 23.96–7).

Contrary to Rousseau, Collingwood agreed with de Ruggiero and Green that freedom was an achievement, and not an innate attribute of human life. According to de Ruggiero,

> Men are not born free, they become free by means of society and the State ... This is the great distinction between the liberal conceptions of the eighteenth and nineteenth centuries. The one places liberty at the beginning, the other at the end, of the historical process (de Ruggiero, 1959: 32).

As Boucher explains, Collingwood's account of the development of freedom echoed that of the British and Italian idealists. For most of the British and Italian Idealists, the development of freedom was correlative with the development of liberalism in Europe, that is, it made its greatest strides in the latter half of the nineteenth century and in the early part of the twentieth. Liberalism was not equated with economic freedom and was compatible with many measures that abstract theorists may classify as socialist (Boucher, 1989: 147).

Liberalism, according to the Italian and British idealists, is opposed to the authoritarian kind of socialism, or that which impedes the development of the freedom of the will. For them, the individualism of classical liberalism had given way to a more organic conception of society in which the antinomy of individualism and authority is resolved. Hence de Ruggiero argues that liberalism's hostility to the state has diminished as the state has become more capable of synthetically expressing the varied interests in society. The state has become conscious of its duty to broaden and strengthen the energies of individuals and of their free and voluntary associations. As Boucher points out, therefore,

> Collingwood's own account of the development of the freedom of the will and its gradual elimination of capriciousness is a theoretical and extended articulation of de Ruggiero's point that freedom is an achievement rather than an endowment (Boucher, 1989: 149).

According to Collingwood, then, classical social contract theory is deficient as an account of society. In order to combat both the abstract rationalism that undermines human self-understanding and irrationalism (of which fascism was a prime example), Collingwood found it necessary, as I will now illustrate, to overcome the inadequacies of social contract theory in a dialectical account of liberalism.[2]

Collingwood's dialectical account of liberalism involves a distinction between society and community. The word 'society' in modern European languages is borrowed from the vocabulary of Roman law. Society, or *societas*, is a relation between *personae*, that is, people who are capable of free will and joint action, and comes into existence through a 'social contract', which is a simple agreement of will between two *personae*. Both the Roman and the modern use of the word 'society' try to safeguard the idea that a contract must be the joint activity of free agents (NL, 19.5–58). Variations of the term society that disregard the idea of free will are dismissed as being perversions of its true meaning. In its 'true and proper sense', society is constituted by free activity on the part of its members (NL, 19.11 and 19.81).

A community, on the other hand, is a state of affairs in which something is divided or shared by a number of human beings. A

---

[2]   As Boucher remarks, the lack of a theory of the non-social community is not only a defect of the classical politics: it is also a defect of liberalism (Boucher, 1989: 154).

society is a kind of community where the members share a social consciousness or a will (NL, 20.12–2). Social consciousness, Collingwood explains, is an act of deciding to become a member and go on being a member:

> A society or partnership is constituted by the social will of the partners, an act of free will whereby the person who thereby becomes a partner decides to take upon himself a share in a joint enterprise (NL, 20.22).

Although every society is a community, a community may exist that has not yet become a society, that is, a non-social community (NL, 20.31–2). In every community something is divided among the members, and everybody gets their share. The establishment and maintenance of this allotment of shares is called ruling. Whereas a society is a self-ruling community, a non-social community needs for its existence to be ruled by something other than itself (NL, 20.34–36).

Something capable of ruling itself may sometimes give authority to something else to rule over it. For example, B is a surgeon who undertakes to remove C's appendix. He receives authority to do so from A, which is the society of which B and C are members. The decision to take out the appendix is a joint decision of the surgeon and patient, where the patient is adult and of a sound mind (NL, 20.45–47). If the patient is a child, the decision is taken by the surgeon and the patient's parent. From the child's point of view, the removal of the appendix is an act of force (NL, 20.49). For Collingwood, 'force' in a social or political context always means 'moral force' or relative mental strength: 'When a man suffers force the origin of the force is always something within himself, some irresistible emotion which makes him do something he does not intend to do' (NL, 20.59).

The idea of oneself as having a will is correlative to the idea of something other than oneself as having a will (NL, 21.14). Collingwood insists that the individual will only emerges in the context of the recognition of other wills (cf. McIntyre, 1996: 121). He declares:

> No man has any idea of himself as a free agent, without an idea of free agents other than himself and of social relations between them. No man has an accurate idea of himself as a free agent without an accurate idea of free agents other than himself and of social relations between them (NL, 21.19).

As McIntyre indicates, then, contrary to foundational social contract theory, Collingwood claims that free will is not constitutive of society, but develops only within a pre-existing society (McIntyre, 1996: 121).

The development of free will, or the conversion of a non-social community into a society, is never complete. Something of the non-social element always remains, out of which society develops (NL, 21.5–55). The law of primitive survivals, therefore, which operates in relation to the development of mind, also pertains to societies (cf. Connelly, 2003: 214–5). As Boucher demonstrates, this complements Collingwood's argument in the 'Fairy Tales' manuscript (1936–37), according to which modern societies retain traces of the primitive societies out of which they grew. Thus, in order to understand our own culture, we must 'face the savage within us' (Boucher, 1989: 156).

Whereas authority and initiative are an important part of social life, in a non-social community there is force instead of authority (NL, 21.7–72). In a non-social community, A forces B to do something by promise of reward or threat of punishment. The first arouses an irresistible desire in B, the second an irresistible fear. If B is sufficiently foolish he or she can be controlled by an insincere promise, or fraud, that is, '… a special form of force specially adapted for use against fools' (NL, 21.74). Reward and punishment, Collingwood asserts, are useless against people of free will.

The exercise of force is either voluntary or involuntary. If it is involuntary, the slave-driver sinks to the mental level of the slaves he or she drives, and the exercise of force, or the 'corrupting influence of power', undermines a person's will. According to Collingwood, 'Slave-driving is compatible with freedom only if the slave-driver retains the conviction of his own freedom by consorting with other men whom he recognizes as free' (NL, 21.76). The idea of oneself as a free agent can only be retained by discussing one's intentions on equal terms with one's equals.

A free agent may be unable to prevent a certain passion or desire from taking charge, and his or her will may be said to 'crack' (NL, 21.81). If this occurrence is sufficiently widespread, a society may break down into the non-social community out of which it has arisen. As a last resort against this, societies use criminal law. Accordingly, a person whose will has cracked is forcibly prevented from impeding the other members of the society from living socially or politically. Crime, then, is an action by one member of a society prejudicial to the pursuit of the self-appointed task of the society as a whole and by lapsing into criminality a person ceases to function as a member of society (NL, 21.84–88).

Collingwood points out that 'Most communities, if not all, are mixed communities ...' (NL, 22.11). As an example, he discusses the family. One part of a family is a society, and the other part is a non-social community. The nursery is a non-social community because the children do not join it of their own free will; they are drafted into it when they are too young to consent. If nurseries are to exist, there must be nurses to run it and parents to replenish it. In the simplest and commonest case, the 'typical family', the same persons discharge both functions (NL, 22.1–19). When children reach physical and mental maturity, they become able to fend for themselves, to have their own children and organise them into a nursery (NL, 22.28). In so-called 'savage' life puberty marks the end of childhood and the initiation into adulthood. Because European life is more complicated, the educational or nursery period is longer (NL, 22.31–3).

According to European ideas, marriage is a social contract whereby a man and woman become partners in the enterprise of producing children (NL, 22.34). A marriage which entails the production of children passes through three phases. Firstly, before any children are conceived, the family is a society working at turning itself into a mixed community. In the second phase the family has transformed itself into a mixed community consisting of a social nucleus of parents and a non-social community of children. The children are engaged in growing up and the parents in helping them to do so. In the third phase the children have grown up to the point of possessing free will, and are incorporated into the family-society (NL, 23.22–8).

According to Collingwood, modern Europeans today think of marriage as having the aim of producing children. Prior to the widespread knowledge and use of contraceptives, the aim of marriage was seen as being the gratification of sexual desire, with the procreation of children as a consequence of this. Knowledge of contraceptives means that most people only have children when they do so of their own free will (NL, 23.48–52).

Children, as members of the non-social family community, are incorporated into the family society, on reaching maturity. In order to reach this stage, a process of education is carried out partly by the child upon itself, and partly by others upon it. The educative process must always hold out the promise of future incorporation into the society. In the family the parents have to make it clear to the child from an early age that he, or she, will be welcomed as an equal as the signs of mental maturity become manifest. This is an aspect of the child's education that parents cannot delegate (NL, 23.62–4; cf. Boucher, 1989: 157).

Collingwood's account of the family as a mixed community prepares the ground for his discussion of the body politic. Collingwood contends that the Greeks saw the body politic as a society of citizens corporately ruling themselves, with non-citizen dependants, such as wives, children and slaves; whereas in the Middle Ages it was regarded as a non-social community, a human herd ruled by strong men (NL, 24.5). Hobbes said that the body politic is both. It changes out of one and into the other. The medieval account of it represents the starting point, and the Greek account the finishing point. It is always moving between these two points.

In Collingwood's view, history records a process whereby a Greek social body politic has turned into a medieval non-social body politic, and from that to a new social kind of body politic, the 'bourgeois' life of the medieval and post-medieval age. Similarly, in political theory, the Greek theory of political life as the theory of a social body politic has turned into the medieval theory of a non-social body politic, and that again into the conception of the 'bourgeoisie' as the root of all princely authority (NL, 24.51–3).

According to Collingwood, 'We are in a world where nothing stays put, but everything moves; the things we say must move, too, in the same rhythm as the things we are talking about' (NL, 24.55). He refers to Plato's distinction between two kinds of discussions: 'eristical' and 'dialectical'. An eristic discussion is one in which each party tries to prove that he was right and the other wrong, whereas:

> In a dialectical discussion you aim at showing that your own view is one with which your opponent really agrees, even if at one time he denied it; or conversely that it was yourself and not your opponent who began by denying a view with which you really agree (NL, 24.58–9).

Plato's belief in the superiority of dialectical discussion, Collingwood asserts, rested on his assumption that there is a dialectic in things. He followed Heraclitus' idea that everything moves and nothing stays still (NL, 24.61–62). A Heraclitean world is a world of change where the positive term in a pair of contradictories is gradually gaining on the negative term. What was not-*x* is turning into *x*. It is like a pot of black paint in which you are mixing more and more white: 'The paint was never either pure black or pure white; it is always turning into a paler and paler grey. And if you settle upon any standard of light-greyness with which at any moment it conforms, you must be ready to give up as a standard which by now has been left behind. This readiness to give up something which at a certain time you settled upon as true is dialectical thinking' (NL, 24.64–5).

For example, the same community could be described as a society or a non-social community, by attending to different elements. But this is only a difference in 'point of view': a dialectical difference (NL, 24.67). As Collingwood explains,

> According to Hobbes … a body politic is a dialectical thing, a Heraclitean world in which at any given time there is a negative element, an element of non-sociality which is going to disappear, or at least is threatened with abolition by the growth of the positive element; and a positive element, an element of sociality (NL, 24.68).

Just as in families children grow up and are incorporated into the family-society: 'By a dialectic of the same kind the subjects in a body politic grow up into sharing the work of rule' (NL, 24.75).

Collingwood attempts to summarise his account of the body politic in what he calls 'the three laws of politics'. Firstly, a body politic is divided into a ruling class and a ruled class. Secondly, the barrier between the two classes is permeable in an upward sense. Members of the ruled class must be susceptible of promotion into the ruling class. Thirdly, there is a correspondence between the ruler and the ruled (NL, 25.7–9). For example, vigorous rulers teach the ruled to develop a vigorous political life: 'Here the freedom whereby the rulers rule percolates, owing simply to the process of ruling, without any intention that it shall do so, downwards through the strata of the body politic' (NL, 25.94). On the other hand, if the rulers are slavish, what will percolate is slavishness:

> In Plato's *Republic* the tyrant is not a skilful and determined politician who seizes power for himself, but a piece of flotsam floating on the political waves he pretends to control, shoved passively into power by the sheer lowness of its own specific gravity. This is quite possible by the inverse working of the third law of politics. Hitler, referring to Plato's sense of the word 'democracy', claims to be a democratic ruler. He claims that he has been, so to speak, ejected by the automatic working of a mob, which elevates to a position of supremacy over itself whatever is most devoid of free will, whatever can be entirely trusted to do what is dictated by the desires which the mob feels (NL, 25.95–8).

Hence, according to the three laws of politics, although the ruling class rules over the ruled class by means of force, the relationship between them cannot merely be based on force. The rulers prepare the ruled for rule by providing exemplars that the ruled will be inspired to follow. Such inspiration will affect only those who have almost reached the level of free will. This requires cooperation rather than confrontation, a dialectical rather than an eristical or adversarial relationship (cf. Boucher, 1989: 160–61).

Connelly rightly points out that Collingwood's conception of the ruling class can be interpreted in two different ways. Sometimes the term 'ruling class' appears to mean those who happen to be rulers in relation to a particular political problem, and at other times it appears to mean those who by virtue of being capable of self-rule are eligible as members of the ruling class. In one sense the ruling class is coextensive with society, and in another sense it is not. Connelly decides that it is best to restrict the term 'ruling class' to the former meaning and distinguishes between the 'ruling class' and 'society' (Connelly, 2003: 221–2). I suggest, however, that the alternative interpretation is at least as valid. If we take the term 'ruling class' to designate a wider group of people than those working in the formal institutions of government (and roughly equate the ruling class with society), this allows for some illuminating comparisons with Ortega y Gasset, which I will discuss further on in this chapter.

In Collingwood's view, then, democracy and aristocracy, properly understood, are not hostile to each other, but mutually complementary. Thinking that every member of a body politic should rule is 'doctrinaire democracy'. Forgetting that the function of ruling must be a function in any body politic, that a body politic must rule itself, is 'doctrinaire aristocracy' (NL, 26.1–12). Democracy and aristocracy give partial answers to the question: 'how shall we make the ruling class as strong as possible?' Democracy answers: 'By enlarging it so far as possible. By recruiting into it, to discharge one or other function, every member of the ruled class who may constitute an addition to its strength'. Aristocracy answers: 'By restricting it so far as is needful. By excluding from its membership everyone who does not or would not increase its strength' (NL, 26.14–15). In the dialectical process of recruitment of a ruling class, democracy and aristocracy are positive and negative elements in that process. When the two elements are considered in false abstraction from this dialectical process, and then considered eristically as two competing views, what follows is 'doctrinaire democracy' and 'doctrinaire aristocracy' (NL, 26.16–17). No pure democracy or pure aristocracy has ever existed. Every body politic is composed of a ruling class and a ruled class. The ruling class may contain persons not capable of ruling, who need to be excluded, and the ruled class may contain persons capable of ruling, but debarred from it on frivolous grounds, who need to be promoted (NL, 26.23–27).

Collingwood contends that political thought in the nineteenth century allowed itself to be dazzled by the French Revolution and failed to apprehend its continuity with the long historical process out of which it had grown. The word 'revolution' had been borrowed towards the end of the seventeenth century by the vocabulary of politics from the vocabulary of literary criticism (NL, 26.7–71). This indicated and perpetuated a superficial concept of history, as it implies that history normally flows uniformly in a straight line, then it waggles and you are surprised (NL, 26.75–6). Thus, for Collingwood, 'If a twentieth-century reader of history came to an incident that surprised him, he would know what to call it. He would call it a piece of bad history: something his author had failed to explain' (NL, 26.77).

The word 'revolution' has no scientific significance, therefore, only an emotional one:

> It means an event whereby the mighty are put down from their seat and the humble and meek exalted. It is uttered, if you are one of the mighty, with intent to freeze your blood; if you are one of the humble and meek, to give you opium-dreams of coming felicity (NL, 26.82).

Misled by the false view of 'revolution' in general, and the French Revolution in particular, nineteenth-century observers thought that democracy had defeated aristocracy and established itself as the only political system rational in theory and tolerable in practice. But the dialectical process of political life had not come to an end: both democratic and aristocratic elements had been present in the French and American revolutions (NL, 26.9–92).

Hence political life, like family life, contains an indispensable element of force. Children have to be looked after without their consent, and similarly the ruled, so far as they are not capable of ruling themselves, must be ruled without their consent (NL, 27.1–13). This involves the use of force and fraud. Force and fraud on the part of the rulers is necessary if it is for the good of the ruled or for the facilitation of ruling (NL, 27.21–29). However, Collingwood explains, force and fraud are used by a capable ruler only upon those of his subjects most backward in political education. For the less childish, they are differentially replaced by 'induction' and other forms of partial and progressive sharing in the liberty of the ruler (NL, 27.38). The principle of aristocracy is the principle of force, and the principle of democracy is the principle of self-government (NL, 27.47).

According to Collingwood, throughout the history of Europe the democratic principle and the aristocratic principle have always been positive and negative elements in the dialectical process of recruiting to and excluding from the ruling class (NL, 27.5). However, in the nineteenth century, there arose the idea that democracy and aristocracy were in an eristical and not a dialectical relation. Constitutional history had been a battle between the two, which the French revolution had settled in favour of democracy (NL, 27.51). The supposed victory in an imaginary eristic of one false abstraction over its opposite means the replacement of a dialectical process in which the two co-operate by a continuation of the imaginary eristic. The eristic is imagined to proceed pendulum-wise. In the make-believe disputation of false abstractions, the vanquished abstraction draws strength from its defeat and comes back re-invigorated to the imaginary fight. The real dialectic of harmonious co-operation between contradictory principles is imagined as being replaced by a false dialectic of oscillating conflict between false abstractions. The whole mistake is the logical consequence of making false abstractions (NL, 27.53–57).

The illusion that democracy had triumphed over aristocracy gave rise to the opposite illusion in the twentieth century that the reassertion of aristocracy was imminent. Tyranny arose in Germany and Italy, because democracy had been introduced in Germany in a doctrinaire spirit and under the strain of military defeat and into nineteenth-century Italy, which was inadequately grounded in the tradition of political dialectic (NL, 27.6–62). Collingwood goes on to claim that

> This is why, as an anti-dialectical system of politics, it has succeeded in overwhelming France, where the dialectic of political life has never been well understood; for the defeat of France in 1940 was not a strictly military defeat but a defeat in the realm of political ideas (NL, 27.63).

Similarly it failed to conquer England, because the English retained the mental vigour to hold on to the lesson that political life is essentially dialectical (NL, 27.64).[3]

As an example of dialectic in political life Collingwood refers to nineteenth century English politics, which was dominated by two parties, Liberal and Conservative. The aim of the Liberal party was to hasten the percolation of liberty throughout the body politic, and the aim of the Conservative party was to retard it. The relation between them was consciously dialectical. They were not fundamentally in disagreement. Both agreed that the process of percola-

---

[3]   There is a touch of English nationalism in Collingwood's views here: something which Eric Voegelin castigates Collingwood and others for in 'The Oxford Political Philosophers' (1953). Voegelin's argument is challenged by J.D. Mabbott (1954).

tion must go on and both tried to find the optimum rate of progress. Collingwood cites Disraeli's Reform Bill of 1867 as an example of the agreement between the two parties (NL, 27.79–83). Disraeli boasted that he had 'dished the Whigs', meaning that under his leadership the Conservative party, by extending the franchise, was adopting the traditional Liberal policy. Another Conservative said that he was a brake on the vehicle of progress. The policy of the Conservatives was not to stop the vehicle but to slow it down when it seemed likely to go too fast (NL, 27.84). Thus, the two parties may be compared to two barristers who agree that justice shall be done, but they show the court what is to be said for the plaintiff and for the defendant respectively (NL, 27.89).

The failure to understand the dialectic of politics is also used to explain the decline of the Liberal party in the early twentieth century:

> In a dialectical system it is essential that the representatives of each opposing view should understand why the other view must be represented. If one fails to understand this, it ceases to be a party and becomes a *faction*, that is, a combatant in an eristical process instead of a partner in a dialectical process (NL, 27.92).

Liberals pictured themselves as dragging the vehicle of progress against the dead weight of human stupidity, the Conservatives being a part of that dead weight. Whereas Conservatives understood that there must be a party of progress, Liberals never understood that there must be a party of reaction. Therefore the Liberal party was replaced by the Labour party, which the Liberal party would have absorbed had it understood the dialectic of English politics (NL, 27.94–7).

As well as providing an account of the dialectical process by which non-social communities are converted into societies, Collingwood stressed that the principles of liberalism needed to be extended more fully into the sphere of international relations. Collingwood argues that there are three logically distinct stages in political life. The first stage is society, in which a number of persons immanently rule themselves. The second stage is internal politics, where a society rules over a dependent non-social community. The third stage is external politics, whereby a body politic deals with problems arising out of its relation with other bodies politic. These three stages exist in a logical series. Internal politics presupposes the existence of a social will. Problems connected with the rule of one class over another are envisaged by the rulers as problems confront-

ing their joint social consciousness. Similarly external politics presupposes internal politics (NL, 29.1–17).

Each of these stages has its own dialectic. Each is a Heraclitean
world, where everything moves and nothing rests. The dialectic of
society is the conversion of a non-social community into a social
community. People find themselves in a non-social community and
form a society by a joint act of will, by deciding to do so. The
non-social element is never completely eliminated. It is just prevented from impeding social life. The dialectic of internal politics
converts the ruled class into collaborators with the rulers. Freedom
percolates throughout the body politic from the ruling class merely
by their act of ruling, so long as they have free will. If the ruling class
do not have free will, and their ruling is an involuntary act due to
irresistible passion or desire, what percolates through the body politic will be servility. In proportion as the ruling class fails to make
itself a society, it cannot lift its subjects to the level of co-operators
(NL, 29.2–44).

Collingwood's dialectical conception of liberalism is also applied
to international politics. The dialectic of external politics, he
explains, is where differences between bodies politic are converted
from non-agreement into agreement, rather than hardened into disagreement. For resolving differences between bodies politic, conflicts of interests, conflicts of rights, or conflicts of duties, making
war is the alternative to dialectic. War is a state of mind which consists in believing that such differences have to be settled eristically. It
does not necessarily involve the employment of military force.
Yielding to a threat of armed conflict (real or bluff) is war, regardless
of whether the threat is implicit or explicit. Similarly it is war
whether the force used is military force, or the force of economic or
religious sanctions (NL, 29.5–69).

War is a reversal of the dialectical methods hitherto employed in
the dialectic of society and the dialectic of internal politics. Social life
only exists because persons deliberately aim at agreeing together.
Bodies politic only exist because the so-called 'pugnacious instinct
of mankind' has been twice overcome (NL, 29.7–82). Similarly in
'Man Goes Mad', Collingwood rejects the notion that '… roots of war
are a combative instinct inherent in human nature'. Conflict is '… a
condition of all life: but conflict and war are not the same things, and
combative instinct, if there is such an instinct, no more entails the use
of battleships than daggers in the street' (MGM, 15).

Collingwood argues that war cannot be blamed entirely on one party (NL, 29.85). Any aggressor can argue that he fights only because he is forced to fight:

> If A attacks B because he is afraid of B and is convinced that he must hit first, the blame is shared. A is acting, admittedly, like a criminal lunatic; but B is to blame for having been so foolish as to frighten him into a fit of aggressiveness (NL, 29.88).[4]

A breakdown in the dialectic of external politics is caused by the internal condition of a body politic being unsound, where the rulers are unskilful and unsuccessful at ruling (NL, 30.3–35). War makes rule easier for an incompetent and heavy-handed ruler, increasing loyalty among the ruled and justifying rigorous demands being made of them. The reason why the rulers rule badly is because of disharmony among the rulers. War masks the disharmony and inward corruption in a body politic. Thus, the ultimate cause of war is that traces of non-sociality are not completely overcome by the 'dialectic of society' whereby a ruling class harmonises itself (NL, 30.35–39). No society ever totally leaves behind the 'Yahoo herd' that it has emerged from. War, therefore, can never be abolished. Any individual case of a defect in sociality can be removed by the various techniques for coming to agreement. But with the curing of one defect, another comes into existence: defect is infinitely changeable (NL, 30.8–86).

Collingwood asserts that a body politic would be justified in making war upon another if it is itself intent on peace, and the other body politic has already reduced itself so far as possible to the level of the 'Yahoo herd'. The second body politic, by its very existence, would constitute a threat to the first. War is a form of disagreement where the disagreement cannot be reduced to agreement because one party will not argue or listen to reason. He must be reduced to the state of somebody prepared to listen to reason before the dialectic can begin (NL, 30.9–98). According to Collingwood,

> War serves the cause of peace, and is therefore politically justified, when it is the only available method of discouraging a people who are individ-

---

[4]   This does not mean that a partial acceptance of blame should lead one to desist from responding to aggression. Pacifism, Collingwood argues, is 'war-mongery complicated by defeatism' and promotes war by ensuring that war-makers shall have their reward: 'Not realizing that modern war is a neurotic thing, an effect of terror where there is nothing to fear and of hunger where the stomach is already full, he proposes to deal with it by throwing away his arms so that the war-makers shall not be afraid of him, and giving up what they would snatch (from him or others) so that their hunger shall be appeased' (NL, 29.9–97; cf. Boucher, 1989: 184–5).

ually the victims of their own emotions, and collectively a prey to the tyrannous but popular 'rule' of a sub-man whom they hail as a super-man, from pursuing abroad an aggressively belligerent policy, the natural extension of the tyranny to which they are accustomed at home, and forcing them to realize that the only way to prosperity at home is through peace abroad (NL, 30.99).

Collingwood argued in 'Man Goes Mad' that the failure to extend the principles of liberalism into international relations[5] had given rise to international anarchy, militarism and Fascism in the 1930s (EPP, 185). Militarism, in Collingwood's view, was one of the signs of madness in our civilisation (MGM, 3), and the dialectical understanding of liberalism was the solution.

As we have seen, then, Collingwood found classical social contract theory to be deficient because of its failure to attach a positive meaning to the phrase 'state of nature' (NL, 33.18). In particular, Collingwood criticises the Germans in this respect. Unlike Western Europe, Collingwood argues, Germany and Prussia lacked the experience of political and social life that was necessary to understand the classical politics (NL, 33.21–25). Rousseau's German readers misunderstood 'the natural condition of mankind' to mean, not the nursery where babies are born, but the cave or 'savage' life; not the opposite of society, but the opposite of civilisation (NL, 33.2). The phenomenon observed by Machiavelli had never occurred in eighteenth-century German consciousness: the spontaneous creation by subjects of a social order capable of protecting their rights against a prince inclined to override them (NL, 33.26). The classical politics was interpreted as a theory of law and morals for a subject who never did anything except what was prescribed by convention or what was ordered by the prince and his servants (NL, 33.31).

Collingwood accuses the Germans of 'herd-worship', a form of communal self-adoration, which expresses a man's feeling of powerlessness in the grip of a non-social community of which he is a member (NL, 33.35–6). Kant and Hegel are accused of promoting 'herd-worship' by rejecting Hobbes' notion of the commonwealth as an 'artificial Man', characterised by joint social activity. For them, the state is natural in its origin and divine in its essence (NL, 33.41–2). There has been a tension in political and social sciences, Collingwood argues, between the Western European scientific tradition and German 'herd-worship' (NL, 33.7). For example, Nietz-

---

[5]   Collingwood also argued in 'Man Goes Mad' that the principles of liberalism needed to be extended into economic life, but this is something that I will discuss in the next chapter.

sche perceived a divided consciousness in German intellectual life, rejected the nationalism which was deliberately emphasising all that was anti-rational in the German tradition, and exhorted his country-men to be 'good Europeans' (NL, 33.72). According to Collingwood, when Marx calls for a revolution and property to be transferred to 'the state', by 'state' he means 'non-social community' (NL, 33.79). Marx is accused of embracing 'materialism' because it involved denying the existence of free will, and of hating the bourgeois, because he thought of the bourgeois as a man specially addicted to entering into free partnerships (NL, 33.97–9).

As I have illustrated, then, the deficiencies of social contract the-ory are overcome in an account of liberalism where the non-social community is converted by a dialectical process into society. As Boucher remarks, Collingwood's theory attempts to locate the state of nature, or the non-social aspects of life, within the framework of the body politic itself (Boucher, 1989: 166). According to K.B. McIntyre, Collingwood's elucidation of the necessary social ele-ment within the concept of freedom echoes the critique of contract theory offered by the German and British idealists of the nineteenth century, and that his unusual appropriation of the vocabulary of social contract theory is best understood as a rhetorical manoeuvre designed to undermine the validity of the concept of the atomistic individual which grounds social contract theory (McIntyre, 1996: 117). McIntyre explains that

> For Collingwood, the notion of the pre-social individual is a myth which he supplants with a conception of the continuous conversion of the non-social community into membership in society. This conversion does not involve the voluntary consent of the converted. It is a decision based upon the political context of the particular body politic (McIntyre, 1996: 131).

Social contract, for Collingwood, is a continuing and continuous process. Society and political entities such as the state and the nation are continuously made and remade.

The concept of the state designates the ruling class within the body politic (NL, 25.23). For Collingwood, like Croce, Boucher explains, there exists 'not the State, but political actions', and the State 'is not a substance but an activity' (Boucher, 1989: 167).[6] The

---

[6] When we understand the State philosophically, rather than as substance, Collingwood believes, the State cannot confine itself to the making and admin-istering of rules or laws. It must to some extent interest itself in economic and moral questions as well, but for political, and not for economic or moral, reasons (Boucher, 1989: 171). The promotion, maintenance, and protection of the politi-

state does not have a monopoly of political action. Political action is identical with action in general in so far as it organises itself: 'Political action is therefore bound to overflow the limits of the state and to appear wherever there is action of any kind' (EPP, 113). The administration of criminal law by the state does not take away the right and duty of every citizen to keep his own peace (EPP, 114).[7] Collingwood's view, contrary to foundational social contract theory, that political systems are continuously made and remade is illustrated in 'Political Action':

> When the political spirit of a society is no longer satisfied with its existing structure, no longer finds that structure to express its own political aspirations, it alters it. And this process is really going on at all times. To speak of a stable political system as 'existing', and then as suddenly altered with a jerk by a so-called reformation or revolution, is to be deceived by appearances. Every fresh political action is in reality a modification of the whole political poise and attitude ('constitution') of the agent. (EPP, 102)

Similarly, in *An Essay on Metaphysics* Collingwood argues that Locke's political theory is outdated, and to retain it unmodified is an example of 'reactionary anti-metaphysics' (EM, 97–8). The Lockian theory, as we have seen in Part Two, assumed that nationality was an absolute presupposition. For the contemporary historian or political theorist, however, it is a relative presupposition: nationality is constantly destroyed and remade (EM, 99). For Collingwood, society and the state are not things, but processes. The aim of these processes, as I will now explain, is the achievement of civilisation, or civility.

Collingwood's dialectical account of politics and reform of social contract theory culminates with his theory of civilisation and barbarism. Civilisation, according to Collingwood, is a process of approximation to an ideal state; it is to approach nearer to an ideal state of 'civility' and recede from the opposite ideal state of 'barbarity' (NL, 34.5–51). No actual state is purely civil or purely barbarous, and is always a mixture of the two (NL, 34.52). When the process of civilising is at work, the civil elements in the life of a community are gradually predominating and the barbarous elements are being prevailed over (NL, 34.55). Repeating the argument of *An Essay on Philosophical Method*, Collingwood argues that all mental processes have

cal good of orderliness is the justification for political, or state, intervention. The state should intervene to alleviate poverty because it is an offence against order (EPP, 97; Boucher, 1989: 172).

[7] The role of the state is something that I will discuss in more detail in the final chapter.

this approximative character. A mental process from ignorance to knowledge or from fear to anger or from cowardice to courage never begins simply at the first term, but always at the first term with a mixture of the second; and never ends simply at the second term, but always at the second term qualified by the first. The process does not begin in pure ignorance and end in pure knowledge (NL, 34.58–59).

Collingwood argues that there are three senses in which the term civilisation has been used. Firstly, it refers to the process itself. Secondly, the term civilisation is used to refer to the condition which is achieved as the result of undergoing the process of civilisation. Thirdly, the ideal of civilisation itself, towards which the process of civilisation aims, is often referred to as civilisation. For the sake of symmetry, Collingwood believes that it is justifiable to use three corresponding senses of the term barbarism: as a name for the process of barbarising, as a name for the condition to which that process leads, and as an equivalent to 'barbarity' (NL, 34.7–79; cf. Boucher, 1989: 209).

In 'What Civilisation Means'[8] Collingwood points out that whereas 'civility' is a certain state or condition of society, 'civilization' implies something more, namely the act of bringing about that state or condition. Civility has a static implication, civilisation a dynamic (NL, 481–2). Every society is at a stage between civilisation and barbarism, moving away from barbarism and attempting to move closer to civility (NL, 487–8). Collingwood argues that the simplest way of conceiving the relation between civilisation and barbarism is to regard them as two contradictory entities separated by a dichotomy. This understanding is outmoded and the result of obsolete conceptions of historical change (NL, 485–6; cf. Boucher, 1989: 209).

A second view of the relation between civilisation and barbarism arises out of late eighteenth-century historical thought, which viewed every period as one of transition. According to this view, each existing society stands on a scale somewhere between the absolute zero of barbarism and the infinity of civilisation, and is civilised to some degree relative to the ideal. The idea of degrees of civilisation presupposes that there is one universal civilising process through which all communities go, and reflects the monism of historical thought in the nineteenth century.

In terms of *An Essay on Philosophical Method*, as Boucher indicates, this view is deficient. Although the ideal of civility, as the generic

[8] This appears in Appendix 2 of the revised edition of *The New Leviathan*: pp. 480–511.

essence, is recognised to be manifest in differing degrees, the manifestations are not acknowledged to be different in kind. Also all of
the intermediate forms on the scale are mutually exclusive. This
view of the relation between barbarism and civilisation denies the
overlap of forms. Opposition and distinction are thought to be
mutually exclusive types of relation, whereas an adequate understanding of the concept of civilisation must exhibit it as a fusion of
opposites and distincts (NL, 487–8; Boucher, 1989: 210).

Twentieth-century historians, Collingwood claims, have rejected
historical monism and embraced historical pluralism. They recognise that at various times different communities have followed their
own ideals and instituted different processes to achieve them, and
are not therefore embodiments of different degrees of one single
ideal (NL, 488–9). Each civilisation attempts to live a different kind
of civilised life. However, this view does not imply historical relativism: 'The plurality of civilizations does not exclude a sense in which
civilization is one' (NL, 490).

Each civilisation is both and ideal and a fact. In so far as each will
have achieved a certain kind and degree of civilisation, it actually
exists and is a fact. The fact is itself an ideal, in that the degree and
kind of fact achieved will have been conceived as something desirable and worth aiming for, and its continuing existence is dependant
upon its continuing to be thought of as an ideal worth pursuing (NL,
490; cf. Boucher, 1989: 211).

The attainment of a certain kind and degree of civilisation implies
the concept of a further ideal that is as yet unrealised. As well as ideals that are facts, or ideals of the first order, there are also ideals that
are recognised but not realised, or ideals of the second order. The
extent to which the second-order ideals differ from those of the first
will vary considerably from person to person and from society to
society. But even second-order ideals are only partial. For example,
the ideal English gentleman might not behave with equal gentility
on all occasions. Beyond first- and second-order ideals is a third
order. This is the ideal of universal civility – not civility on this or that
occasion, but civility on each and every occasion. All particular ways
of behaving civilly presuppose the ideal of behaving civilly without
any limit whatever (NL, 492–4).

Collingwood argues that the discrepancies between its achievements and its second-order ideal are elements of barbarism in a
civilisation. However, the failure to realise the second order ideal is a
failure only to realise that part of the second order ideal that goes
beyond the first order ideal. According to the nineteenth-century

conception of progress, the source of this failure is a time-lag between the formation and execution of a plan (NL, 495). Each stage of progress demolishes a piece of barbarism, and man becomes more and more civilised as time passes. In the twentieth century we recognise that elements of barbarism that exist are not relics of a past age (as claimed by the nineteenth century concept of progress), but new creations, for example, the wretchedness of poverty and the horrors of twentieth century war. These barbarisms are products of the civilising process (NL, 496). Every advance in the civilising process gives opportunity for barbarism as well as for civilised behaviour.

According to Collingwood, man creates his own posterity. The facts of a situation determine the agent's opportunities, but they cannot determine his or her choice among those opportunities: 'His awareness of himself as a free agent is an awareness of these alternative possibilities for action which arise from the situation, and awareness of his power to choose between them' (NL, 497). He inherits certain facts – economic facts, social facts, legal facts and so forth – but he makes his will for himself.

Ideals are not inherited, only the fact that certain ideals were pursued. The heirs to the ideals decide whether the same ideals will continue to be pursued. The achievements of civilisation, inherited in the form of fact, are always opportunities to build a new civilisation or a new barbarism (NL, 497). Opportunities progress, but the human will is just as capable of using opportunities for good or ill as always. The greater the opportunities it inherits, the greater the temptation to abuse them, and this temptation is the origin of barbarism (NL, 498). While man makes his will for himself, the civilising will (or the willing of civilisation) inextricably linked with historical self-consciousness. The act of becoming historically self-aware is an act of will: an idea, as we have seen, that Collingwood illustrates in the concept of duty.

For Collingwood, the civilising process leads to what he calls the dialectic of discontent. 'Dialectic' here means contradictory propositions about the right method of treating a thing with which you are discontented. 'Discontent' refers to the discrepancy between what is realised in your society and what you would wish to be realised; between 'first order ideal' and 'second order ideal' (NL, 498). In the work of practical rationality, which we call civilisation, people are more discontented with their achievements the more they have achieved. Discontent means being aware of the barbarous elements in one's own civilisation. This leads to two attitudes: the reforming attitude and the conservative attitude. The reforming attitude demands their removal, the altering of institutions so that the barbarous elements are left out. The conservative attitude is to accept them as necessary evils, and because one cannot see how they can be left out, to argue that they cannot be altogether evil (NL, 499).

The reforming attitude is justified, as civilisation is an activity and cannot exist statically. The will to be civilised is the will to become more civilised. The conservative attitude is justified, in that advancement in civilisation is not made by throwing away what one has acquired because it is imperfect. The spirit of reform unchecked by the spirit of conservatism would lead to retrogression by destroying these foundations and thus produce effects as disastrous as its intentions are admirable. The spirit of reform is the first attitude towards recognised imperfection. The spirit of conservation is man's second thoughts about the same problem. Thus, many people take up the reforming attitude when young, and move towards conservatism as they grow older. Without this dialectical interaction between the two, the spirit of reform becomes Utopianism, and the spirit of conservation becomes reaction (NL, 500). A wise discontent is one which asks, not merely 'what ideal do we want to realize?' but 'what ideal can we realize here and now?' (NL, 501).

For Collingwood, civilisation presupposes society, and there is an integral relation between mind, society and civilisation. Collingwood argues that there are two constituents of civilisation. The first constituent of civilisation is concerned with the relation of a community to itself, the relation of its members to one another. The second constituent concerns the relation of the community to what is outside the community. This can be subdivided into relations with the natural world and relations with other communities (NL, 35.3–34).

In relations between members of a community, 'civilization' means behaving 'civilly' to one another. Acting civilly is to refrain from acting in a way that would arouse a strong passion or desire in another individual strong enough to diminish that person's self-respect—'that is threaten his consciousness of freedom by making him feel that his power of choice is in danger of breaking down and the passion or desire likely to take charge' (NL, 35.41). The word 'civil' came to have this meaning in ancient Latin (NL, 35.42). However, complete civility between all members of a community is only a council of perfection.

> Civilization is not civilization but barbarity unless it insists that you shall treat every member of your community as civilly as possible; it is not civilization but utopia unless it distinguishes occasions on which

you simply must be civil from others on which you may (and indeed, even for civility's sake, must) be uncivil (NL, 35.49).

A community that is civil in relation to the natural world is one which gets from the world of nature what it needs in the way of food, clothing and other satisfactions, as the fruit of its own industry, and through intelligent labour, directed and controlled by a scientific understanding of the natural world (NL, 35.5). The difference between a 'civil' community and a 'savage' community is that the civilised community has learned to save its muscles by using its brains in getting what it can out of the natural world (NL, 35.53). This is a modern sense of the word 'civil', and is found in derivatives of the Latin word such as 'civilité', 'civilità', 'civility', a Renaissance group of words whose central idea is that by coming to a better understanding of the natural world, man can increase his ability to get what he needs out of it, and become more civilised in relation to it (NL, 35.55).

Need, in this respect, is not a fixed entity, and needs change in accordance with expectations.

> What man needs of the natural world is what he thinks he can get from it. His catalogue of these needs undergoes expansion as his consciousness of power over the world of nature expands. As men become, in this second sense of the word, more 'civilized', what passed for luxuries are constantly being transferred into the list of necessaries, and new luxuries are constantly being invented. And what is a luxury to a higher civilization is not a luxury to one at a lower level of development … (NL, 35.58–9).

The question of whether civilisation means an increase in civility towards members of other communities depends on how any given community answers the question: 'Are foreigners human?' If the answer is 'yes', then civility requires that we treat them civilly. If the answer is 'no', then foreigners are part of the natural world and are scientifically exploited (NL, 35.6–64). The conviction that foreigners are human arises through experience of common action with them, setting up a social consciousness in virtue of which we recognise them as part of ourselves (NL, 35.68). The process of civilisation regarding the relation of a community to members of other communities is one where, originally treating people outside the community as natural things to be exploited, they come to consider them as human beings entitled to civility (NL, 36.14).

Although a historicist, therefore, Collingwood's perspective is universalist.[9] Historicism and universalism, in Collingwood's thought, are complementary. This is clear from his early manuscripts on logic onwards. As I indicated in Part Two, Collingwood argued in *Libellus de Generatione* that the world changes through and through, although in this incessant change it remains unalterably the same (Collingwood 1920a: 56). The historicist nature of Collingwood's universalism is also evident in the fact that the existence of the ideal of universal civility is not separate from the holding of the ideal. The ideal is not something transcendent and detached from the world of becoming and change: instead, it is an historical fact within that world, and a presupposition of particular ways of behaving civilly. For Collingwood, in comparing and evaluating civilisations and ideals of civility, different civilisations can be judged by the same standard, but it must be a standard that each civilisation regards as valid (see Connelly, 2003: 276–7). Furthermore, the transition from seeing foreigners as other to recognising them as one of us exemplifies Collingwood's conception of dialectic as stages in the development towards a wider truth.

To define the essence of civilisation, Collingwood explains, we must find the connection between a spirit of civility towards our fellow human beings and a spirit of intelligent exploitation of the natural world (NL, 36.25–6). The intelligent exploitation of the natural world involves 'natural science', which in this case means the handing on from generation to generation of knowledge which it is useful for a farmer, sailor, hunter, fisherman or the like to have. This is the kind of 'natural science' which was mostly discovered during the Neolithic Age, and of which the masters among ourselves are what we call 'unskilled agricultural labourers' (NL, 36.3–32). To have achieved any degree of civilisation relative to the natural world, a community must have acquired and conserved an incredible amount of this sort of natural science (NL, 36.33). According to Collingwood,

---

[9]   Boucher contends that Collingwood's ideas are close to those of Michael Walzer, who suggests that the thin morality we claim to be universally valid among human beings by the very fact that they are human, and among different states as the instruments through which they act on the world stage, is a projection of the thick morality that pertains in civilised communities. According to this view, '... there is an international society which is grounded, not on a natural or hypothetical contract in a Rawlsian original position, but on norms that have become commonly acknowledged by leaders of states and their citizens' (Boucher, 2000: 199). For Collingwood, on this view, it is by means of some form of common action that we develop our social consciousness and recognise foreigners not as other, but as one of us.

The mainspring of the whole process is the spirit of agreement. So vast a body of knowledge (I call it knowledge, but it is not the kind of thing logicians call knowledge; it is practical knowledge, knowing how to tie a bowline, knowing how to swim, knowing how to help a lambing ewe, how to tickle a trout, where to pitch a tent, when to plough and when to sow and when to harvest your crop) can only be brought together in a community (for it is too vast for the mind of one man) whose custom is that everybody who does not know a thing that may be useful for the betterment of living shall go frankly to one who knows it, and listen while he explains it or watch while he shows it, confident by custom of a civil answer to a civil question (NL, 36.46).

The connection between the two above characteristics of civilisation is civility. Civility between human beings not only constitutes civilisation relative to the human world; it is also what makes possible a community's civilisation relative to the natural world (NL, 36.5–51). The condition for the build up of knowledge in a community is that inventions are not hoarded but taught. It depends on a desire for knowledge and a desire to impart knowledge (NL, 36.59–64). But, as well as this 'dialectic of knowledge', which is the origin and essence of civilisation, there is also an 'eristic of knowledge': the monopolising of knowledge to gain power over people (NL, 36.65–6).

The trends towards the destruction of civilisation are incorporated in the concept of barbarism. For Collingwood, civilisation can be promoted unconsciously. Barbarism, however, can never be promoted unconsciously, because it entails a clear conception of what it is revolting against in order to flourish. Barbarism cannot win in its revolt against civilisation because 'there is no such thing as civilization' (NL, 41.68). All we have are various approximations to the ideal, with infinite capacities for modifying their civilisations and inventing new channels of development as soon as barbarism attacks (cf. Boucher, 1989: 240–41).

As I have argued, therefore, for Collingwood, the deficiencies in human self-understanding due to abstract rationalism are overcome in a dialectical theory of politics and civilisation, and this involved resolving the inadequacies of classical social contract theory. As we have seen in the previous chapter, Ortega y Gasset, like Collingwood, argues for a rapprochement between theory and practice. Therefore Ortega, along with Collingwood, also develops a dialectical account of society and politics, which was an integral part of a historicist response to the crisis of Western civilisation. Ortega emphasises the dynamic and dialectical character of European liberalism but, unlike Collingwood, he outrightly rejects social contract theory.

As we have seen, Collingwood's interpretation of social contract theory rejects the traditional idea of atomistic individuals and a foundational contract. Instead the contract is a continuous socialising process. The rationalism of traditional social contract theory, then, is assimilated and transcended in a dialectical manner. Thus, importantly, Collingwood's position means that 'the Western European scientific tradition' (NL, 33.7) is to some degree vindicated and absorbed, and not simply discarded. Although it is true that Ortega's philosophy also absorbs and transcends rationalism, this dialectical approach is not quite as explicit in Ortega's treatment of social contract theory.

Whereas Collingwood distinguishes between society and community, Ortega rejects social contract theory and instead draws a distinction between association and society. In 'Unity and Diversity of Europe',[10] Ortega argues that Europe since the Middle Ages has existed as a common space or environment, and coexistence and society are equivalent terms (HS, 49). For Ortega, society, unlike association, (and like Collingwood's conception of community) is that which is produced automatically by the simple fact of coexistence, and it secretes customs, habits, language, law and public power. It is a 'modern' error, Ortega asserts, to think that society is brought about by willed agreement. Any such agreement presupposes the existence of people living together under certain customs, and the agreement can only determine one form or another of this coexistence. The idea of a social contract is an attempt 'to put the cart before the horse' (HS, 50).

Ortega criticises rationalistic conceptions of the origin of society in 'The Sportive Origin of the State'. He argues that primitive tribes are divided into the social classes of youth, maturity and old age, and are dominated in power and authority by youths, whose primary concern is to fight. But: 'War calls for a leader and necessitates discipline, thus bringing into being authority, law, and social structure' (HS, 28). The aggression of youths, Ortega argues, provides the irrational historical origin of the state:

> It is not the worker, the intellectual, the priest, properly speaking, or the businessman who started the great political process, but youth, preoccupied with women and resolved to fight – the lover, the warrior, the athlete (HS, 32).

---

[10]   This essay is published in *History as a System and other essays toward a philosophy of history*, (1961) pp. 43–83.

However, despite the different interpretation of the word 'society' and the refusal to engage with social contract theory, Ortega's argument does to some extent complement Collingwood's criticism of social contract theory for not sufficiently taking into account what the latter calls the non-social part of the body politic, and its dynamic or dialectical relationship with society proper.

For Ortega, it is a symptom of crisis in a civilisation when societal circumstances do not favour the emergence of the excellent human being. Thus Ortega's dialectical liberalism was integrally related to promoting the conditions favourable to the emergence of cultural elites.[11] While Collingwood distinguishes between a society and a non-social community (or a ruling class and a ruled class), Ortega argues in *The Revolt of the Masses* that society is always a dynamic unity of two component factors: minorities and masses (RM, 13). Those who belong to a 'select minority' demand more of themselves than others, even though they may not themselves fulfil those higher exigencies. There is a distinction between

> ... those who make great demands on themselves, piling up difficulties and duties; and those who demand nothing special of themselves, but for whom to live is to be every moment what they already are, without imposing on themselves any effort towards perfection; mere buoys that float on the waves (RM, 15).

According to Ortega, the mass-man does not accept authority external to himself, unless his surroundings force him to do so, and today his surroundings do not so force him. On the contrary the excellent man is urged, by interior necessity, to appeal from himself to some standard beyond himself, whose service he freely accepts. Contrary to what is usually thought, it is the man of excellence, and not the common man, who lives in essential servitude. When, by chance, such necessity is lacking, he grows restless and invents some new standard, more difficult, more exigent, with which to coerce himself.[12] Ortega refers to Goethe: 'To live as one likes is plebeian; the noble man aspires to order and law' (RM, 63). Noble life stands opposed to the common or inert life, which reclines statically upon itself, condemned to perpetual immobility, unless an external force compels it to come out of itself: 'Hence we apply the term mass to

---

[11] For Ortega, capitalism promotes the wrong kind of aristocracy. He argues instead for a hierarchy of culture, divided into better and worse rather than rich and poor (cf. Dobson, 1989: 53).

[12] Likewise, in *Beyond Good and Evil*, Nietzsche declares 'Under conditions of peace the warlike man attacks himself' (Nietzsche, 1990: 76).

this kind of man – not so much because of his multitude as because of his inertia' (RM, 65).

Ortega argues that mass-man is hermetically enclosed within himself, incapable of submitting to anything or anybody, believing himself to be self-sufficient (RM, 66). On the other hand, he cannot control by himself the process of civilisation. He has learned to use much of the machinery of civilisation, but is ignorant of its very principles (RM, 67). Something paradoxical, but natural, has happened. From the very opening-out of the world and of life for the average man, his soul has shut up within him (RM, 68). The individual finds himself with a stock of ideas. He decides to content himself with them and regard himself as intellectually complete (RM, 69). The mass-man has 'ideas', Ortega asserts, but they are not genuine ideas, nor is there possession culture (RM, 71). According to Ortega,

> It is no use speaking of ideas when there is no acceptance of a higher authority to regulate them, a series of standards to which it is possible to appeal in a discussion. These standards are the principles on which culture rests … There is no culture where there are no principles of legality to which to appeal. There is no culture where there is no acceptance of certain final intellectual positions to which a dispute may be referred. There is no culture where economic relations are not subject to a regulating principle to protect interests involved. There is no culture where aesthetic controversy does not recognise the necessity of justifying a work of art (RM, 71–2).

Instead there is barbarism, which is the absence of standards to which appeal can be made (RM, 72).

With Syndicalism and Fascism, Ortega argues, there appeared for the first time in Europe a type of man who does not want to give reasons or to be right, but simply shows himself resolved to impose his opinions (RM, 73). Hence the 'new thing' in Europe is 'to have done with discussions', and detestation is expressed for all forms of intercommunion which imply acceptance of objective standards, ranging from conversation to parliament and science. Normal processes are suspended, and hermetism of the soul urges the masses to intervene in public life by direct action (RM, 74):

> Restrictions, standards, courtesy, indirect methods, justice, reason! Why were all these invented, why all these complications created? They are all summed up in the word civilisation, which, through the underlying notion of the word *civis*, the citizen, reveals its real origin. By means of all these there is an attempt to make possible the city, the community, common life. Hence if we look into all these constituents of civilisation just enumerated, we shall find the same common basis. All, in fact, presuppose the radical progressive desire to take others into consideration. Civilisation is before all, the will to live in common. A man is uncivilised,

barbarian in the degree in which he does not take others into account (RM, 75–6).

In Ortega's view,

> The political doctrine which has represented the loftiest endeavour towards common life is liberal democracy. It carries to the extreme the determination to have consideration for one's neighbour and is the prototype of 'indirect action'. Liberalism is that principle of political rights, according to which the public authority, in spite of being all-powerful, limits itself and attempts, even at its own expense, to leave room in the State over which it rules for those to live who neither think nor feel as it does, that is to say as do the stronger, the majority (RM, 76).

Liberalism is the supreme form of generosity. It announces the determination to share existence with the enemy–with an enemy which is weak:

> It was incredible that the human species should have arrived at so noble an attitude, so paradoxical, so refined, so acrobatic, so anti-natural. Hence, it is not to be wondered at that this same humanity should soon appear anxious to get rid of it. It is a discipline too difficult and complex to take firm root on earth (RM, 76).

According to Ortega, the mass-man believes that the civilisation into which he was born and which he makes use of, is as spontaneous and self-producing as nature (RM, 89). The principles on which the civilised world is based and by which it has to be maintained have no interest for him. Civilisation becomes more complex and difficult in proportion as it advances, and today man is unable to keep pace with the progress of his own civilisation. As civilisation advances, each new generation needs a great deal of experience, or history. 'Historical knowledge is a technique of the first order to preserve and continue a civilisation already advanced' (RM, 91). It does not give us positive solutions to the new aspect of vital conditions, but it prevents us from committing the mistakes of other times.

Thus, there is not anything 'new' in Bolshevism or Fascism. The future must overcome the past by swallowing it. If it leaves anything outside it is lost. An advance must be made on the liberalism of the nineteenth century, but this is not to be done by being anti-liberal (RM, 94). Liberalism had its reason, which will have to be admitted. It is the part that it not reason that must be taken from it. Europe needs to preserve its essential liberalism, as a condition for superseding it (RM, 95). For Ortega, then,

> There is no hope for Europe unless its destiny is placed in the hands of men really 'contemporaneous', men who feel palpitating beneath them the whole subsoil of history, who realise the present level of existence,

and abhor every archaic and primitive attitude. We have need of history in its entirety, not to fall back into it, but to see if we can escape from it (RM, 96).

According to Ortega, a superabundance of resources does not favour existence. Instead it produces deformities (RM, 100). Human life has arisen and progressed only when the resources it could count on were balanced by the problems it met with.[13] Ortega argues that the average man

> ... finds himself surrounded by marvellous instruments, healing medicines, watchful governments, comfortable privileges. On the contrary, he is ignorant of how difficult it is to invent those medicines and those instruments and to assure their production in the future; he does not realise how unstable is the organisation of the State and is scarcely conscious to himself of any obligations (RM, 101–2).

People lose contact with the very substance of life, which is made up of absolute danger, and is radically problematic. Hence, Ortega explains, we must accept our true destiny, and the destiny of the European today is to be a liberal (RM, 102–3).

According to Ortega, the scientist is the prototype of mass-man (RM, 108–9). In order to progress, science demanded specialisation. Hence the scientist has been gradually restricted and confined into narrower fields of mental occupation, and has progressively lost contact with other branches of science, and with it that integral interpretation of the universe which is the only thing deserving the names of science, culture, and European civilisation (RM, 109–10). The specialist knows very well his own tiny corner of the universe, but he is radically ignorant of the rest. In politics, in art, in social usages, and in other sciences, he will adopt the attitude of the primitive, ignorant man; but he will adopt them forcefully and with self-sufficiency. By specialising him, civilisation has made him hermetic and self-satisfied within his limitations; but the very inner feeling of dominance and worth will induce him to wish to predominate outside his speciality (RM, 112). Science, therefore, needs from time to time, as a necessary regulator of its own advance, a labour of reconstitution, an effort towards unification, without which the progress of science itself is not assured (RM, 113). The specialist is radically ignorant of the historical conditions requisite for the con-

---

[13] This resembles John Ruskin's view, according to which wealth is not automatically equivalent with possessions and production, for of these some are wealth and some are 'illth'. Wealth is determined by the 'intrinsic value' of a thing, not its exchange value, and 'intrinsic value' rests in the fitness of such labour or commodity as a means to 'the joyful and right exertion of perfect life in man' (see Williams, 1993: 142).

tinuation of science; that is to say, how society and the heart of man are to be organised in order that there may continue to be investigators (RM, 114).

Ortega's political theory, therefore, like Collingwood's, is a vindication of liberalism and the idea of freedom, and it constitutes a specifically historicist response to the ills of modernity. Although not using the language of social contract theory, Ortega affirms the idea that society and the state are the products of an open-ended dialectical process of human construction. However, as I indicated in Part One in the discussion of the relation between artist and community, Ortega's elitism is slightly different from Collingwood's. Ortega's distinction between the minority aristocracy and the masses is far more rigid than Collingwood's distinction between society and the non-social community. While Collingwood emphasises the importance of members of the non-social community being gradually incorporated, through education, into society and mental maturity, Ortega provides few explicit ideas about how and whether members of the masses could achieve a fuller more developed rationality. In this respect, Ortega's theory is less dynamic and dialectical than Collingwood's.

As we have seen, Collingwood's dialectical and developmental theory of society and politics led him to argue that different societies that embody different ideals of civilisation are attempts to achieve the ideal of universal civility. In Ortega's case, the dialectical view of politics led to the argument that the individual European nation-state constitutes a movement towards European unity.

During the Modern Age, Ortega asserts, Europe exercised authoritative influence over the rest of the world (RM, 126). Europe had been the ruler of the world, but now she is no longer sure that she is or will continue to be the ruler (RM, 131). But, Ortega argues, this apparent decadence may be a beneficial crisis which will enable Europe to be really, literally Europe:

> The evident decadence of the *nations* of Europe, was not this *a priori* necessary if there was to be one day possible a United States of Europe, the plurality of Europe substituted by a formal unity? (RM, 139).

Europe's loss of command is a worry because there is no other group of countries to take its place. If the European grows accustomed to not ruling, it will lose the discipline of responsibility that can keep Western minds in tension:

> If this is lacking, the European will gradually become degraded. Minds will no longer have that radical faith in themselves which impels them,

energetic, daring, tenacious, towards the capture of great new ideas in every order of life (RM, 144).

According to Ortega, European decadence manifests itself in the fact that the nation-state has become obsolete. European nations, he asserts, face economic difficulties because they are limited by the political frontiers of the respective states (RM, 146). The European has lost respect for national states, and has discovered that to be English, German or French is to be provincial (RM, 148–9). The state is the result of movement, struggle and effort, where man strives to escape from the natural society of which he has been made a member by blood. In its origins it is crossbred and multilingual:

> There is no possible creation of a state unless the minds of certain peoples are capable of abandoning the traditional structure of one form of common life, and in addition, of thinking out another form not previously existing (RM, 155).

The state begins by being a work of imagination. It is not a thing, but a movement. It is at every moment something which *comes from* and *goes to*. Its unity consists precisely in superseding any given unity (RM, 163).

As Europeans, Ortega argues, we are more influenced by what is European in us than by what is special to us as Frenchmen, Spaniards, and so on (RM, 180). According to Ortega, therefore, the grave demoralisation which manifests itself as a rebellion of the masses has its origin in the demoralisation of Europe:

> No one knows towards what centre human things are going to gravitate in the near future, and hence the life of the world has become scandalously provisional … The European cannot live unless embarked upon some great unifying enterprise. When this is lacking, he becomes degraded, grows slack, his soul is paralysed (RM, 181–2).

What are known as nations arrived in the nineteenth century at their highest point of expansion:

> Nothing more can be done with them except lead them to a higher evolution. They are now mere past accumulating all around Europe, weighing it down, imprisoning it … Everyone sees the need of a new principle of life … Only the determination to construct a great nation from the peoples of the Continent would give new life to the pulses of Europe. She would start to believe in herself again, and automatically to make demands on, to discipline, herself (RM, 182–3).

Ortega argues that Europe has been left without a moral code. No new morality has appeared to replace the old antiquated one (RM, 187). Modern culture and civilisation tend to belief in the amorality of life. 'Europe is now reaping the painful results of her spiritual conduct. She has adopted blindly a culture which is magnificent, but has no roots' (RM, 189).

Ortega's promotion of the idea of a united Europe, then, is explicitly connected with the development of historical and dialectical reason. In 'Unity and Diversity of Europe', he points out that the shape of this super-national state would be very different from those to which we are accustomed, just as the national state differed from the city-state of ancient times. To conceive of reality as dynamic, Ortega argues, was never easy for Greco-Roman thought. It was not able to detach itself from the visible. The corporeal object was for them the essential 'thing' (HS, 53). To the European mind, on the other hand, everything visible seems simply the apparent mask of a hidden force which is constantly producing it and is its true reality. For centuries the peoples of Europe have lived under a public power so purely dynamic that it can be characterised only by names like 'European balance' and 'balance of power' (HS, 54). Europe is not a 'thing' but a balance (HS, 55).

According to Ortega: 'Aligning oneself with the left, as with the right, is only one of the numberless ways open to man of being an imbecile: both are forms of moral hemiplegia' (HS, 70). In contemporary civilisation the whole of life tends to be absorbed by politics, and this total 'politicalism' is one and the same phenomenon as the revolt of the masses: it drains people of solitude and intimacy (HS, 71). From the eighteenth century onwards it became a general belief throughout most of Europe that the only method of solving great human problems was the method of revolution, to change everything at a single blow and in all spheres of life (HS, 76–7). However, in revolutions the abstract tries to rebel against the concrete. Human affairs are historical and therefore in the highest degree concrete. The only method of thinking about them with some chance of hitting the mark is 'historic reason' (HS, 78).

Three centuries experience with 'rationalism' and Cartesian 'reason' enable us to realise its failure in the realm of strictly human affairs, and demand that it be integrated in the more deep-rooted system of 'historic reason'. Historical reason, Ortega argues, demonstrates the futility of all general revolutions, of all attempts to bring about a sudden change of society and begin history anew. It opposes revolution with continuity (HS, 80). The method of continuity is '… the only one that can avoid, in the course of human affairs, that pathological element that makes history a notorious, constant struggle between paralytics and epileptics' (HS, 83).

For Collingwood, therefore, a dialectical and historical theory of liberalism is an important part of his philosophical response to the crisis of modernity. As the comparison with Ortega helps us to understand, however, Collingwood's response to cultural crisis (with its overlap of philosophy and political theory) ought to be seen as playing a salient role in the wider context of the development of early twentieth-century historicism and 'crisis' thought. In the final chapter, I will discuss how dialectical and historical philosophy is used by Collingwood to respond to particular examples of cultural crisis, namely the problems of economics and of bureaucratic administration.

Chapter Ten

Civilisation, Capitalism and the Bureaucratic State

From the dialectical nature of civilisation, described in the previous chapter, it follows that, for Collingwood, particular elements of civilisation are also to be understood dialectically. In *The New Leviathan* the elements, or properties, of civilisation are described as wealth, education, 'law and order', and 'peace and plenty'. Regarding the role of wealth (but also, to some degree, in relation to the other elements) in civilisation, Collingwood's dialectical philosophy implies a critique of industrialism and laissez-faire capitalism. As is the case with Collingwood's theory of art, and the Romantic theory of 'culture', which I outlined in Part One, the critique of capitalism develops from a holistic point of view. According to Boucher,

> Collingwood's concern with the larger questions in social and political theory allies him much more closely with modern theorists, such as Hannah Arendt, Charles Taylor, Alasdair MacIntyre, and Richard Rorty, who have sought to uncover the fundamental forces serving to corrupt contemporary civilisation, than with those who explore issues of social justice and economic redistribution (Boucher, 2000: 187).

However, as I will argue, for Collingwood, issues of social justice and economic redistribution were interconnected with fundamental forces serving to corrupt Western civilisation.

As we have seen, Collingwood argues that what a community needs from the natural world changes according to its power to get things from the natural world. What people have no power to get from the natural world they learn to do without, docking their needs to match their powers: 'Man's demands upon the natural world, if his mastery of 'natural science' ... is increasing, increase concurrently with his power to satisfy them; and it makes no difference whether civilization is defined in terms of increased demand or increased power to satisfy demand' (NL, 38.12–13 and 35.58). Wealth, then, is a comparative term. One community A may be wealthier than another community B, but each may be 'worse off' as compared with a still wealthier community C. 'How much a community demands of nature and how much it gets from nature is the measure of its wealth, and thus one measure of its civilization' (NL, 38.21–29).

In both *The New Leviathan* and 'What Civilization Means', Collingwood distinguishes between wealth and riches. He argues that the adjective 'wealthy' applies primarily to a community, whereas 'rich' applies in the first instance to individuals. Also wealth is a comparative term, which involves reference to a standard, whereas 'rich' is a relative term (NL, 38.3–38). If every member of a community is sufficiently fed, clothed, and housed to a standard it is satisfied with, it is wealthy (NL, 38.5–51).

To be rich is to be rich in relation to another party who is poor. The relation between rich and poor in economic relations is a relation of power. Riches and economic force are the same thing. Uncomplicated by force, an economic transaction is freely entered into and viewed as mutually beneficial. The exercise of force in a transaction introduces an element of compulsion which undermines the free will of the individual. A person is forced to sell something for less than he or she regards as a just price, a 'just price' being that for which I am willing to exchange something when I am not forced to do so (NL, 38.6–65).

The distinction between a 'fair price' and 'the price a thing will fetch' is a moral distinction. It is an application to exchange of the distinction between free action and forced action. Exchanges involving a fair price, because they involve no force, are wholly civil (NL, 505). Thus to take advantage of one's economic power by paying low wages to a labourer is to exploit the latter's economic weakness. Collingwood, however, doubts that law can prevent this from happening:

> I suspect that ... once the contrast between riches and poverty is allowed to exist a force is set up which henceforth it is idle to resist. However men work to minimize the result, there will always be one law for the rich and

another for the poor; for that is what being rich and being poor are (NL, 38.67–71).

The existence of the contrast between rich and poor is an offence against the ideal of civility, as it implicitly involves the constant use of force by the rich in economic dealings with the poor (NL, 38.74). However, any civilisation is only an approximation to the ideal of civility, and in many respects so far departs from it as to permit the use of force:

> Those responsible for the institutions of a particular civilization, then, must recognise clearly that the existence of a contrast between rich and poor, even a slight contrast, is an element of barbarity in it; but if it is only a slight contrast they may judge it sufficiently paid for by the service done to the whole community by the rich as the class charged with maintaining the communal wealth. The community in which the contrast between rich and poor exists, therefore, will not, if it is wise, waste the ingenuity of its lawyers in trying to abolish the evils resulting from that contrast. It will examine its economic life very carefully, to decide whether that contrast is necessary to the preservation of what it regards as a tolerable standard of living. If it decides that the contrast can be diminished (for it can never be wholly abolished, any more than any other of the forms in which force appears as a feature in political life) without a greater inroad on its income or capital than it can afford, it will take the necessary steps to that diminution (NL, 38.77–38.8).

According to Collingwood,

> ... the *raison d'être* not only of bodies politic but of every community is that men should live, as Aristotle says, a good life; and in our terminology Aristotle's 'good life' is called civilization. This is the only motive for which men accumulate wealth: in order to pursue civilization. To accumulate wealth in order to create by its means a contrast between rich and poor is to use it for the destruction of civilization, or the pursuit of barbarism (NL, 38.81–3).

The wealth of one member of society, Collingwood explains, tends to promote the wealth of every other member with whom he is in exchange (NL, 505). The *laissez-faire* economics of Adam Smith is justified as a theory of wealth, but is folly when applied to the relation between rich and poor. Because it is a moral distinction, the distinction between riches and wealth has not always been understood by economists and the general public, thus leading to a confusion of terms:

> The confusion affects not only theory and vocabulary, it affects economic life too. There is some reason to think that in the countries which call themselves civilized the pursuit of riches though incompatible with the very idea of civilization, has sheltered itself behind the pursuit of wealth, which is an integral part of civilized life, and in this concealed

position has grown into a monstrous parasite upon civilization itself (NL, 506).

Christian moral theology denounced avarice as a deadly sin. Certain thinkers at certain times have interpreted this as implying that economic life as such is sinful, and there was an opposite reaction to this in Calvinist influenced countries. But, Collingwood argues, 'avarice' means the pursuit of riches, not wealth (NL, 507).

Collingwood's dialectical account of wealth, then, implies a critique of capitalism. Capitalism can be understood here in terms of how it is described by Max Weber, who contrasted modern capitalism with traditional types of economic activity. According to Weber, in communities where modern productive organisations have not previously been known, workers are interested, not in maximising their daily wage, but only in earning enough to satisfy their traditionally established needs. The regular reproduction of capital, involving its continual investment and reinvestment for the end of economic efficiency, is foreign to traditional types of enterprise (Weber, 1992: xi–xii).

In *The Protestant Ethic and the Spirit of Capitalism*, Weber traces the connections between Puritanism (especially the ideas of predestination and the 'calling') and modern capitalism. For Weber, the 'spirit of capitalism' is represented by the accumulation of wealth and the negation of worldly pleasures. The accumulation of wealth combined with the strict avoidance of all spontaneous enjoyment of life is thought of as an end in itself. According to Weber,

> ... from the point of view of the happiness of, or utility to, the single individual, it appears entirely transcendental and absolutely irrational. Man is dominated by the making of money, by acquisition as the ultimate purpose of his life. Economic acquisition is no longer subordinated to man as the means for the satisfaction of his material needs. This reversal of what we should call the natural relationship, so irrational from a naïve point of view, is evidently as definitely a leading principle of capitalism as it is foreign to all peoples not under capitalistic influence (Weber, 1992: 53).

In so far as attempting to diminish the contrast between rich and poor hinders the increase of communal wealth, capitalism means tolerating this contrast to a greater extent. Hence, capitalism, or the perpetual demand for more and more wealth, is, in Collingwood's terms, uncivilised. For Collingwood (and, it seems, for Weber), the accumulation of wealth cannot be an end in itself, but only a means to the end of civilised life. According to Collingwood, the obsession in Western civilisation with justifying every act, custom and institution by showing its utility (EPP, 197–8) means that we neglect the question of substantive ends.

As Collingwood argues, if nothing is good except in so far as it is useful, there is no utility and therefore no goodness (EPP, 147). Sooner or later the judgement that something is good because it is useful rests on the judgement that something is good in itself, irrespectively of whether or not it is also useful. For Collingwood, the utilitarian trick of judging all human activities by assessing their utility is therefore logically nonsensical and the first step on the road to moral bankruptcy (EPP, 148). Our civilisation has adopted as the first maxim of wisdom the rule: 'take care of the means, and the ends will take care of themselves'.[1] 'Obedience to this rule is the method in the madness of modern civilization' (MGM, 9).

Similarly, according to Peter Drucker, capitalism has been successful purely as an economic system, but people lose faith in it because it does not lead to a free and equal society. Drucker argues that Henry Ford forgot that economic increase and expansion are not ends in themselves: they make sense only as means to a social end (Drucker, 1939: 35). George Orwell argues that there is a need for spiritual brotherhood as an antidote to the ills of modern civilisation:

> Man is not an individual, he is only a cell in an everlasting body, and he is dimly aware of it. There is no other way of explaining why it is that men will die in battle ... the Kingdom of Heaven has somehow got to be brought on to the surface of the earth ... man does not live by bread alone ... a world worth living in cannot be founded on 'realism' and machine-guns (Orwell, 1996: 17–8).

For Collingwood, then, as it is for Weber, Orwell and Drucker, the emphasis on increasing material wealth and the neglect of the social aspect of civilisation contribute greatly to the crisis of the West. In Collingwood's view, the excesses of free-market capitalism point to an increase in civility in terms of human control over nature, but, crucially, a decrease in terms of relations between people.

For Collingwood, the problem that capitalism poses can be seen in the context of the failures of liberalism. Modern liberalism has failed, Collingwood argues, to diffuse wealth adequately in order to reduce the contrast between rich and poor. In clinging to the distinction between public and private, the liberal state preferred not to intrude in economic life if nothing illegal was being done. Just as there had

---

[1]   Similarly, as we have seen, Ortega y Gasset argues that the meaning and final cause of technology lie outside itself, namely in the use man makes of the unoccupied energies it sets free (HS, 118).

been anarchy among liberal polities in international relations, anarchy was also the principle by which the economy operated internal to the state. According to Collingwood, 'This was tolerable in theory only because of the extraordinary doctrine, learnt from Adam Smith, that free pursuit of individual interest best subserved the interest of all; in practice it was soon found wholly intolerable, and the misery of the weaker, to which it gave rise, was the source of modern socialism' (EPP, 185). The solution to this problem, he argues is the more complete application of liberal principles.

Like Collingwood (and Ortega, Orwell and Drucker), Croce argues that the problems of suffering, hardship and the desire for better conditions can only be stated and solved on the plane of moral liberty, and not with materialistic schemes such as *laissez-faire* or communism or intermediates between these extremes. Rather than with such abstract schemes, these problems can be solved as they arise on the moral plane, with due regard for the facts of the situation. The solutions will vary from time to place, the only constant criterion being that of moral liberty and the advance of civilisation (Croce, 1949: 107–8). Thus liberalism must be free from economic prejudice, and Croce is emphatic in his distinction between political, or moral, liberalism and economic liberalism, or *laissez-faire* (Croce, 1949: 28–9).

Collingwood's dialectical account of wealth also complements his account of the crisis of Western civilisation which I outlined in Part One. Throughout his writings, then, Collingwood seems to attack industrialism and capitalism from at least two standpoints. On the one hand, capitalism is uncivilised and un-dialectical in so far as it leads to an increase in the contrast between rich and poor. On the other hand, industrialism and consumerism are responsible for the suppression of emotion, something which threatens human sanity and self-knowledge.

As we have seen, for Collingwood, emotion is the dynamo that drives practical life (PA, 68–9). Failure to express emotions leads to the 'corruption of consciousness' and has grave consequences for civilisation. In 'Fairy Tales', Collingwood argues that our civilisation has suppressed emotion by the cultivation of a thick-skinned or insensitive attitude towards it. Our civilisation's obsession with utilitarianism means that whatever cannot be justified in utilitarian terms it tends to suppress. In particular, art and religion are distrusted as things not altogether respectable: 'To live within the scheme of modern European-American civilization involves doing a certain violence to one's emotional nature, treating emotion as a thing that must be repressed, a hostile force within us whose out-breaks are destructive of civilized life' (Collingwood, 2004: 206–7; EPP, 197–8).

As a result, the role of magic in society has been misunderstood as pseudo-science. Its influence has been suppressed and the ritualised and conventionally accepted ways of discharging emotions into practical activities have been undermined. Our utilitarian civilisa-tion prides itself on eradicating superstition and 'irrational' emo-tions and does not realise that the denial of such emotions amounts to a corruption of consciousness (cf. Boucher, 2000: 202).

Collingwood argued that the rise of industrialism led to the replacement of art proper with the pseudo-art of amusement, and the corruption of Western civilisation. Whereas art proper is the expression of emotion, amusement involves the discharge of emo-tion, and has a corrupting effect when it discharges emotions needed in ordinary life. The suppression of emotion resulting from industri-alism and capitalism creates a desire for the drug of amusement art as 'an escape from the all-pervading gloom and squalor of our urban civilization' (PAE, 436). Also, as I indicated in Part One, Collingwood regarded the suppression of emotion as manifesting itself in the destruction of the countryside by industrialisation.[2]

According to Collingwood's dialectical philosophy, therefore, the pursuit of wealth is one aspect of civilisation, but civilisation as a whole includes emotional expression through art and religion, and the historical thinking and dialectical interaction of social life. The accumulation of wealth is important, but if it is pursued at the cost of undermining society and suppressing emotion, it is a manifestation of the crisis of civilisation. The solution to the crisis is the cultivation of forms of emotional expression and the further development of historical and dialectical thinking.

Along with wealth, Collingwood describes the properties of civili-sation in *The New Leviathan* as education, 'law and order' and 'peace and plenty'. In his discussion of these properties, especially educa-tion, Collingwood again demonstrates that modernity has reached a

---

[2] For Orwell also, modern capitalism implies the suppression of emotional ex-pression. Referring to his return from Burma and five years service in the Indian Imperial Police, Orwell wrote: 'At that time failure seemed to me to be the only virtue. Every suspicion of self-advancement, even to 'succeed' in life to the ex-tent of making a few hundreds a year, seemed to me spiritually ugly, a species of bullying' (Orwell, 1989: 138). Orwell refers to industrialism as an unhealthy way of living: the modern industrial technique provides cheap substitutes for everything. Thus 'We may find in the long run that tinned food is a deadlier weapon than the machine gun' (Orwell, 1996: 91).

point of crisis because of an over-reliance on forms of thought derived from natural science, and the solution is the cultivation of forms of emotional expression and dialectical thinking.

For Collingwood, education is one of the most important properties of civilisation, and this is something he emphasises throughout his writings. In order to keep itself alive from one generation to the next, a civilisation must provide sufficient education to keep in perpetual motion the conversion of non-social members into social members of the community. In a body politic those entrusted with the task of bringing about the civilising, or socialising, process are the rulers. Political activity and political education are correlative. 'In the case of the family, the agent in this process is the parental society, and the name of the process is education' (NL, 40.63). In a family, the nursery must be converted from a non-social community into a society, and this is the process of civilising the children (NL, 37.31). Education develops the mind up to the level of mental maturity, through various stages of consciousness, emerging into the life of rational consciousness, and, as we have seen, the specifications of the number and nature of the level of consciousness are articulated in *The Principles of Art* and modified in *The New Leviathan* (see Boucher, 1995b: 272).

As for the content of education, Collingwood never systematically addressed the question of what it should be, except in relation to the place of art in education, but we can construct an answer from his many and varied comments on such matters. Education should attempt to provide an understanding of all the forms of experience. In *Speculum Mentis* these forms of experience were art, religion, science, history and philosophy, all of which constituted a linked hierarchy, and each of which represented a different stage of mental development. All of the forms of experience were seen by Collingwood as having an important place in the education of a civilised community (cf. Boucher, 1995b: 283–4; Hughes-Warrington, 1996: 222–6).

However, although Collingwood never fully and formally presented his ideas on the content of education, he did write a remarkable account of its manner. Collingwood argues that the civilising or educating of children is better done by parents than by specialists or public education institutions (NL, 37.32–3). The parent has greater power over the child and, to the child, stands for omnipotence as a specialist can never do. Also the parent has the resourcefulness and versatility of a non-specialist in finding and allowing the child to find new subjects to study. The parent is tied to no particular methods and is judged by no particular results (NL, 37.34–37). According to Collingwood,

> It is pitiable to see men who have 'devoted their lives to education' struggling against overwhelming odds to run schools in such a way that in favourable cases, and granted exceptional ability on their own part, they can excite in pupils a very small fraction of the enthusiasm and the self-confidence that any ordinary parent can excite in his own very ordinary children by taking hardly any trouble at all; and to hear their admirers hailing them as great reformers in the world of education (NL, 37.38).

Plato is 'the man who planted on the European world the crazy idea that education ought to be professionalized', and that the profession ought to be a public service (NL, 37.4). For Collingwood,

> The loss of power and efficiency it has brought about is beyond my calculating; I will only suggest that this is what is wrong with European civilization. It has entrusted the conservation of its own traditions to a class of persons who, owing to their position, have not the power to conserve them (NL, 37.41–2).

Collingwood refers to William Cobbett, who brought up his children, 'as "savages" bring up theirs', by joining in their daily lives and encouraging them to join in his own (NL, 37.43). The children pursued 'the deeply interesting and never-ending sports of the field and pleasures of the garden', and they took naturally to book learning, which he accommodated with 'a large strong table' and stationery. A child 'learned to ride, and hunt, and shoot and fish, and look after cattle and sheep, and to work in the garden, and to feed his dogs, and to go from village to village in the dark' (NL, 37.44–48). This, of course, corresponds to what Collingwood calls practical 'natural science' in his definition of 'the essence of civilization' (NL, 36.3–46).

To the objection that, while Cobbett made his living by farming and writing at home, his method of education could not be employed in a world of 'office-drudges' and 'factory-drudges', Collingwood responds that this is '… a good reason for smashing a world of office-drudges and factory-drudges … a world unfit for men to live in' (NL, 37.56). Like Max Weber, Collingwood criticises the Marxist alternative as leading to even greater bureaucratisation (although, unlike Weber, Collingwood regards bureaucracy as inefficient). Collingwood argues that Marxism leads to

> … a world committed not only to the first Platonic error of professional education but to the second Platonic error of bureaucratising the educators. Any relics of efficiency left intact by the first error will inevitably be dissipated by the second. Nor do I advocate standing bogged in the

world of capitalism bolstered up by what they call cold socialism; a world infested by the Juggernauts of big business preserved from the bankruptcy fairly earned through their own incompetence by subsidies paid for out of taxation (NL, 37.58-6).

Collingwood puts forward a number of suggestions to help reduce the influence of what he calls the 'Old Man of the Sea', the professional educator (NL, 37.65). Whatever is done must be done individually.

There must be no waiting for legislative help, and no attempt to do what we want by legislative action. Legislation is controlled by the Old Man of the Sea in his own interest. The sort of professionalized, bureaucratised education ... is the only kind politicians can produce (NL, 37.7-73).

A wise person will not ask politicians to help to get rid of a politician's system of education, a point which also applies to the totalitarians and the communists:

The 'Revolution' of one kind and another, which these gentry agree in proclaiming, is only fire to your frying-pan; it is in either case only the event piously expected by herd-worshippers when the herd shall be all in all and the Old Man of the Sea shall rivet every one of us in permanent chains (NL, 37.79).

Collingwood declares

But there is a vast region of experience in which the irresponsible attitude of doing things for fun resists all the onslaughts of professionalism. For every man who indulges himself in games and sports and pastimes, this region includes all those things. For almost every human being it includes eating and sleeping and making love (NL, 37.83-4).

This region is to be defended and enlarged. Parents should arrange matters so that they can spend more time with their children, and are urged to be irresponsible about them and do nothing for them except what they find it fun to do themselves. Teaching children is not so important as 'all modern children are grossly and criminally overtaught' (NL, 37.9-94).

However, despite the seemingly extreme nature of Collingwood's views, he is not opposed to professional education as such. Collingwood argues that, having being rendered 'harmless', professional teachers can go on teaching. When there are things a child wants to know which the parents cannot teach, it can be sent to learn them from a professional teacher, and the parent, if it wants, can go too (NL, 37.97). The expertise of professional teachers would therefore be solicited rather than imposed. This would leave professional educators with more time to conduct research (cf. Hughes-

Warrington, 1996: 228). As many educational institutions as are needed for the purpose should be kept,

> ... partly as teaching institutions where specialized teaching is on tap for all comers who want it, and partly as institutions of research where science and learning shall be kept alive instead of being, as they too often are in our educational institutions of today, dead (NL, 37.98).

Collingwood, then, takes a holistic approach to education. Education is a philosophical concept. As we have already seen, he distinguished philosophical concepts from non-philosophical empirical concepts. An empirical concept applies to specific classes of facts, whereas a philosophical concept is inter-connected with reality as a whole (EPM, 35). Education proper is conducted by society in general, not merely by specialist educational institutions. Specialist educational institutions have a role to play within the context of education in general. As Hughes-Warrington argues,

> For Collingwood, however, *any* social institution is a potential educator. If, he argues, education is a matter of inculcating education to help students to pass examinations, then we should look no further than the public school of the early 20th century (1939, ch 2). If, on the other hand, education is seen as the process of socialisation, then any individual, group or institution that contributes to the development of rational consciousness should be recognised as educative .... What Collingwood asks us to do is to look beyond the contributions of institutions to recognise the role that individuals, parents and communities can play in the life of the mind (Hughes-Warrington, 1996: 232).

For the British Idealists also, education, as well as having a narrow institutional meaning, had a broader sense in which the organised will of society was at once the exemplar and facilitator of virtue fulfilling the educative function of the state (cf. Boucher, 1995b: 271).

As Hughes-Warrington indicates,[3] Collingwood is influenced by Hegel and Green in being aware of the importance of mediating communities between the individual and the largest social communities. For Green the state grows directly out of the primitive community, differing from it in the degree of freedom it allows, and this means that, at least potentially, the family-community plays an important part in the process of self-realisation (Hughes-Warrington, 1996: 230). But, because of class divisions, according to Green, education is best carried out by a state-run system and could not be left in the hands of parents:

[3]   Hughes-Warrington's interpretation of Collingwood's theory of education is presented in more detail in *'How Good an Historian Shall I Be?': R.G. Collingwood, The Historical Imagination and Education* (2003).

... it is doubtful whether under the modern system of labour in great masses, which draws all who have to work for their living more and more away from their homes, the fate of children can ever with safety be left solely in the hands of the parents (cited from Hughes-Warrington, 1996: 230; Boucher, 1995b: 294);

and 'all questions of education are complicated by questions of class' (cited from Boucher, 1995b: 293).

According to Boucher, Collingwood's own educational experience instilled in him a blind optimism regarding the capabilities of parents and he did not address the plight of those children born to uneducated, ignorant, and uncaring parents (Boucher, 1995b: 293; 1989: 223–4). Collingwood, Boucher argues, was divorced from the poverty and deprivation prevalent among large sections of the community, and was far less sensitive to the social condition of England than idealists such as Green, D.G. Ritchie, Bernard Bosanquet, and Henry Jones (Boucher, 1995b: 293). British idealists saw a role for the state to play in education in order to counteract the consequences of such conditions for the child. State education was needed to overcome class divisions in society and the condition of the poor. Whereas Collingwood criticised the 1870 Education Act, British idealists praised it as contributing to the breaching of class barriers. The extension of the school leaving age and provision for continuing education were seen by them as an enhancement of individual liberty (cf. Boucher, 1995b: 291).

However, what Collingwood seems to say is that the professional or state educator is a good servant, but a bad master. Collingwood was not opposed to professional education as such, but, unlike the British idealists, he argued that the parent, not the state, is to have authority. Parents are more able to focus on the development of consciousness than professional educators because they are free from demands simply to inculcate information (Hughes-Warrington, 1996: 231). It seems that, for Collingwood, when the state, and not parents, has ultimate authority in educational matters, and when education is confined to educational institutions, there may be a tendency for education to become regarded as a means to an end and to become confused with the teaching of skills.

In 'The Place of Art in Education' Collingwood asserts that education is directed to the betterment of human nature in its universality, although there is 'a danger that the necessity of such a general education, as distinct from vocational training, may be overlooked or denied under the stress of our economic scramble for existence' (PAE, 435). As Ridley argues, education, unlike vocational training, or the learning of crafts, has to do with self-knowledge. The student is introduced to books, ideas, theories, works of art, formulae; not in the hope, primarily, that they might prove useful later, as ways of getting things done, but in the hope that they will be understood. When it is properly so-called education is aesthetic; it is something 'of which there can be no technique' (Ridley, 1998: 50–1).[4]

Ridley contends that, with higher education in Britain today, unclear political thinking has led to the pernicious doctrine that education, if it is to be worthwhile, must impart something called 'transferable skills'. The difference between getting 'a certain thing' right and getting 'a thing of a certain kind' right is abolished; and so the distinction between education and vocational training collapses (Ridley, 1998: 51). Under these conditions, the effect is to drive education properly so-called underground. Education still goes on only under a corrupt misdescription. The official ideology means denying students an education. According to Ridley,

> Collingwood's philosophy of art shows with exemplary directness what sort of ethical and conceptual muddle lies at the heart of all this. The mistaking of purposeful activity for technical activity, the confounding of success with the successful realization of a preconceived end, the confusion of the hard task of clarification for the relatively easy one of classification: every element repeats the errors of the technical theory of art, and for just the same reasons (Ridley, 1998: 52).

The confusion of education with vocational training leads to the 'profoundly vicious' idea that art is an ornament or a form of escape from the practical strain of everyday life (PAE, 437). According to Collingwood, we must recover the conviction that the function of art in life is not ornamental, but structural (PAE, 439).

As Hughes-Warrington points out, another reason that, for Collingwood, education should be left primarily to parents is because they have a stronger relationship with very young children. Also, the family is the form of community out of which the social community grows, and a state-centred system weakens the bond between the family and the social community (Hughes-Warrington, 1996: 231).

For Collingwood, parents should carry out education at the initial stages of mental development, or education of the emotions. According to Collingwood, art is the 'initial state' in the formation of knowledge, and out of art, the primary activity of mind, all others grow. Art is imagination, and 'imagination is a fundamental mode of mind's activity, and the right training of imagination is therefore a

---

[4]   This is also consistent with Oakeshott's views in *Rationalism in Politics* (1962).

fundamental part of education' (PAE, 442). Art is also the expression of emotion, something which is necessary for knowledge of emotions, and hence it is a form of self-understanding. According to Collingwood in *Speculum Mentis*, 'Art is the foundation, the soil, the womb and the night of the spirit; all experience issues forth from it and rests upon it; all education begins with it; all religion, all science, are as it were specialized and peculiar modifications of it' (SM, 59).

Collingwood also saw compulsory state education as part of a wholesale destruction of the countryside by town-dwellers. Our vital emotional attachment to the land was being eroded by the values of a utilitarian civilisation. The imposition of the standards of the town by a uniform education system was a threat to the emotional foundations of our civilisation (cf. Boucher, 1995b: 294–5).[5] If, on the other hand, education cultivates self-expression, children 'need no longer experience that boredom of school' which is the product of a utilitarian, industrialised civilisation, and are given the foundations of a sane and rational life (AM, 15). Collingwood's focus is on the development of the child, rather than the formal subject matter of the curriculum. In this respect, Boucher suggests that Collingwood's views on the role of parents in education echo the modern move to transfer the authority of the teacher to the parent, and in this respect he stands in the tradition of Rousseau and Dewey (Boucher, 1995b: 270).

Because Collingwood equated education with the civilising process, and argued that 'the life of politics is the life of political education' (NL, 32.34), he regarded education as something needed by adults as well as children. Adults need political education, and education at the higher levels of mental development. This kind of education is carried out by society in general and not necessarily by public education institutions. In *An Autobiography*, he criticises the *Daily Mail* for not living up to its educational responsibilities (A, 155). Members of the public need to be kept adequately informed on public questions and imbued with public spiritedness to do their work creditably. Parliamentary democracy depends on a politically educated public opinion (A, 153–4).

---

[5]   Boucher also indicates that Collingwood's intense distrust of the specialist is echoed by Hans-Georg Gadamer and Ronald Beiner, who take the technological revolution not as evidence of liberation from the drudgery of everyday life, but as the rejection and denial of our vital human capacities. For them, and for Collingwood, our ever-increasing reliance upon experts or technocrats subdues our critical faculties, and leads to the denial of emotions in our civilisation (Boucher, 1995b: 292).

Through education people are made conscious of their freedom and stimulated to develop their self-respect. To think of oneself as free is correlative with thinking of others as being free, and as people with whom social relations exist. Rational consciousness, as we have seen, is correlative to social consciousness. In a society each mentally adult person recognises the freedom of others, and acknowledges the wills of others as a source of rules binding on everyone (NL, 21.77). Political education also involves converting occasions of non-agreement into occasions of agreement, and not allowing them to harden into disagreement. This means developing in people a social consciousness which gradually renounces eristic or adversarial methods of resolving disputes, and adopts a dialectic or conciliatory approach to overcoming differences. Education has the role of refining social relations and prompting mutual respect, in order that society approximates to civility (cf. Boucher, 1995b: 279–81). Regarding the question of education being complicated by class divisions, a civilised society will not tolerate a great contrast between rich and poor (NL, 38.77–83). But, for Collingwood, diminishing the contrast between rich and poor is not best pursued by a policy of compulsory state education.

As we have seen, then, Collingwood's support for parental control over education is connected with his belief in the cultivation of forms of emotional expression as a solution to the crisis of Western civilisation. However, his views about education are also related to the role of dialectical thinking. For Collingwood, excessive reliance on state bureaucracy stifles the dialectical interaction and spontaneity of civilised life. This is also evident in his discussion of the other properties of civilisation: 'law and order' and 'peace and plenty'.

According to Collingwood, through the rule of law people develop and strengthen their wills. People become more and more capable of controlling their desires and passions and less and less likely to succumb to the threats of those who would cajole and frighten them into doing things that they would not do of their own free will. Hence, 'law and order mean strength' (NL, 39.92; cf. Boucher, 1989: 230). 'Peace and plenty' are the fruits of civilisation, and a consequence of 'law and order'. Peace does not mean a life of stagnation and quiescence. It is 'a dynamic thing' and 'a strenuous thing' whereby the process is checked by which non-agreements are hardened into disagreements, and it involves the 'dialectical labour' whereby non-agreements are converted into agreements (NL, 40.24).

Collingwood argues that keeping the peace is not solely the business of the rulers. In a community which consists of a social ruling class, and a non-social ruled class, a dialectical process is set up whereby the non-social community changes by degrees into a society (NL, 40.6–62).

> It is by the operation of the Third Law of Politics that the non-social community gradually approximates to the character of a society. So far as this happens, every member of the ruled class comes to share in the civilization of the community as a whole and hence in the work of keeping the peace. To throw the whole work of keeping the peace upon the shoulders of 'the state' means that 'the state' is conceived as doing its work so inefficiently that the Third Law of Politics never comes into operation, and no share in that work is ever taken by the ruled. This is fully recognized by the tradition of English Law: which makes a distinction between the king's peace and the peace of the individual subject, and requires every man to keep his own peace and thus co-operate in keeping the peace of the community. To take the education of children out of their parents' hands and put it in the hands of the king (or, as we nowadays say, 'the state') demonstrates a charming loyalty to the king and trust in his omnipotence; but it is taking a job away from those who can do it and handing it over to those who cannot. This dodge for the avoidance of responsibility … I shall call … 'passing the baby' (NL, 40.65–40.7).

A community among which the peace is adequately kept by converting occasions of non-agreement into occasions of agreement and thus averting quarrels before they happen, is called a well-mannered community (NL, 40.71). According to Collingwood, 'in each case the tradition of good manners is an outcome of a tradition that in one way or another men keep their own peace' (NL, 40.76). A tradition of good manners is easy to maintain, including in a public house:

> It is not (as might be thought by confirmed baby-passers) that the chucker-out keeps men polite, any more than the policeman keeps them honest. They keep themselves polite and honest. They have been civilized up to that point; and being civilized they value their civilization and keep themselves by their own free will up to the standard they now recognize (NL, 40.78–9).

As with keeping the peace, so with the procuring of plenty, there are some things that can be done publicly and there are some things that can only be done privately. The labour of procuring plenty, or thrift, means restricting consumption, increasing production and improving distribution (NL, 40.91–2). Collingwood distinguishes between the king's thrift and private thrift:

> If the ruled class in the community had remained utterly non-social and uncivilized through bestiality in itself and incompetence in its rulers, there would be no private thrift; whatever plenty the community enjoyed would have to be procured solely by the rulers, and 'the king's thrift' would be all the thrift there was …. From this Yahoo condition they would by degrees be elevated through the work of any body politic worthy of the name. From a brutally passive or non-social condition the mere fact of being ruled, if it were done with the least competence, would to some extent civilize them, socialize them, and endow them with a conviction (or as it is called a 'sense') of responsibility. However little way this process went, it would lead them to distinguish what I have called 'the king's thrift' from 'private thrift' and to see that, just as every man has a peace of his own, so every man has a plenty of his own to procure by his own thrift … (NL, 40.94–97).

Like Collingwood, Ortega y Gasset also regards excessive reliance on the bureaucratic state as symptomatic of the crisis of modernity and he proposes dialectical thinking as a solution. Ortega refers to the state as 'the gravest danger now threatening European civilisation' (RM, 117). The contemporary state has become a formidable machine capable of exercising overwhelming power on any portion of the social framework. But mass-man

> is not conscious of the fact that it is a human creation invented by certain men and upheld by certain virtues and fundamental qualities which men of yesterday had and which may vanish into air tomorrow (RM, 119–20).

The mass-man will tend to demand that the state intervene immediately to solve any problem or difficulty in public life, leading to the danger that it will absorb all spontaneous social effort and historical action, 'which in the long run sustains, nourishes, and impels human life' (RM, 120).

There is a danger that, through the state, the mass will tend to crush any creative minority which disturbs it. Spontaneous social action will be broken up, and society will have to live *for* the governmental machine: 'The people are converted into fuel to feed the mere machine which is the State. The skeleton eats up the flesh around it. The scaffolding becomes the owner and the tenant of the house' (RM, 121–2). An example of this is the enormous increase in the police force of all countries, made necessary by the increase of population. The Conservative government in England in the early nineteenth century refused to establish a police force considering disorder the price to pay for liberty.[6] As we have seen, to the problem

---

[6] Ortega cites John William Ward: 'In Paris they have an admirable police force, but they pay dear for its advantages. I prefer to see, every three or four years,

of the crisis of civilisation, Ortega regards dialectical thinking and historical thinking as a solution. Furthermore, Ortega's dialectical understanding of liberalism leads him to regard the state as not a thing, but a process, possibly leading to the transcending of the (European) state in a united Europe.

Like Collingwood and Ortega, de Ruggiero also puts forward the idea of a dialectical political life as a solution to the overweening influence of the bureaucratic state. De Ruggiero argues that democracy, although compatible with liberalism, implies a strong emphasis on the collective or social elements in political life at the expense of the individual element (de Ruggiero, 1959: 370–2). Democracy is impatient towards gradual individual development from within and tries to determine social development from without. Hence, self-government is permitted only to the highest ranks of the social hierarchy, but denied to subordinate associations and individuals, and this leaves society a prey to bureaucracy and demagogues. State interference is the 'open sesame' of the democratic mind, destined to make good every lack of experience and of energy (de Ruggiero, 1959: 373–4).

For de Ruggiero, 'the democratic worship of the state', through the social contract, confers upon citizens a general will, in practice the will of the numerical majority, and threatens the rights of minorities (de Ruggiero, 1959: 374–5). The evil of democracy is not the triumph of quantity, but the triumph of bad quality. Lack of education on the part of the masses and the omnipotence of the state widen the gulf between the actual majority and the majority of representatives, and threaten to make democracy a tyranny over the many in the interests of the few. Democratic tyranny finds a spy in every citizen, and knows no limit to its extension. The liberal, in contrast, knows that the autonomy of his own consciousness possesses an absolute spiritual value which is the very source of political progress (de Ruggiero, 1959: 376–7).

These consequences also partially result from industrial evolution, which by degrees has reduced the margins of individual independence. The rigid and unintelligent application of the principle of equality tends to diffuse mediocrity, and reduces the practical opportunities for individual independence, self-government and resistance to oppression by the central power (de Ruggiero, 1959: 378). It is therefore necessary to liberalise the structure of democratic

half a dozen people getting their throats cut in the Ratcliffe Road, than to have to submit to domiciliary visits, to spying, and to all the machinations of Fouché' (RM, 124).

society, to vitalise its elements from within, and to make them into centres of spontaneous co-operation. The feasibility of such a task, de Ruggiero declares, depends on the original unity of liberalism and democracy, and the dialectical character of the opposition between them (de Ruggiero, 1959: 379).

This synthesis, liberal democracy, aims at instilling a sense of autonomy into the masses, and at paving the way for self-government of the state by means of varied and independent forms of particular and local self-government. Its execution cannot be entrusted to state providence, and can only be effected by patient and assiduous education (de Ruggiero, 1959: 379). Liberal parties can fulfil a function of critical examination, or opposition, within democratic society:

> Unable to compete with democracy in the work of electoral campaigns among the masses, they may carve from the great common territory a small district to be cultivated in their own way, as a nursery garden of freedom (de Ruggiero, 1959: 380).

In de Ruggiero's view, a practical demonstration must be given of the origin and development of aristocracies of freedom, or social elites, so that the entire block of the masses may by degrees shape itself into a multiplicity of definite forms and figures (de Ruggiero, 1959: 380).

For Collingwood, de Ruggiero and Ortega y Gasset, then, dialectical thinking is seen as a solution to the crisis of modernity. One of the symptoms of crisis is the overweening influence of bureaucratic administration and a dialectical political life is the solution. This is quite different from the view of Weber, however, for whom bureaucratic administration is a symptom of the crisis of modernity but who does not regard dialectical thinking as a solution.

For Weber, rationality is problematic in the modern world. The process of rationalisation appears in terms of a reversal of the relation between means and ends: that which was originally a mere means becomes an end in itself. This reversal marks the whole of modern civilisation, whose arrangements, institutions and activities are so 'rationalised' that they enclose and determine humanity like an 'iron cage' (Lowith, 1993: 68). According to Weber,

> No one knows who will live in this cage in the future, or whether at the end of this tremendous development entirely new prophets will arise, or there will be a great rebirth of old ideas and ideals, or, if neither, mechanized petrification, embellished with a sort of convulsive self-importance. For of the last stage of this cultural development, it might be truly said: 'Specialists without spirit, sensualists without heart; this nullity

imagines that it has attained a level of civilization never before achieved'
(Weber, 1992: 182).

Rationalisation is associated with bureaucratic administration. For
Weber, once it is fully established, bureaucracy is 'a form of power
relation ... that is practically unshatterable' (Weber, 1970: 228).
Bureaucratic rationalisation is something from which escape is ever
more improbable (cf. Sayer, 1991: 144).

Similarly, (following on from Weber's analysis of rationalisation)
Horkheimer and Adorno put forward a critique of 'Enlightenment':
'For the Enlightenment, whatever does not conform to the rule of
computation and utility is suspect' (Horkheimer and Adorno, 1973:
6). According to Horkheimer and Adorno, with 'Enlightenment'
rationalisation, 'Being is apprehended under the aspect of manufacture and administration' and everything is converted into a repeat-
able, replaceable process (Horkheimer and Adorno, 1973: 84).

The pessimistic analysis of modern, rational society, put forward
by Weber, and further developed by the Frankfurt school of Adorno
and Horkheimer, had Nietzschean roots.[7] According to Nietzsche,
the 'herd' was increasingly subject to the state, which was the new
idol (replacing a dead God) that would rob people of their freedom.
In Nietzsche, according to Lowith, 'we can see Weber's anxieties
about the slavery of modern people within the bureaucratic machine
of the modern state and about the possibilities of personal autonomy
in a world which had been transformed by the processes of rationalisation' (Lowith, 1993: 10). For Nietzsche, 'when empires were
doomed they had many laws' (Nietzsche, 1968: 745).

Orwell (another member of the Romantic tradition) refers to
bureaucratic administration as one of the most problematic features
of modernity. Referring to broadcasting, Orwell complains that
'More and more the channels of production are under the control of
bureaucrats whose aim is to destroy the artist or at least castrate him'
(Orwell, 1996: 335). However,

> the huge bureaucratic machines of which we are all part are beginning to
> work creakily because of their mere size and their constant growth. The
> tendency of the modern state is to wipe out freedom of the intellect ...
> (Orwell, 1996: 335).[8]

---

[7]   Weber ranked Nietzsche with Marx as the dominant interpreters and critics of
        modernity. He claimed that the probity of the modern scholar could be judged
        by the extent to which they acknowledge that their work would not be possible
        without Marx and Nietzsche (Owen, 1995: 3n; Lowith, 1993: 2).

[8]   While discussing the privateness of English life Orwell declares: 'It is obvious
        that this purely private liberty is a lost cause. Like all other modern peoples, the

As I have indicated, then, the extensive bureaucratisation and rationalisation of life is regarded as symptomatic of a crisis of the West not only by Collingwood, Ortega and the Italian Idealists, but also by such thinkers as Nietzsche and Weber. However, unlike the latter, Collingwood and Ortega regard *dialectical thinking* as the solution.[9] For Collingwood, Ortega and de Ruggiero, abstract rationalism can be transcended and overcome through dialectical and historical reason: it might be suggested that their arguments could be applied in political theories of civil association, agonistic liberalism, and pluralist participatory democracy. With dialectical and historical thinking, therefore, something of what might be called the 'Enlightenment project' can be salvaged, and civilisation is provided with a way forward.

English are in the process of being numbered, labelled, conscripted, "co-ordinated" ... in all societies the common people must live to some extent *against* the existing order' (Orwell, 1996: 59). Orwell criticises the attempt of the modernist writers, Lawrence, Yeats, and Pound, to escape the homogenising and centralising pull of industrialised civilisation as hopeless yearning (in 'Socialism and the English Genius' and 'Inside the Whale'). Nevertheless, he praises Yeats for being 'too big a man to share the illusions of liberalism' (Orwell, 1996: 273).

[9]   The relative merits or defects of the solutions proposed by Nietzsche and Weber will not be assessed in this study, which is specifically concerned with Collingwood's solutions to the crisis of modernity.

Conclusion

The argument of this book has been that Collingwood's philosophy ought to be understood as a diagnosis of and a response to a crisis of Western civilisation. The theme of the crisis of civilisation has not been explicitly discussed in much detail by commentators on Collingwood's philosophy. Hence this work, in discussing 'crisis' thought, places Collingwood's philosophy in a wider context than that in which it is usually placed.

The theme of the crisis of modernity is crucially important not only in twentieth-century philosophy, but also in social and political thought and literary and artistic discourse. It is pivotal to Romanticism, historicism and most of twentieth-century continental philosophy in terms of the development of alternatives to positivism and hegemonic modes of thinking derived from natural science. This study, therefore, locates Collingwood's philosophy in the wide context of the emergence, in the late nineteenth- and twentieth century, of philosophies of process and becoming and the understanding of truth and meaning as historically contextual and contingent. Historicism seeks to reconcile the quest for truth with historical change and process, and this problem, which Dilthey tried to solve, continued into the twentieth century (see Meyerhoff, 1959: 16–8) and still goes to the heart of contemporary philosophical debate.

The argument that I have presented not only adds to our understanding of Collingwood by placing his philosophy in the context of Romanticism, historicism and 'crisis' thought, but it also enhances our comprehension of these philosophical movements by enabling us to see Collingwood as providing a key contribution to them. One of Collingwood's principal aims was to develop a new kind of philosophy which would understand history. It would be devoted to both epistemological problems, such as how historical knowledge is possible, but also 'metaphysical problems, concerned with the nature of the historian's subject-matter: the elucidation of terms like event, process, progress, civilization, and so forth' (A, 77). Collingwood's philosophy is not a last word on these subjects, and it provides a fertile ground for future explorations of these themes. This work has argued that one of the key contributions of his philosophy lies in tracing a common ground between a variety of intellectual traditions: between the development of a philosophy of art, following from the Romanticism of John Ruskin, and the emergence of a dialectical and historical philosophy, as is particularly evident in the thought of the Italian Idealists and Ortega y Gasset.

As I have argued, the conception of the crisis of civilisation and the specific solutions that Collingwood advocated for it take a variety of complementary forms. In Part One, I first discussed Collingwood's early conceptualisation of the crisis of civilisation in terms of the separation of the forms of experience from one another. Influenced by Romanticism and Ruskin, Collingwood's proposed solution to this problem was the re-union of the forms of experience in 'a complete and undivided life'. Following *Speculum Mentis*, however, Collingwood's view of the forms of experience came to be modified in important ways, and greater emphasis was placed on his philosophies of art and of historical and dialectical thinking, which became related solutions to the crisis of civilisation.

As I argued in Chapter Two, for Collingwood, the crisis of civilisation reveals itself first in aesthetic activity. Collingwood argued that Western culture is afflicted by the suppression of emotion. Symptoms of this include the confusion of art with craft, the predominance of the pseudo-art of amusement over art proper, the destruction of the countryside and the hegemony of values associated with industrialism. Collingwood's solution for this problem is a theory of art as the expression of emotion. Art proper is distinguished from craft. Whereas crafts (such as magic and amusement) represent, describe and generalise, art, on the other hand, is the expression of emotions in their unique individuality. Through expressing his or her emotions, the artist enables others to express their emotions. Through the development of this theory of art and the critique of the dehumanising effects of industrialism, Collingwood assimilates and extends the Romantic tradition of Ruskin and D.H. Lawrence.

Chapter Three explored Collingwood's philosophy of art in more detail. Art, in Collingwood's view, was revealed to be identical with consciousness and language and was explained as providing the raw material on which intellect can build. Art provides the concrete individual points between which it is the business of intellect to establish or apprehend relations. Through artistic activity we both create the world and become conscious of it. Hence art provides a solution to the corruption of consciousness and an antidote to the crisis of civilisation. By expounding the conception of art as the expression of emotion and the consciousness of truth, Collingwood draws together various strands of Romantic and modernist ideas about art into a systematic and comprehensive philosophy.

Chapter Four demonstrated that the kind of solution that Collingwood developed in his philosophy of art for the crisis of modernity becomes clearer in his account of the interaction between artist and audience. This was an addition to the theory of art that he had hitherto developed and provides an indication of the kind of solution to the crisis of the West that Collingwood put forward in his logic and metaphysics. As I explained in this chapter, then, for Collingwood, artistic production necessarily involves collaboration between artist and audience. The artist is the spokesperson for his or her audience, and art is the community's medicine for the corruption of consciousness. The dialectical interaction between innovation and tradition in Collingwood's philosophy of art complements and, in some ways, improves on the philosophies of art put forward by Ruskin, Eliot and Ortega y Gasset by being more completely dialectical or historical. All of this, of course, prefigures Collingwood's dialectical view of logic and metaphysics, which I expounded in part Two.

Part Two demonstrated that, for Collingwood, the suppression of emotion was a symptom of a deeper malaise. Collingwood argued that the philosophical foundations of Western civilisation were unsustainable because of a reliance on the Platonic philosophy of being. The solution, he argues, is a dialectical logic and metaphysics and a philosophy of history that reconciles normative standards with the process of becoming. Collingwood's dialectical logic, as I explained in Chapter Five, transcends the coherence theory of truth, replacing it with an account of truth as that which includes within itself most successfully diverse and by themselves conflicting points of view. This is a dialectical process, therefore, that leaves out the Hegelian Absolute and where further dialogue, criticism and counter-criticism is always possible.

Collingwood's dialectical logic is inextricably linked with an ontological claim that reality is dialectical. Therefore, his promotion of dialectical logic as a solution to the ailments of Western civilisation is paralleled by a reform of metaphysics. Hence Collingwood's dialectical logic (or logic of question and answer), as I argued in Chapter Six, cannot be separated from his account of metaphysics as a historical science which uncovers absolute presuppositions. The meaning of a set of absolute presuppositions, I contended, can only fully be understood in the context of the complex of questions and answers that it gives rise to. Contrary to the views of some commentators, I argued that Collingwood's reform of logic and metaphysics is more than hermeneutics because it also includes an ontological claim about the nature of reality. For Collingwood, spiritual or intellectual changes transform the nature of reality as much as physical changes do.

Chapter Seven demonstrated in more detail how Collingwood's philosophy responded to cultural crisis by reconciling normative thinking with historical change. Collingwood's historical metaphysics became more clearly defined through its rejection of both reactionary traditional philosophy and irrationalism. But, in Collingwood's view, the advancement of science and civilisation are not achieved by metaphysics alone. Metaphysics, I argued, must be supplemented by a broader philosophy of history which gives an account of the sciences and practices (with their questions, answers and relative presuppositions) that absolute presuppositions have given rise to and thus determining if an example of progress has occurred. Like the emotions that an artist expresses, the absolute presuppositions that the metaphysician reveals are not in themselves 'better' or 'worse' than another set of absolute presuppositions, but the act of uncovering them and clarifying what they are is indispensable for the advancement of science and civilisation.

For Collingwood, as I explained, there can be progress in a civilisation, not in terms of individual appetites and desires, but in terms of shared practices or a 'way of life' considered as a whole. However, our knowledge of whether one period of history taken as a whole showed progress over its predecessor may be limited – depending on how much we know of each period as a whole. Nevertheless, we make changes in social and cultural life only because we have faith that they are advances. According to Collingwood's philosophy, then, the criteria for value and truth are located not in a transcendent world removed from human experience, but in a 'way of life' considered in its widest context. But a culture or way of life is not static or complete: it has value only in so far as it assimilates and explains what is outside and different. In this respect, Collingwood's philosophy of history moves beyond the coherence theory of truth and Ruskin's more static view of culture.

Chapter Seven also included a comparison of Collingwood with Ortega y Gasset and Nietzsche. These comparisons place Collingwood in the context of historicism and the development of 'crisis' thought more generally. Ortega and Nietzsche are also significant because both advance philosophies which place value less on fundamental principles or individual judgements in themselves, but on their ability to generate vitality and enhance life as a whole. Unlike Collingwood and Ortega, however, Nietzsche is more sceptical about reason. Thus his more severe diagnosis of and proposed remedies for the nihilism confronting civilisation are rejected by the dialectical approach of both Collingwood and Ortega.

Part Three examined the way in which Collingwood's solution to the crisis of modernity in his philosophy of art, logic, metaphysics and philosophy of history manifests itself in a dialectical account of morality, politics and civilisation. For Collingwood, there is an intimate relation between theory and practice. As I explained in Chapter Eight, the historicist phenomenology of mind developed in *The New Leviathan* modifies and extends the theory of mind put forward in *The Principles of Art*, providing a more detailed account of the levels of consciousness and the dialectical development from one level to the next. The phenomenology of mind culminates with an account of morality as duty, and duty, as the practical aspect of historical thinking, transcends the inadequacies of utility and right. Duty, as the highest form of freedom and rationality, excludes the freedom of caprice and is completely determined by one's consciousness of obligation. In this respect, Collingwood's conception of duty constitutes a solution to the rationalism of modernity and overlaps with the Romantic idea of authenticity and the theories of Ortega and Nietzsche. Collingwood, however, differs from Nietzsche in insisting on the word 'morality' to describe authentic action. Hence his theory is an extension to the history of Western moral philosophy rather than a rejection of it.

As I demonstrated in Chapter Nine, Collingwood's view that the advancement of civilisation depends on dialectical thinking and historical self-consciousness becomes further elucidated in his theory of society and politics. Collingwood sought to reform traditional social contract theory by providing an account of how members of the non-social community could be educated into society, mental maturity and free will. Political life, Collingwood argues, proceeds through dialectical discussion, which through free discussion of opposing views finds some common ground on which to act — as opposed to eristical or adversarial discussion, where one party tries to prove that he or she is right and the other wrong. In the dialectical process of recruiting people into the ruling class, democracy and aristocracy are complementary positive and negative elements in that process. Contrary to foundational social contract theory, then, in Collingwood's view, society and the state are not things, but processes. Political systems are continuously made and remade.

The aim of these processes is the achievement of civilisation, or civility. Acting civilly, according to Collingwood, means refraining from diminishing a person's self-respect or threatening their consciousness of freedom. However, it also denotes a scientific exploitation of the natural world. The process of civilisation towards foreigners or strangers is one where, originally regarding them as natural things to be exploited, we come to consider them as human beings entitled to civility. Despite the existence of a plurality of civilisations and ideals of civility, each ideal presupposes a further ideal of universal civility: that of behaving civilly without any limit whatever. Civility between human beings also makes civility towards the natural world possible through the dialectical sharing of knowledge.

Part Three unites many of the concerns of Part One and Part Two. The articulation of a philosophy of art as the expression of emotion and consciousness of truth as an antidote to the corruption of consciousness is complemented by the development of a dialectical philosophy which is neither relativist nor removed from the world of historical change. Collingwood's historicist theory of mind, society and civilisation, a focal point of which is the account of how human beings can move from the lower levels of consciousness to the higher, illustrates how his solutions to the crisis of civilisation examined in Part One and Part Two include one another.

In particular, the examination of Collingwood's account of capitalism and bureaucratic administration in the final chapter demonstrates that the aesthetic and the dialectical understandings of the crisis of civilisation in his philosophy are intertwined. For Max Weber, like Collingwood, as I have explained, bureaucratic rationalisation was a symptom of a crisis in modern Western civilisation: something which Weber described as an 'iron cage'. Bureaucratic administration was also one of the problematic features of modern civilisation which Horkheimer and Adorno analysed under the rubric of 'Enlightenment'.

However, the solution proposed by Collingwood (and to some extent by the similar philosophies of Ortega y Gasset and the Italian Idealists) is a specifically dialectical, historicist and Romantic philosophy where faith is placed in the ability of human beings to over-come rationalism through dialectical/historical thinking and aesthetic self-expression. As Collingwood argued in 'The Present Need of a Philosophy', philosophy could help to solve the ills of con-temporary civilisation by providing a reasoned conviction that human progress is possible and that the problems of moral and political life are in principle soluble (EPP, 169). Nietzsche, Weber, and the Frankfurt School represent an alternative approach that is rejected by Collingwood.

Nevertheless, the importance of Nietzsche cannot be ignored, in particular because of his seminal articulation of the problem of nihil-ism in the late nineteenth century, and because of his huge influence on 'crisis' theory in the twentieth century. Similarly, Weber's theory of rationalisation and bureaucratic administration and the critique of Enlightenment by Horkheimer and Adorno (each of which had Nietzschean origins) illustrate the wider context of Collingwood's concern with the bureaucratic state as a symptom of the crisis of the West and provide a counterpoint to Collingwood's dialectical solu-tion.

Throughout the book I have pointed out that Collingwood's dia-lectical response to the crisis of civilisation is a salient part of a wider development of historicism in the early twentieth century, where both Collingwood and Ortega y Gasset play a key role. Both attempt to develop historical thinking and to make an advance on Dilthey's distinction between *Geisteswissenschaften* and the natural sciences. In Graham's view, Collingwood and Ortega can be regarded as virtual co-founders of a new 'critical' philosophy of history, replacing the older speculative philosophies of history (Graham, 1997: 140). The comparison with Ortega, then, illustrates the point that Collingwood's response to the crisis of the West should be seen as more than simply an Idealist response. Collingwood's response, like Ortega's, to some extent transcends both Idealism and realism to play a key role in the development of early twentieth-century philos-ophy.

Ortega's pivotal role as a 'crisis' thinker has already been men-tioned – however, as Graham indicates, Ortega's treatment of crisis connects more visibly with the old speculative philosophies of his-tory than Collingwood. While Dilthey and Collingwood concen-trated more on historical knowledge, Ortega stressed the ontological aspects of history more (Graham, 1997: 135 and 152).

Also Ortega emphasises the aristocratic aspect of the dialectical solution to the crisis of modernity, particularly in his conceptions of art, culture and politics. His concern is the somewhat Nietzschean one of trying to resurrect an aristocracy of culture from within the mediocrity and rationalism of mass society. (Unlike Nietzsche, of course, Ortega's solution embodies a faith in dialectical reason.)

It is here that Collingwood differs from Ortega. There seems to be greater faith in Collingwood's philosophy in the ability of human beings to move from the lower types of consciousness to the higher. The artistic self-expression that Collingwood champions includes that of ordinary persons whose understanding of art is rudimentary but whose emotional self-expression can develop through education. For Collingwood, the expression of emotion and the understanding of art are potentially open to all whose consciousness can develop and not only to those who, as Ortega argues, are members of the excellent minority or the cultured few. In this respect, as I argued in Chapter Nine, Collingwood's philosophy seems more completely dialectical and he is more optimistic about the ability of dialectical thinking to counteract the rationalism of modernity.

In any case, Collingwood's theory of society is one where the barrier between the ruling class and ruled class (or, in Ortega's terms, between the excellent minority and the masses) is more permeable in the upward sense (NL, 25.8) than in Ortega's philosophy. This difference between Collingwood and Ortega is also especially pronounced in their political philosophies in general. Ortega has less to say about how one could join the minority aristocracy and seems to take a less optimistic view about the prospects for liberalism in a mass society.

For Ortega, then, (because of his less dialectical view of the relation between elites and the masses) there is less emphasis on both the philosophy of art and political philosophy in providing a solution to the ills of contemporary civilisation. The solution that Ortega proposes is more concentrated on the philosophy of historical reason than Collingwood's. The more completely dialectical response to the crisis of modernity that we can see in Collingwood's philosophy is multi-faceted: a solution that embraces not only logic, metaphysics and the philosophy of history, but one that is also expressed or intimated in a philosophy of art (where, to some extent, all of us are artists, unlike Ortega's theory, where only an elite few are artists) and is made explicit in a theory of mind, society, politics and civilisation. *The New Leviathan* thus represents a kind of culmination in Collingwood's treatment of the theme of crisis, especially, as I have argued, in his controversial and seemingly eccentric views about the education of children. Despite the controversial nature of these views, Collingwood's account of education and of capitalism and the role of the state in general in Part III of *The New Leviathan* effectively draws together the response to cultural crisis in his aesthetics and the attempt to work out a philosophy of becoming (reconciling normative thinking with historical development) in his logic and metaphysics. Throughout the various aspects of Collingwood's philosophy, it becomes clear that the individual development of consciousness from the lower levels to the higher has a fundamental importance.

Collingwood, therefore, inherits a philosophical outlook from Ruskin, Hegel and Dilthey and attempts to develop an improved response to the key problems that they confronted: the corruption of Western civilisation (as explicitly concerned Ruskin) and the working out of a more completely dialectical and historical philosophy (than was achieved by Hegel and Dilthey). The comparisons with Ortega y Gasset, and to a lesser extent with Nietzsche and Weber, provide key contextualisations to Collingwood's arguments and help us to situate Collingwood's concerns, as well as to appreciate the persuasiveness of his solutions. Other comparisons with literary figures such as Orwell and the modernist writers, Lawrence, Pound, and Eliot have also been used. Like Collingwood, writers such as Lawrence and Pound thought that reason must be supplemented by emotion in order to save European civilisation from degeneration, but (being, first and foremost, artists and not philosophers) they seem more to provide inspirational examples of the expression of emotion, rather than fully worked-out philosophies.

To follow Collingwood, then, the solution to the problem of the crisis of civilisation is both the cultivation of forms of emotional expression and the development of historical and dialectical thinking. If the modern West is identified with the term 'Enlightenment', then Collingwood demonstrates that, through a re-conceptualisation and transcending of Enlightenment, Western civilisation can endure and we can afford to be hopeful about its future prospects.

References

Collingwood References

Collingwood, R.G., 1916, *Religion and Philosophy*, London: Macmillan; abbreviated as RP.

Collingwood, R.G., 1917, *Truth and Contradiction*, Chapter II, Unpublished Manuscript, Bodleian Library, Dep. 16/1; abbreviated as TC.

Collingwood, R.G., 1919, 'A Footnote to Future History', Unpublished Manuscript, Bodleian Library, Dep.12; abbreviated as FFH.

Collingwood, R.G., 1919, 'Lectures on the Ontological Proof of the Existence of God', Unpublished Manuscript, Bodleian Library, Dep. 2.

Collingwood, R.G., 1920a, *Libellus de Generatione*, Unpublished Manuscript, Bodleian Library, Dep. 27.

Collingwood, R.G., 1920b, 'Notes on Hegel's Logic', Unpublished Manuscript, Bodleian Library, Dep. 16/2.

Collingwood, R.G., 1920–21, *Draft of an opening chapter to a 'Prolegomena to Logic'*, Unpublished Manuscript, Bodleian Library, Dep. 16/5.

Collingwood, R.G., 1921, Lectures on Moral Philosophy, Unpublished Manuscript, Bodleian Library, Dep. 4.

Collingwood, R.G., 1923, 'Action: A Course of Lectures (16 lectures) on Moral Philosophy', Unpublished Manuscript, Bodleian Library, DEP 3.

Collingwood, R.G., 1924, *Speculum Mentis*, Oxford: Clarendon Press; abbreviated as SM.

Collingwood, R.G., 1925, *Outlines of a Philosophy of Art*, London: Oxford University Press; abbreviated as OPA.

Collingwood, R.G., n.d., c.1926, 'Art and the Machine', Unpublished Manuscript, Bodleian Library, Dep. 25/8; abbreviated as AM. (Published in *The Philosophy of Enchantment*, 2004).

Collingwood, R.G., 1926, 'The Place of Art in Education', *Hibbert Journal*, Vol. 24, 434–48; abbreviated as PAE.

Collingwood, R.G., 1929, Lectures on Moral Philosophy, Unpublished Manuscript, Bodleian Library, Dep. 10.

Collingwood, R.G., 1933, *An Essay on Philosophical Method*, Oxford: Clarendon Press; revised edition with an Introduction and additional material edited by James Connelly and Giuseppina D'Oro, 2005; abbreviated as EPM.

Collingwood, R.G., 1934, 'The Nature of Metaphysical Study', Unpublished Manuscript, Bodleian Library, Dep. 18/2; part of lecture 1 and all of lecture 2 is published in *An Essay on Metaphysics*, revised edition, edited with an Introduction by Rex Martin, Oxford: Clarendon Press, 1998, 356–78; abbreviated as NMS.

Collingwood, R.G., 1935, 'Method and Metaphysics', Unpublished Manuscript, Bodleian Library, Dep. 19/3; abbreviated as MM. (Published in *An Essay on Philosophical Method*, revised edition, 2005, pp. 327–55).

Collingwood, R.G., 1936a, 'Man Goes Mad', Unpublished Manuscript, Bodleian Library, Dep. 24/4; abbreviated as MGM. (Extract published in EPP; Published in full in *The Philosophy of Enchantment*, 2004).

Collingwood, R.G., 1936b, 'Realism and Idealism': 'Central Problems in Metaphysics' – Lectures written April 1935 for delivery T.T. 1935, Unpublished Manuscript, Bodleian Library, Dep. 20/1; abbreviated as RI.

Collingwood, R.G., 1936–37, 'Fairy Tales', Unpublished Manuscript, Bodleian Library, Dep. 21. (Extract published in EPP; Published in full in *The Philosophy of Enchantment*, 2004).

Collingwood, R.G., 1938, *The Principles of Art*, Oxford: Clarendon Press; abbreviated as PA.

Collingwood, R.G., 1939, *An Autobiography*, London: Oxford University Press; abbreviated as A.

Collingwood, R.G., 1945, *The Idea of Nature*, Oxford: Clarendon Press; abbreviated as IN.

Collingwood, R.G., 1964, *Essays in the Philosophy of Art*, edited with an Introduction by Alan Donagan, Bloomington: Indiana University Press; abbreviated as EPA.

Collingwood, R.G., 1965, *Essays in the Philosophy of History*, edited by W. Debbins, Austin, University of Texas Press; abbreviated as EPH.

Collingwood, R.G., 1989, *Essays in Political Philosophy*, edited with an Introduction by David Boucher, Oxford: Clarendon Press, 1989; abbreviated as EPP.

Collingwood, R.G., 1992, *The New Leviathan*, revised edition with an Introduction and additional material edited by David Boucher, Oxford: Clarendon Press; first published 1942; abbreviated as NL.

Collingwood, R.G., 1993, *The Idea of History*, Oxford: Clarendon Press, revised edition with an Introduction by W.J. van der Dussen; originally published 1946; abbreviated as IH.

Collingwood, R.G., 1995, 'Ruskin and the Mountains', introduced by James Connelly, *Collingwood Studies*, Vol.2, 1995, 185–9; originally published in *Oxford and Cambridge Mountaineering* 1921, Cambridge: Marshall, 21–26.

Collingwood, R.G., 1998, *An Essay on Metaphysics*, revised edition, edited with an Introduction by Rex Martin, Oxford: Clarendon Press; first published 1940; abbreviated as EM.

Collingwood, R.G., 2001, Review of J.N. Figgis, *The Will to Freedom: or the Gospel of Nietzsche and the Gospel of Christ*, Longmans, Green & Co.,

Collingwood and British Idealism Studies, Vol.8, 146; originally published in *Oxford Magazine*, 31/5/18, 299.

Collingwood, R.G., 2004, *The Philosophy of Enchantment: Studies in Folktale, Cultural Criticism, and Anthropology*, edited by David Boucher, Wendy James, and Philip Smallwood, Oxford: Clarendon Press.

Other References

Adas, Michael, 1989, *Machines as the measure of men: science, technology and ideologies of Western dominance*, Ithaca: Cornell University Press.

Beaney, Michael, 2001, 'Collingwood's Critique of Analytic Philosophy', *Collingwood and British Idealism Studies*, Vol. 8: 99–122.

Beaney, Michael, 2005, 'Collingwood's Conception of Presuppositional Analysis', *Collingwood and British Idealism Studies*, Vol. 11, No. 2: 41–114

Beiner, Ronald, 1983, *Political Judgement*, London, Methuen.

Boucher, David, 1985, *Texts in Context*, Dordrecht, Martinus Nijhoff.

Boucher, David, 1989, *The Social and Political Thought of R.G. Collingwood*, Cambridge: Cambridge University Press.

Boucher, David, 1992, 'Editor's Introduction', R.G. Collingwood, *The New Leviathan*, revised edition, Oxford: Clarendon Press.

Boucher, David, 1995a, 'The Life, Times and Legacy of R.G. Collingwood', *Philosophy, History and Civilization: Interdisciplinary Perspectives on R.G. Collingwood*, edited by Boucher, Connelly and Modood, Cardiff, University of Wales Press: 1–31.

Boucher, David, 1995b, 'The Place of Education in Civilization', *Philosophy, History and Civilization: Interdisciplinary Perspectives on R.G. Collingwood*, edited by Boucher, Connelly, and Modood, Cardiff, University of Wales Press: 269–97.

Boucher, David, 1997, 'Introduction', in David Boucher (editor), *The British Idealists*, Cambridge: Cambridge University Press.

Boucher, David, 2000, 'R.G. Collingwood: The Enemy within and the Crisis of Civilisation', in David Boucher and Andrew Vincent, *British Idealism and Political Theory*, Edinburgh: Edinburgh University Press: 185–209.

Browning, Gary, 1995, 'New Leviathans for Old', *Collingwood Studies*, Vol. 2, 89–106.

Browning, Gary, 2004, *Rethinking R.G. Collingwood: Philosophy, Politics and the Unity of Theory and Practice*, Basingstoke: Palgrave Macmillan.

Carey, John, 1992, *The Intellectuals and the Masses*, London, Faber and Faber.

Connelly, James, 1995, 'Art Thou the Man: Croce, Gentile or de Ruggiero?' *Philosophy, History and Civilization: Interdisciplinary Perspectives on R.G. Collingwood*, edited by David Boucher, James Connelly, and Tariq Modood, Cardiff: University of Wales Press, 92–114.

Connelly, James, 2003, *Metaphysics, Method and Politics: The Political Philosophy of R.G. Collingwood*, Exeter: Imprint Academic.

Coyle, Michael, 1995, *Ezra Pound, Popular Genres and the Discourse of Culture*, Pennsylvania: The Pennsylvania State University Press.

Croce, Benedetto, 1934, *History of Europe in the Nineteenth Century*, translated by Henry Furst, London, Unwin; reprinted in 1965.

Croce, Benedetto, 1949, *My Philosophy and other essays on the moral and political problems of our time*, translated by E.F. Carritt, London: Allen and Unwin.

Dobson, Andrew, 1989, *An Introduction to the Politics and Philosophy of José Ortega y Gasset*, Cambridge, Cambridge University Press.

Diffey, T.J., 1995a, Review of *Outlines of a Philosophy of Art*, by R.G. Collingwood, *Collingwood Studies*, Vol. 2, 234–242.

Diffey, T.J., 1995b, 'Aesthetics and Philosophical Method', *Philosophy, History and Civilization: Interdisciplinary Perspectives on R.G. Collingwood*, edited by David Boucher, James Connelly, and Tariq Modood, Cardiff: University of Wales Press, 62–78.

Dilworth, John, 1999, Review of *R.G. Collingwood: A Philosophy of Art*, by Aaron Ridley, *Journal of Aesthetics and Art Criticism* 57, no. 3, 390–2.

Donagan, Alan, 1962, *The Later Philosophy of R.G. Collingwood*, Oxford: Clarendon Press.

Donagan, Alan, 1964, 'Introduction', R.G. Collingwood, *Essays in the Philosophy of Art*, Bloomington: Indiana University Press

D'Oro, Giuseppina, 1999, 'How Kantian is Collingwood's Metaphysics of Experience?', *Collingwood Studies*, Vol. 6: 29–52.

D'Oro, Giuseppina, 2000, 'On Collingwood's Rehabilitation of the Ontological Argument', *Idealistic Studies*, Vol. 30, no.3: 173–88.

D'Oro, Giuseppina, 2002, *Collingwood and the Metaphysics of Experience*, London: Routledge.

Drucker, Peter, 1939, *The End of Economic Man*, London: Heinemann.

Eliot, T.S., 1962, *Notes Towards the Definition of Culture*, London: Faber and Faber; first published in 1948.

Ferrater Mora, José, 1963, *Ortega y Gasset: An Outline of his Philosophy*, New Haven: Yale University Press.

Gadamer, Hans-Georg, 1981, *Reason in the Age of Science*, Massachusetts: MIT Press.

Graham, John T., 1997, *Theory of History in Ortega y Gasset: 'The Dawn of Historical Reason'*, Columbia, University of Missouri Press

Haddock, Bruce, 1980, *An Introduction to Historical Thought*, London, Edward Arnold.

Helgeby, Stein, 1994, 'Action, Duty and Self-Knowledge in R.G. Collingwood's Philosophy of History', *Collingwood Studies* Vol. 1, 86–107.

Helgeby, Stein, 2004, *Action as History: The Historical Thought of R.G. Collingwood*, Exeter: Imprint Academic

Hinz, Michael, 1994a, *Self-Creation and History: Collingwood and Nietzsche on Conceptual Change*, Lanham, University Press of America

Hinz, Michael, 1994b, 'Process and Progress: Metaphysics as a Science of Mind', *Collingwood Studies*, Vol. 1: 124–42.

Horkheimer, Max, and Adorno, Theodor W., 1973, *Dialectic of Enlightenment*, translated by John Cumming, London: Allen Lane.

Hughes, H. Stuart, 1959, *Consciousness and Society: The Reorientation of European Social Thought 1890–1930*, London: MacGibbon and Kee.

Hughes-Warrington, Marnie, 1996, 'How Good an Historian Shall I Be? R.G. Collingwood on Education', *Oxford Review of Education*, 22, no. 2, 217–35.

Hughes-Warrington, Marnie, 2003, *'How Good an Historian Shall I Be?' R.G. Collingwood, the Historical Imagination and Education*, Exeter: Imprint Academic.

Iiritano, Massimo, 2002, 'From the principle of non-contradiction to contradiction as a principle: The beginning of Collingwood's revolution in logic', *Collingwood and British Idealism Studies*, Vol. 9, 45–69.

Johnson, Peter, 1998, *R.G. Collingwood: An Introduction*, Bristol: Thoemmes Press.

Johnston, William M., 1967, *The Formative Years of R.G. Collingwood*, The Hague: Martinus Nijhoff.

Larmore, Charles, 1996, *The Romantic Legacy*, New York: Columbia University Press.

Lawrence, D.H., 1955, *Selected Literary Criticism*, edited by Anthony Beal, London: William Heinemann.

Levenson, Joseph R., 1965, *Confucian China and Its Modern Fate: The Problem of Intellectual Continuity*, London: Routledge and Kegan Paul

Lewis, Peter, 1995, 'Art, The Community's Medicine', *British Journal of Aesthetics*, Vol. 35, no. 3, July, 205–16.

Lowith, Karl, 1993, *Max Weber and Karl Marx*, edited by Tom Bottomore and William Outhwaite, London and New York, Routledge.

Lund, James, 1998, 'The Idea of the History of Philosophy: Beginnings', *Collingwood Studies*, Vol. 5: 1–27

Mabbott, J.D., 1954, 'Note on "The Oxford Political Philosophers"', *The Philosophical Quarterly*, Vol. 4, No. 16: 258–61.

Martin, Rex, 1998a, 'Editor's Introduction', R.G. Collingwood, *An Essay on Metaphysics*, revised edition, Oxford: Clarendon Press

Martin, Rex, 1998b, 'Collingwood's Logic of Question and Answer, its Relation to Absolute Presuppositions: a Brief History', *Collingwood Studies*, Vol. 5: 122–33.

Marcus, John, T., 1962, 'The Consciousness of History', *Ethics*, Vol.73, Issue 1, 28–41.

McIntyre, K.B., 1996, 'Collingwood, Oakeshott, and the Social Contract', *Collingwood Studies*, Vol.3, 117–36.

Meyerhoff, Hans (editor), 1959, *The Philosophy of History in our Time*, New York, Doubleday.

Miller, Eugene F., 1972, 'Positivism, Historicism, and Political Inquiry', *The American Political Science Review*, Vol. 66, Issue 3, 796–817.

Mink, Louis, 1969, *Mind, History and Dialectic: The Philosophy of R.G. Collingwood*, Bloomington: Indiana University Press.

Mink, Louis, 1972, 'Collingwood's Historicism: A Dialectic of Process', *Critical Essays on the Philosophy of R.G. Collingwood*, edited by Michael Krausz, Clarendon Press, Oxford: 154–78.

Modood, Tariq, 1989, 'The Later Collingwood's Alleged Historicism and Relativism', *Journal of the History of Philosophy* 27: 101–25.

Modood, Tariq, 1995, 'Collingwood and the Idea of Philosophy', *Philosophy, History and Civilization: Interdisciplinary Perspectives on R.G. Collingwood*, edited by Boucher, Connelly and Modood, Cardiff: University of Wales Press, 32–61.

Nietzsche, Friedrich, 1968, *The Will to Power*, translated by Walter Kaufmann and R.J. Hollingdale, edited with notes by Walter Kaufmann, New York: Vintage Books.

Nietzsche, Friedrich, 1969, *Thus Spoke Zarathustra*, translated with an introduction by R.J. Hollingdale, Harmondsworth: Penguin.

Nietzsche, Friedrich, 1990, *Beyond Good and Evil*, translated by R.J. Hollingdale with an Introduction by Michael Tanner, London, Penguin.

Oakeshott, Michael, 1962, *Rationalism in Politics and other essays*, London: Methuen.

Oldfield, Adrian, 1995, 'Metaphysics and History in Collingwood's Thought', *Philosophy, History and Civilization: Interdisciplinary Perspectives on R.G. Collingwood*, edited by Boucher, Connelly and Modood, Cardiff, University of Wales Press: 182–202.

Ortega y Gasset, José, 1932, *The Revolt of the Masses*, anonymous translation, New York, Norton; abbreviated as RM.

Ortega y Gasset, José, 1957, *Man and People*, translated by Willard R. Trask, New York, Norton; abbreviated as MP.

Ortega y Gasset, José, 1958, *Man and Crisis*, translated from the Spanish by Mildred Adams, New York and London: Norton; abbreviated as MC.

Ortega y Gasset, José, 1960, *What is Philosophy?* Translated by Mildred Adams, New York: Norton

Ortega y Gasset, José, 1961, *History as a System and other essays toward a philosophy of history*, translated by Helene Weyl, New York and London: Norton; first published in 1941; abbreviated as HS.

Ortega y Gasset, José, 1946, 1963, *Mission of the University*, translated with an Introduction by Howard Lee Nostrand, London: Routledge & Kegan Paul; abbreviated as MU.

Ortega y Gasset, José, 1968, *The Dehumanization of Art and other essays on art, culture, and literature*, translated by Helene Weyl, New Jersey: Princeton University Press; abbreviated as DA.

Orwell, George, 1989, *The Road to Wigan Pier*, Harmondsworth: Penguin; first published by Victor Gollancz Ltd 1937.

Orwell, George, 1996, *The Works*, Vol.11, edited by Sonia Orwell and Ian Angus, London: Secker and Warburg; first published in 1968.

Ouimette, Victor, 1982, *José Ortega y Gasset*, Boston, Twayne.

Owen, David, 1995, *Nietzsche, Politics and Modernity*, London: Sage.

Parker, Christopher, 2000, *The English Idea of History from Coleridge to Collingwood*, Aldershot: Ashgate.

Peters, Rik, 1995, 'Collingwood on Hegel's Dialectic', *Collingwood Studies*, Vol. 2, 107–27.

Peters, Rik, 1999, 'Collingwood's logic of Question and Answer, its Relation to Absolute Presuppositions: another Brief History', *Collingwood Studies*, Vol. 6, 1–28.

Pound, Ezra, 1954, *Literary Essays of Ezra Pound*, edited with an introduction by T.S. Eliot, London: Faber and Faber.

Rader, Melvin, 1967, 'Art and History', *The Journal of Aesthetics and Art Criticism*, Vol. 26, Issue 2, 157–168.

Raley, Harold C., 1971, *José Ortega y Gasset: Philosopher of European Unity*, University of Alabama Press.

Redman, Tim, 1991, *Ezra Pound and Italian Fascism*, Cambridge: Cambridge University Press.

Ridley, Aaron, 1998, *R.G. Collingwood: A Philosophy of Art*, in The Great Philosophers Series no. XXI, edited by Ray Monk and Frederic Raphael, London: Phoenix Press.

Rubinoff, Lionel, 1970, *Collingwood and the Reform of Metaphysics*, Toronto: University of Toronto Press.

Ruggiero, Guido de, 1959, *The History of European Liberalism*, translated by R.G. Collingwood, Boston, Beacon Press; first published by Clarendon Press 1927.

Ruskin, John, 1907, *Unto this Last; The Political Economy of Art; Essays on Political Economy*, London: Dent; reprinted 1968.

Ruskin, John, 1908, *The Crown of Wild Olive and the Cestus of Alglaia*, London: Dent.

Sayer, Derek, 1991, *Capitalism and Modernity, An excursus on Marx and Weber*, London and New York: Routledge.

Shipley, Glenn, 2001, Review of *An Essay on Metaphysics*, revised edition, in *Collingwood and British Idealism Studies*, Vol.8: 166–80.

Tanner, Michael, 1990, 'Introduction', Friedrich Nietzsche, *Beyond Good and Evil*, translated by R.J. Hollingdale, London: Penguin.

Taylor, Charles, 1991, *The Ethics of Authenticity*, Cambridge and London, Harvard University Press.

Taylor, Donald, 2000, 'Collingwood's Developing Aesthetic: Artists and Audiences', *Collingwood and British Idealism Studies*, Vol.7, 32–44.

Thatcher, David, 1970, *Nietzsche in England 1890–1914*, Toronto: University of Toronto Press.

Van der Dussen, Jan, 1995, 'Collingwood on the Ideas of Process, Progress and Civilization', in *Philosophy, History and Civilization: Interdisciplinary Perspectives on R.G. Collingwood*, edited by Boucher, Connelly and Modood, Cardiff, University of Wales Press: 246–68.

Vanheeswijck, Guido, 1994, 'The Function of "Unconscious Thought" in R.G. Collingwood's Philosophy', *Collingwood Studies*, Vol.1, 108–123.

Vanheeswijck, Guido, 1996, 'R.G. Collingwood, T.S. Eliot, and the Romantic Tradition', *Collingwood Studies*, Vol. 3, 76–95.

Vanheeswijck, Guido, 1997, 'Collingwood's Metaphysics: Not a Science of Pure Being, but Still a Science of Being', *International Philosophical Quarterly*, 38, no. 2: 153–75.

Voegelin, Eric, 1953, 'The Oxford Political Philosophers', *The Philosophical Quarterly*, Vol.3, No.11: 97–114.

Weber, Max, 1970, *From Max Weber*, edited by H. Gerth and C. Wright Mills, London, Routledge.

Weber, Max, 1992, *The Protestant Ethic and the Spirit of Capitalism*, London and New York: Routledge.

Williams, Raymond, 1993, *Culture and Society: Coleridge to Orwell*, London: The Hogarth Press; first published in 1958.

Winchester, Ian, 2004, 'Collingwood's Notion of a Work of Art', *Collingwood and British Idealism Studies*, Vol. 10, 62–70.

Index